WHITE ALLIES

in the Struggle

for Racial Justice

WHITE ALLIES
in the Struggle for Racial Justice

Drick Boyd

ORBIS BOOKS
Maryknoll, New York 10545

ORBIS BOOKS
Maryknoll, New York 10545

Fathers and Brothers MARYKNOLL

Founded in 1970, Orbis Books endeavors to publish works that enlighten the mind, nourish the spirit, and challenge the conscience. The publishing arm of the Maryknoll Fathers and Brothers, Orbis seeks to explore the global dimensions of the Christian faith and mission, to invite dialogue with diverse cultures and religious traditions, and to serve the cause of reconciliation and peace. The books published reflect the views of their authors and do not represent the official position of the Maryknoll Society. To learn more about Maryknoll and Orbis Books, please visit our website at www.maryknollsociety.org.

Published by Orbis Books, Box 302, Maryknoll, NY 10545-0302.

Manufactured in the United States of America

Library of Congress Cataloging-in-Publication Data

White allies in the struggle for racial justice / [edited by] Drick Boyd.
pages cm
Includes bibliographical references and index.
ISBN 978-1-62698-149-2 (pbk.)
1. Civil rights workers—United States—Biography. 2. Whites—United States—Biography. 3. African Americans—Civil rights—History. 4. Civil rights movements—United States—History. 5. Civil rights—Religious aspects—Christianity. 6. Racism—United States—History. 7. Antislavery movements—United States. 8. Abolitionists—United States—Biography. 9. Christians—United States—Biography. 10. United States—Racerelations. I. Boyd, Drick, editor.
E185.98.A1W54 2015
323.092'2—dc23
[B]

2015019274

Contents

Contemporary White Allies

Foreword

Rev. C. T. Vivian

The Rev. C. T. Vivian was a friend and associate of Dr. Martin Luther King Jr. in the Southern Christian Leadership Conference (SCLC) during the civil rights movement. He participated in his first sit-in in 1947, and has been a lifelong activist, author, and minister. He helped found the Nashville (TN) Christian Leadership Conference and helped organize the lunch counter sit-ins of 1960. Along with 4,000 demonstrators he marched on the Nashville city hall and prodded Mayor Ben West to publicly agree that racial discrimination in retail establishments was morally wrong. In 1961 he participated in the Freedom Rides after the original riders had been beaten and were unable to continue, and rode from Montgomery, Alabama, to Jackson, Mississippi, to complete the ride. In the mid-1960s he helped design Upward Bound, a program to help low-income youth go to college, and implemented the first Upward Bound program in Alabama. During the civil rights era he helped organize several SCLC campaigns in the South and is featured prominently in the civil rights documentary Eyes on the Prize. *In 1970 he became the first member of Martin Luther King's staff to write about the civil rights movement when he published* Black Power and the American Myth. *On November 20, 2013, President Barack Obama presented Rev. Vivian the Medal of Freedom for being a "champion for justice and equality." Below he shares examples from his experiences of how Whites participated as allies of African Americans in the struggle for racial justice during that period.*

During the civil rights era there were many in the White community who said they believed in racial justice but failed to act on those beliefs. Despite the general passivity of these well-meaning Whites, there were some who were willing to step forward and join the movement. Here are a few significant instances I remember.

All White people were not cruel racists. Some White people could be educated beyond racism. I discovered that the higher their education level, the less racist the individual. When in high school, I remember a White classmate, Don Coghill, telling me, "I would invite you to my party but my mother won't let me. All of our classmates want you to be there. We all would, if we could." I then knew that a new generation was coming, and they did come.

One time my wife, Octavia, and I were having lunch with Mrs. Rosa Parks in a Tennessee restaurant when a young White man came up to us and asked Mrs. Parks to forgive him. We were surprised and listened as he continued. "It was my uncle who put you off that bus in Montgomery. When I saw you, I knew I had to at least ask you to forgive me," he said. I knew then that a new generation could grow up in the South.

In the late 1970s I was startled when Governor George Wallace invited ten of us who led the 1965 march from Selma to Montgomery to come to his office with ten of his staff members. I was startled because years earlier when a group of us made that same trek, Governor Wallace refused to meet with us. This time, after meeting he asked all of us to stay for friendly conversation. I had a seat directly across from him where I could see his eyes. Someone asked him the question we all wanted to ask. "If you could go back and relive your past, would you have been a racist?" His demeanor changed. He looked down rather sadly and slowly pointed up while sitting in his wheelchair and slowly said, "No, I would not." Pointing upward toward the sky, he continued, "We all want to go up there."

Since then, men and women, ministers and lay persons, Black and White, from all over the nation, from both the North and South, have helped in the struggle against racism. Anne Braden, a White woman, became a leader in the Southern struggle. She and her husband helped in the fight to end housing discrimination against Blacks in Louisville, Kentucky. Mr. Braden was jailed for taking that stand. They both struggled for racial justice, not on one occasion, but for a lifetime. A White Lutheran preacher, Rev. Robert Graetz, accepted a pulpit in a Black church in Montgomery, Alabama. Even though his home was bombed, he stayed to pastor and wrote a book that still speaks to ministers, Christians, and those who suffer with the condition of believing they can be racist Christians.

During the civil rights movement while in Mississippi, I had been punched by a police officer and then thrown in jail. A White doctor was sent to examine me. The doctor had to touch me and care for my injury but all the while, he continually looked back at the prison guards wondering what they would think of him, or how they might even harm him, if he showed compassion for me while doing his job. I realized the doctor and I were both prisoners of racism and Southern tradition. Decent Southerners were silent and held some fear but were waiting to be free—free to be decent and compassionate people. Their freedom would help free us.

It is the stories of White people like these that Drick Boyd tells in this book. They stood by us, walked with us, and in some cases suffered with us in our struggle for justice, equality, and freedom.

Acknowledgments

White Allies in the Struggle for Racial Justice comes out of my own journey to live and work in solidarity with my brothers and sisters of color toward building a more racially just society. Since my introduction to the life and work of Dr. Martin Luther King Jr. in the early 1970s, I have aspired to live with the kind of commitment to racial justice exemplified by the people whose stories are told in this book. Many of these stories have guided me in my own journey, and have been shared in abbreviated form with friends and students for years. A few years ago Ra Mendoza, one of the students in my Race and Ethnic Relations class, suggested I write these stories down. Her suggestion gave birth to this book. In the process of my research I have learned about so many more White allies than I imagined existed; only a small percentage of the stories that could have been told are related here.

I thank Robert Ellsberg, Maria Angelini, and the staff at Orbis Books for agreeing to work with me on this project. Robert's input and ideas have improved the original project immensely. I also thank my graduate assistant, Jess Lamson, and my daughter, Phoebe Boyd, for their invaluable feedback as they proofread the original drafts. I am particularly grateful to Rev. C.T. Vivian for agreeing to write the foreword and to his daughter Kira for her persistence and help in making it happen. I appreciate the encouragement and insights from my colleagues Dr. Kimberlee Johnson, Dr. Nathan Corbitt, and my brother Winton Boyd; they kept urging me on when I felt stuck. Dr. Todd Allen, founder of the Return to the Roots Civil Rights Tour, provided valuable insights and connections. I am also thankful also to my wife Cynthia, who patiently allowed me the time to work on this important project.

In my journey there have been many guides and mentors. My friends and colleagues in NewCORE (New Conversations on Race and Ethnicity) have shown me repeatedly the impact of a good story told well. Calenthia Dowdy, Conrad Moore, and the other facilitators at Roots of Justice, have shaped my understanding of the complex nature of racism and how to combat it. Dr. James Tillman, who taught the first course I have ever took on racism, set me on the course on which I have travelled ever since.

Finally, I want express my gratitude to the students in the Urban Studies masters program, whose passion for justice continues to feed my soul. These stories were written with them in mind. Their energy and persistent questions help me to stay conscious and vigilant in my own struggle with racism. I often feel I gain as much or more than my students when we struggle together with the issues of race and difference. My hope is that these stories can guide and inspire them and others like them, as together we yearn and work for the actualization of Dr. King's vision of the Beloved Community.

Drick Boyd
Philadelphia, PA

Introduction

The Need for Role Models

We Are All Human Beings

One day in the 1850s, a young girl named Abbie Whinnery was swinging on the iron gate in front of her house. Abbie was the daughter of John Whinnery, one of the stationmasters of the underground railroad in the staunchly abolitionist town of Salem, Ohio. The night before, a group of runaway slaves had been shepherded into Salem and, at that very moment, were hiding in the Whinnerys' attic until the evening fell when they would be moved farther north in the network of safe houses that had been developed through Ohio from Kentucky to Canada. As Abbie played in her front yard, a marshal and two deputies rode up to the house. Even though Ohio was considered a "free state," the Fugitive Slave Law empowered law enforcement officials from the slaveholding states to seek and arrest slaves who had escaped north to places like Ohio.

Approaching the young girl in pigtails, the marshal asked Abbie, "You folks got any slaves in your house, Miss?" Without batting an eye, Abbie replied, "Not a one." Because Abbie and her family were Quakers, and Quakers were known not to lie, the marshal said, "Come on then, men. She's a Quaker," and went on their way.

After the men had departed, Abbie's father who had overheard the whole conversation came out to the gate. "Abbie," he said, "I heard what thou said to the men who came here. Thou knows there are six men hidden in our attic this minute. Did thou tell an untruth?"

Again without hesitation Abbie responded, "Oh no, Papa. He asked about slaves, but thou told me that no human beings are ever slaves. They are free men to us, aren't they?"[1]

[1] Dale Shaffer, *Salem: A Quaker City History* (Charleston, SC: Arcadia, 2002), 43.

Whether this story is true or apocryphal, it illustrates that, despite the racism that prevailed throughout the United States of the 1850s in both the North and South, there were White[2] people like the Whinnery family who were able to transcend the attitudes of their time and who risked arrest, ostracism, and in some cases even death in order to oppose that racism and to ally themselves with those brutalized and degraded by it. All too often the stories of these brave antiracist allies such as Abbie Whinnery are left untold.

A Legacy of Racism

Despite the fact that nearly 150 years ago racial slavery was abolished and made unconstitutional in the United States, the sordid history of White racism still haunts the Western world, and in particular the United States. The origins of modern racism can be traced to the persecution of Jews by European Christians during the late Middle Ages. Most historians believe that the concept of race developed sometime between the sixteenth and eighteenth centuries and that it was used by the British to distinguish themselves from the Irish, and by continental European Christians to justify their inhumane treatment of Jews and Turkish Muslims. These same attitudes were then transferred to African slaves leading to mass deportation from their homeland and enslavement in the colonies of North America and the Caribbean. The European settlers brought their White supremacist worldview to North America where those same dehumanizing, racist attitudes were projected onto Native Americans, Mexican peasants, Chinese and Japanese laborers, and East European miners. Although the legal justifications for slavery were abolished in the early nineteenth century in England and in 1865 in the United States, the legacy of racist policies and practices continued into the twentieth century with Jim Crow segregation, and the eugenics movement culminating in Nazi genocide against six million Jews in the 1930s and 1940s. The horrific aftermath of the Nazi death camps, coupled with the burgeoning US civil rights movement led US political leaders to eventually overturn policies of segregation and discrimination against all races with the Civil Rights Act of 1965. Policies such as affirmative action were designed to correct

[2] Because the terms "White," "Black," and "People of Color" are used to describe people who have been defined by the social construct called race, I have chosen to treat these words as artificial titles and thus capitalized them for effect. The only exception to this practice is that when I have quoted a source that have kept these terms in the lower case, I have maintained the author's preferred form of expression.

the abuses of the past and paved the way for all sorts of legislation at federal, state, and local levels that made discrimination on the basis of race and/or ethnicity a criminal offense.[3]

In the last fifty years it has become legally and morally unacceptable in general US society for White persons to purposefully and openly speak or act toward Persons of Color in derogatory or dehumanizing ways. For this reason most White people in the United States consider racism to be a thing of the past, and no more than a minor issue. With the 2008 election of a biracial president who identified himself as an African American, many Whites proclaimed that the United States had reached a "postracial era." Mark Warren in his book *Fire in the Heart* cites studies in which an overwhelming percentage of Whites believe that Blacks have just as good a chance as Whites to be hired for a job for which they are qualified, receive a quality public school education, find affordable housing and have access to affordable, appropriate health care. Warren concludes that "many whites remain ignorant of the continued existence of racial inequality."[4]

However, persons aware and sensitive to the subtle dynamics of institutional racism have documented that, despite the change in cultural language and the substantial elimination of racist practices in the public square, racism is hardly a thing of the past. Experts in the areas of public education, criminal justice, economics, housing, and law have clearly shown that racist assumptions and proclivities still permeate the systems and institutions that govern everyday life. Moreover, the election of a biracial president has coincided with the rise of White supremacist groups and a conservative backlash whose constituency is overwhelmingly White, and whose objections to President Obama's policies are often expressed in racist code words.[5]

---

[3] For fuller explanation on the history of racism see George Fredrickson, *Racism: A Short History* (Princeton, NJ: Princeton University Press, 2002); Audrey Smedley and Brian Smedley, "Race as Biology Is Fiction, Racism as a Social Problem Is Real: Anthropological and Historical Perspectives on the Social Construction of Race," *American Psychologist* 60, no. 1 (January 2005): 16–26; Audrey Smedley and Brian Smedley, *Race in North America: Origin and Evolution of a Worldview* (Boulder, CO: Westview Press, 2012); Ronald Takaki, *A Different Mirror: A History of Multicultural America*, rev. ed. (New York: Back Bay Books, 2008).

[4] Mark Warren, *Fire in the Heart: How White Activists Embrace Racial Justice* (New York: Oxford University Press, 2010), 3.

[5] See the following sources for studies of institutional racism: Michelle Alexander, *The New Jim Crow: Mass Incarceration in the Age of Colorblindness*

Furthermore, despite the dismantling of segregationist Jim Crow laws, Americans are as residentially and socially segregated in the twenty-first century as they were in the segregated South of the 1950s. This segregation has led White people to be socially and culturally isolated from People of Color in significant ways. Although popular media and music allow Whites, Blacks, Hispanics, Asians, and other ethnic groups to see one another at a distance, the actual personal interaction between Whites and People of Color is relatively low. School segregation today is greater than in the late 1960s, and only 15 percent of Whites report having a close friend who is not White.[6] Thus Whites have grown up in an environment that has largely isolated them from day-to-day interactions with People of Color.

This isolation was brought home to me a few years ago when I was teaching an adult education course on cross-cultural studies in which I assigned students to interview someone from a race or ethnicity different from their own. On hearing this, a White woman in her forties who worked in the professional world informed me she could not complete the assignment because in her words "I don't know anyone who is not white." Now most likely this woman routinely crossed paths with People of Color in her work and daily life, but despite sharing the same space on many occasions with People of Color, she had not interacted to the point of feeling she could complete the assignment. Instead of acceding to her request to be given an alternative assignment, I agreed that indeed she did have a problem and that she needed to figure out when and how she would cross her self-imposed barrier and complete the assignment, which in fact she found a way to do.

Although an extreme case, this story illustrates the degree to which White people are isolated from the vagaries of racism that People of Color must confront daily. As a result, Whites have developed what Peggy McIntosh has called "an invisible knapsack" of White privilege, which enables them to go through their lives oblivious to the status and privilege granted to them by general society simply by virtue of their white skin. Most Whites in the United States are born into a context in which the laws, policies, and general cultural attitudes favor them

(New York: New Press, 2011); Derrick Bell, *Faces at the Bottom of the Well: The Permanence of Racism* (New York: HarperCollins, 1992); Jonathan Kozol, "An Unequal Education," *School Library Journal* 46, no.10 (May 2000): 46–49; John Stapleford, "A Torturous Journey: The Condition of Black America," *Christian Scholars Review* 37, no. 2 (Winter 2008): 231–51; William Julius Wilson, "Inner-City Dislocations," *Society* 35, no. 2 (January/February 1998): 270–77.

[6] Warren, *Fire in the Heart.*

over others. However, because they rarely, if ever, venture beyond their White-dominated enclaves, they come to consider those privileges as normal and something they are entitled to. At the same time, they are socialized to believe that those who do not enjoy those privileges have somehow failed to earn them or deserve not to have them. They may see the disparities in income, education, or housing between Whites and People of Color but are led to believe that such disparities are not due to any structural advantages they enjoy, but rather due to the individual failure of People of Color to earn what Whites already have.[7]

The Need for Role Models

I teach courses in racism and social justice at a small Christian liberal arts university in which I attempt to help my students understand how the dynamics of racism so evident in US history are still at work in our culture today, but in subtle and systematized forms. Although most Whites are less likely to participate in "active racism," they still engage in "passive racism," which is often seen in the conscious and unconscious failure of Whites to confront or call attention to discriminatory acts or policies in order to avoid controversy or criticism from other Whites. As Beverly Tatum says, "Because racism is ingrained in the fabric of American institutions, it is easily self-perpetuating."[8] Although generally unaware of the degree to which their status in society has been granted to them based on their race, I have found that when the evidence is presented to them, many White students are open to exploring the current realities of racism. Although not all White students respond positively when presented with the concepts of White privilege, White power, and the insidious presence of systemic racism, many do.

However, acknowledging the reality of racism and knowing what to do with that awareness are two different things. In her teaching of White college students on issues of racism Tatum found that many of them were bound up with a sense of guilt and hopelessness as to what they should do. Likewise, I have found in my courses that there often comes a point where White students feel caught between an overwhelming

---

[7] Peggy McIntosh, "White Privilege and Male Privilege: A Personal Account to See Correspondence through Work in Women's Studies," in *Critical White Studies: Looking Behind the Mirror*, ed. Richard Delgado and Jean Stefancic (Philadelphia: Temple University Press, 1988), 291–99.

[8] I was first introduced to the terms "active racism" and "passive racism" in Beverly Tatum, *Why Are All the Black Kids Sitting Together in the Cafeteria: and Other Conversations about Race* (New York: Basic Books, 1997), 11.

sense of guilt and shame for the history of White racism from which they have benefited while feeling powerless as to how to proceed in a way that does not perpetuate existing racist policies and laws or cause offense to Persons of Color they know through casual interaction. For many of my White students this is a point at which they feel stuck between the awareness of their need to change and confusion on what or how to change. Tatum refers to this as the "guilty white" model of racial identity, which is "characterized by the heightened awareness of racism and the accompanying shame and embarrassment about being white" and which "interferes with one's ability to take effective action to interrupt the expressions of racism."[9]

In my graduate course on race and ethnic relations, there usually comes a point where I divide the class based on their racial ethnic makeup. One time I divided the students into three groups—people of African descent, Hispanics, and Whites. My instruction to each group was to talk among themselves and to come back in thirty minutes to report on what they celebrated about their racial/ethnic group identity and culture. Although the Black and Hispanic groups were able to share several cultural treasures, the White group reported that they had nothing to share. In fact they confessed that for about half of the allotted the time, they sat silently looking at each other trying to figure out how to start the conversation. When confronted with the reality of their Whiteness, these students were at a loss to see anything positive.

White Antiracist Allies

Reflecting on the research of Janet Helms,[10] Beverly Tatum writes that in addition to opposing racism the "task for Whites is to develop a positive White identity based on reality, not on assumed superiority."[11] The White antiracist activist Tim Wise[12] has pointed out that White people have few models of how they are to live and act against the racism of our day. However, whenever racism is discussed in formal or informal settings, most often the legacies of courageous men and women of color

[9] Beverly Tatum, "Teaching White Students about Racism: The Search for White Allies and the Restoration of Hope," *Teachers College Record* 95, no. 4 (Summer 1994): 471.

[10] Janet Helms, *Black and White Racial Identity: Theory, Research and Practice* (Westport, CT: Greenwood, 1990).

[11] Tatum, *Why Are All the Black Kids*, 94.

[12] Tim Wise, *White Like Me: Reflections on Race from a Privileged Son* (Brooklyn, NY: Soft Skull Press, 2011).

are invoked. Antiracist heroes such as Rosa Parks, Martin Luther King Jr., Septima Clark, Cesar Chavez, Malcolm X, and Fannie Lou Hamer are celebrated, as they should be. These men and women stood up to racist laws and practices despite facing the threat of imprisonment, torture, and even death; for their courage and stamina they are rightly celebrated.

However, there is also a history of Whites who resisted the temptations of White power and privilege, and chose to align themselves with People of Color seeking to bring about racial justice. These White people were moved by the passion and justice of the antiracist cause and transgressed the mores of their time to support the efforts toward dismantling racism that were being led by their brothers and sisters of color. Often their actions were the result of a long process of growing awareness that eventuated in their acting against the formal and informal rules of their racist environment. Many of these folks suffered for their choices, and some even died. These relatively unknown White people provide an alternative model of Whiteness: the model of the White ally.

Tatum defines the White ally as "an antiracist activist, a white man or woman who is clearly identifiable to People of Color in the struggle against racism."[13] Frances Kendall[14] adds that allies are inherently agents of change. Andrea Ayvazian[15] expands on these ideas by adding that the ally works to "dismantle any form of oppression from which she or he receives benefit" and consciously takes responsibility for the changes needed in society to challenge the prevailing patterns of oppression. These actions include making invisible privilege visible and working to facilitate the empowerment of those persons limited or injured by oppressive social structures. In her study of contemporary White antiracist activists, Becky Thompson found that allies were consistently people engaged in a "living practice of crossing borders—racial, cultural, and spiritual."[16] As a Black colleague of Cynthia Brown succinctly put it, the "white ally is one who stands beside you and goes with you as to war."[17]

---

[13] Tatum, "Teaching White Students about Racism," 462.

[14] Frances Kendall, *Understanding White Privilege: Creating Pathways to Authentic Relationships across Race*, 2nd ed. (New York: Routledge, 2012).

[15] Andrea Ayvazian, "Interrupting the Cycle of Oppression: The Role of Allies as Agents of Change," in *Beyond Blackface: Africana Images in US Media*, 2nd ed., ed. Akil Houston (Dubuque, IA: Kendall Hunt, 2007), 625.

[16] Becky Thompson, *A Promise and a Way of Life: White Antiracist Activism* (Minneapolis: University of Minnesota Press, 2001), 329.

[17] Carol Stokes Brown, *Refusing Racism: White Allies and the Struggle for Civil Rights* (New York: Teachers College Press, 2002), 5.

Because by definition the White ally works to dismantle structures that serve his or her racial self-interest and social power, some consider the concept of the White ally to be meaningless, advocating instead for Whites to become "race traitors." From their perspective the only purpose of the social construct of Whiteness has been to exclude those who are not White, and therefore the construct of Whiteness needs to be abandoned because it is inherently problematic for anyone seeking to undo racism and the White supremacy from which it emanates.[18] In a similar vein, Tim Wise[19] calls on Whites to participate in racial treason, suggesting that to work for racial justice is to betray one's allegiance to the White race as it is presently constituted. He further suggests such actions are treasonous because White supremacy is so ingrained in American culture, politics, and economic structure that to oppose White supremacy is to undermine the foundations of American society. Although acknowledging the validity of the analysis that regards antiracist activities by Whites as inherently treasonous and traitorous, Whites who theoretically abolish Whiteness from their minds are still perceived as White by the wider society and enjoy the privileges of Whiteness simply by their participation in that society. Thus, the term "White ally," despite its limitations, seems to be more authentic and realistic, given the status conveyed by Whiteness in North American society.

Mark Warren also sees limitations in the term "White ally" because the term leaves White antiracist activists "stuck in the middle," between being socially and racially identified as White and being politically allied with People of Color. He further points out that the term "ally" assumes the battle against racism is only on behalf of People of Color who suffer the effects of White supremacy and racism, and that Whites are merely supporting someone else's struggle. He argues that the goals of antiracist activism need to go further to the point where Whites seek racial justice in a way that becomes central to their own values and well-being and that they seek to create a common political identity for racial justice that is multiracial.[20]

Dr. Omi Osun Joni L. Jones agrees with Warren's perspective. In a 2011 address before a gathering of members of the Pedagogy and Theater of the Oppressed conference, Dr. Jones described allies as people who recognize that various forms of discrimination (racism, sexism, and

---

[18] Ibid.

[19] Tim Wise, *Speaking Treason Fluently: Anti-Racist Reflections from an Angry White Male* (Brooklyn, NY: Soft Skull Press, 2008).

[20] Warren, *Fire in the Heart.*

homophobia) are largely structurally based and therefore those allies must work with the targets of discrimination to change those structures. However, they do so not only because they simply want to help the "other" but also because they recognize that a world free of oppression is a world of dignity, equality, humanity, and justice, and therefore is a better world for all people, regardless of their social position.[21] As an anonymous Australian aboriginal activist has said, "If you have come here to help me, then you are wasting your time, but if you have come because your liberation is bound up in mine, then let us work together." This is ultimately the position of the ally.

My conviction is that White people who have become sensitized to the challenges of racism can be encouraged by stories of White antiracist allies who have gone before them. These stories provide models and examples as to how Whites today must face the challenges of White privilege and White supremacy. Whites who have become aware of the horrific history of White oppression of People of Color need to know that despite that awful history, there were people who saw beyond their "White blinders"[22] and took actions toward racial justice in their time. These White antiracist allies bucked the trends of their time, and for that they need to be remembered. I am in no way suggesting that they were somehow without prejudices and flaws, for indeed they had their prejudices and flaws. However, despite those flaws, the very fact that they lived as they did can give Whites hope that even though they may still struggle with the effects of conscious and unconscious racism throughout their lives, they too can join the forces for reconciliation and justice.

Telling the Stories

In telling the stories of these White antiracist allies, I do not want to suggest that their efforts surpass the accomplishments of those courageous People of Color who have always had to lead the way. Recently, there have been a number of popular films such as *The Help*, *The Blind Side*, and *Freedom Writers*, which tell the true stories of courageous White people who advocated on behalf of People of Color struggling under the weight of racist oppression. However, too often the implied message of these

---

[21] Omi Osana Jones, "The Role of Allies" (presentation at the Pedagogy and Theater of the Oppressed Conference, Chicago, July 2011).

[22] I first came across this term in reading Spencer Perkins and Chris Rice, *More Than Equals: Racial Healing for the Sake of the Gospel*, rev. and exp. ed. (Downers Grove, IL: InterVarsity Press, 2000).

films has been that those poor People of Color just could not have made it without the help of some good White folks. I want to state emphatically that is not my intent. Rather, I hope to show that throughout the history of racism there have been White folks who have been willing to follow courageous People of Color in their fight for justice, and that they chose to use the power and access that their Whiteness afforded them to work for a racially just society. As will be shown, these persons exhibited many flaws and in some cases only came to their antiracist stance after decades of actively promoting racist structures and enjoying the benefits those structures provided. In some cases aspects of their moral character or emotional health may seem suspect. Yet despite those shortcomings the people highlighted in this book came to a place in their lives where they took an active stance to oppose the racist practices and policies of their day, sometimes at great personal cost.

I also want to say a word about language. In his study of Whites who worked against racism, Warren uses the term "racial justice activist" rather than "antiracist activist," choosing to focus on what the activists were working for rather than what they were working against.[23] I have chosen to use both words, sometimes interchangeably, because in some cases the embedded power and pressure of racism is so great that the best one can do is push back against it. However, as Warren points out, the ultimate goal of all persons fighting racism, regardless of color, is to create a just society where race does not determine one's social position and to move toward Martin Luther King Jr.'s vision of the "Beloved Community."

Finally, I want to make clear that the people whose stories I will tell are part of a personal list of White antiracist allies who have inspired me, and in no way is the list exhaustive. Even my personal list of White allies far exceeds the number of people profiled here. As I have told several people, I began writing this book with the goal of telling fifteen to twenty stories, but I now could tell close to fifty! This is why I provide an appendix at the end of the book with other White antiracist allies whose commitments are also worthy of honorable mention. My hope is that these stories will inspire the telling of other stories, many of which may be known in only limited circles. Moreover, I hope that Whites and People of Color reading this book can see that, despite the horrific history of White racism over the past five hundred years, there is also a legacy of opposition by White antiracist allies from whom we can learn and in whose steps we can follow.

---

[23] Warren, *Fire in the Heart.*

Discussion Questions

1. If you are White: To what extent do you identify with the characterization Tatum gives of the "guilty White person"? If you are a Person of Color: How would you characterize the identity of the White people you know who express concern about racism?
2. Can you think of a nationally known White person who would be considered an antiracist activist? To what extent do you think White people need to learn the stories of White antiracist allies in history?

Bibliography

Alexander, Michelle. *The New Jim Crow: Mass Incarceration in the Age of Colorblindness*. New York: New Press, 2011.

Ayvazian, Andrea. "Interrupting the Cycle of Oppression: The Role of Allies as Agents of Change." In *Beyond Blackface: Africana Images in US Media* 2nd ed., edited by Akil Houston, 233–39. Dubuque, IA: Kendall Hunt, 2007.

Bell, Derrick. *Faces at the Bottom of the Well: The Permanence of Racism*. New York: HarperCollins, 1992.

Brown, Cynthia Stokes. *Refusing Racism: White Allies and the Struggle for Civil Rights*. New York: Teachers College Press, 2002.

Fredrickson, George. *Racism: A Short History*. Princeton, NJ: Princeton University Press, 2002.

Helms, Janet. *Black and White Racial Identity*. Westport, CT: Greenwood, 1990.

Jones, Omi Osana. "The Role of Allies." Presentation at the Pedagogy and Theater of the Oppressed Conference, Chicago, July 2011.

Kendall, Frances. *Understanding White Privilege: Creating Pathways to Authentic Relationships Across Race*. 2nd ed. New York: Routledge, 2012.

Kozol, Jonathan. "An Unequal Education." *School Library Journal*, 46, no. 10 (May 2000): 46–49.

McIntosh, Peggy. "White Privilege and Male Privilege: A Personal Account to See Correspondence through Work in Women's Studies." In *Critical White Studies: Looking Behind the Mirror*, edited by Richard Delgado and Jean Stefancic, 291–99. Philadelphia: Temple University Press, 1988.

Perkins, Spencer, and Chris Rice. *More Than Equals: Racial Healing for the Sake of the Gospel*, rev. and exp. Downers Grove, IL: InterVarsity Press, 2000.

Shaffer, Dale. *Salem: A Quaker City History*. Charleston, SC: Arcadia, 2002.

Smedley, Audrey, and Brian Smedley. "Race as Biology Is Fiction, Racism as a Social Problem Is Real: Anthropological and Historical Perspectives on the Social Construction of Race." *American Psychologist* 60, no. 1 (January 2005): 16–26.

———. *Race in North America: Origin and Evolution of a Worldview*. Boulder, CO: Westview Press, 2012.

Stapleford, John. "A Torturous Journey: The Condition of Black America." *Christian Scholars Review* 37, no. 2 (Winter 2008): 231–51.

Takaki, Ronald. *A Different Mirror: A History of Multicultural America*. Rev. ed. New York: Back Bay Books, 2008.

Tatum, Beverly. "Teaching White Students about Racism: The Search for White Allies and the Restoration of Hope. *Teachers College Record* 95, no. 4 (Summer 1994): 463–76.

———. *Why Are All the Black Kids Sitting Together in the Cafeteria, and Other Conversations about Race*. New York: Basic Books. 1997.

Thompson, Becky. *A Promise and a Way of Life: White Antiracist Activism*. Minneapolis: University of Minnesota Press, 2001.

Warren, Mark. *Fire in the Heart: How White Activists Embrace Racial Justice*. New York: Oxford University Press, 2010.

Wilson, William Julius. "Inner-City Dislocations." *Society* 35, no. 2 (January/February 1998): 270–77.

Wise, Tim. *Speaking Treason Fluently: AntiRacist Reflections from an Angry White Male*. Brooklyn, NY: Soft Skull Press, 2008.

———. *White Like Me: Reflections on Race from a Privileged Son*. Brooklyn, NY: Soft Skull Press, 2011.

Abolitionists and the Underground Railroad

1

JOHN WOOLMAN
(1720–1772)

*A Lone Clear Voice**

A Lone Clear Voice

In 1758 the Philadelphia Yearly Meeting (Society of Friends) met to discuss whether or not as Quakers they should engage in the commonly accepted practice of owning Africans as slaves. The discussion got quite heated and the atmosphere tense, as some members did not like being challenged on something they considered their personal prerogative. In their midst that evening was a man named John Woolman, who was known to be a vocal opponent of slavery and a strong advocate for Quakers relinquishing their slaves. At one point in the meeting, Woolman rose to speak and issued one of the strongest public statements he had ever made on the matter, saying,

> In infinite love and goodness, [God] hast opened our understanding from one time to another concerning our duty towards [the slaves], and it is not a time for delay. Should we now be sensible of what

---

* No known photo of John Woolman is known to exist. The image above depicts, "The Quaker," by Harry Rosin (1942), a statue that stands in the Ellen Phillips Samuel Memorial Garden, Kelly Drive, Fairmount Park, Philadelphia. Photo used by permission of Dr. Nathan Corbitt. The sources used for this chapter are primarily Phillips P. Moulton, "John Woolman's Approach to Social Action—As Exemplified in Relation to Slavery," a paper presented at the American Academy of Religion, 1965; Phillips P. Moulton, ed., *The Journal and Major Essays of John Woolman* (New York: Oxford University Press, 1971); and Michael L. Birkel, *A Near Sympathy: The Timeless Quaker Wisdom of John Woolman* (Richmond, IN: Friends United Press, 2003).

> [God] requires of us, and through a respect to the private interest of some persons or through a regard to some friendships, which do not stand on an immutable foundation, neglect to do our duty in firmness and constancy, still waiting for some extraordinary means to bring about [the slaves'] deliverance, God may by terrible things in righteousness answer us in this matter.[1]

In other words, if we don't do something, God will, and it won't be pretty! That same year the Philadelphia Yearly Meeting passed a resolution expelling members who engaged in the slave trade and appointed a committee to visit slaveholders and persuade them to release their slaves.[2]

The Slave Trade in the Colonial Era

In Woolman's time the Atlantic slave trade was a booming business in England, Spain, Portugal, and their Western colonies. Despite the apparent incongruity of religious leaders owning and endorsing slavery, the Church of England was actively complicit in the trade that brought an estimated 40,000 slaves per year from Africa to England and her colonies during the eighteenth century. The church itself even managed sugar plantations with slaves in Barbados and used the revenue for church activities. Anglican clergymen in the Caribbean were generally indifferent to the indignity suffered by the slaves in their midst. Others, such as the evangelist George Whitfield, expressed disapproval of slavery and yet still owned slaves. Although Baptists and Methodists sought to evangelize the slaves, those efforts did not include a call for masters to grant them their freedom.

The first Africans came to North America at Jamestown, Virginia, in 1621 not as slaves but as indentured servants, who after their designated time of service enjoyed the rights of free citizens. The first Blacks in America were able to purchase land, vote, hold public office, and even own slaves of their own. In 1625 the first census in Virginia registered 23 Blacks as citizens of the new settlement. Colonies from South to North registered among their free citizens former Black indentured servants. Free Blacks were able to vote until the early 1700s in colonies such as Virginia, North Carolina, South Carolina, and Georgia. However, the

---

1 Moulton, "John Woolman's Approach," 401–2.

2 Herbert Aptheker, "The Quakers and Negro Slavery," *Journal of Negro History* 25, no. 3 (1940): 331–62.

status of Blacks began to change in 1660 when both Virginia and Maryland enacted laws making Blacks slaves for life and forbidding interracial marriage. These laws were promoted and driven by the economic interests of the ruling elites and wealthy landowners who wanted to maximize profits with cheap labor. Soon other colonies followed suit, and by 1710 there were approximately 50,000 African slaves in the colonies. By 1776 that number would grow to half a million.[3]

When the slave statutes were first established, the justification given was that Africans were "heathens" and thus not protected by normal Christian theological sentiments. Some religious leaders even went so far as to teach that it was a sin to baptize slaves. However, because by 1660 many of the Africans had already converted to Christianity, this argument lost its weight. The rationale then became that it was a Christian's duty to convert and baptize slaves, but baptism was no longer believed to change their legal status. As Virginia law stated, "The conferring of baptism doth not alter the condition of the person as to his bondage or freedom."[4]

In Woolman's Pennsylvania, slavery had been established by the Dutch and the Swedes before William Penn arrived in 1682. In one of his initial acts Penn declared that Africans would be free after fourteen years, but this decree was never fully observed even by Penn. Among the Mennonites and the Quakers slavery had always been an issue of controversy. At first the Quakers sought simply to regulate slavery so as to retard its growth. The minutes of the yearly meetings in the early 1700s reveal debates among the Friends over the morality and practicality of the slave trade. Even so, the number of slaves in the colony continued to increase from between 2,500 and 5,000 in 1720 to 11,000 or more by 1750. Although some individuals were known to have freed their slaves, no legislation outlawing slavery was passed in Pennsylvania until 1780.[5]

Overall, despite occasional statements expressing disapproval of the practice of slavery, the Quakers were largely silent on the issue, and many Quakers were actually slave owners.[6] In this social and religious

[3] Lerone Bennet, *Before the Mayflower: A History of Black America,* 6th ed. (New York: Penguin Books, 1987), 34–54.

[4] Ibid., 46.

[5] W. E. B. Du Bois, *The Philadelphia Negro: A Social Study* (1899; Philadelphia: University of Pennsylvania Press, 1996), 10–17.

[6] James Walvin, "Slavery, the Slave Trade and the Churches," *Quaker Studies* 12, no. 2 (2008): 189–95.

environment John Woolman is best remembered for having convinced his fellow Quakers to abandon the practice of owning slaves. From 1743 until his death in 1772, Woolman labored tirelessly to influence Quaker slaveholders to set their slaves free and to work for the abolition of slavery throughout the thirteen American colonies. There were some who had spoken against slavery before Woolman. For instance, George Fox, the founder of the Quakers in England, had denounced slavery as early as 1673. Samuel Sewall from Massachusetts published an antislavery tract in 1700, as did a Quaker named Ralph Sandiford in 1729. Quakers in Nantucket, Massachusetts, had voiced opposition to slavery as early as 1706 and in Germantown, Pennsylvania, as early as 1688. During Woolman's lifetime the Philadelphia Quaker Anthony Benezet was considered the most influential voice on the antislavery question. However, most historians today would agree with Frederick B. Tolles when he wrote, "More than any other single influence, it was Woolman's clear and steady voice that woke the conscience of the Quakers and ultimately through them, of the Western world to the moral evil of slavery."[7]

Awakening to the Evil of Slavery

John Woolman was born in 1720, the fourth of thirteen children born to Samuel and Elizabeth Woolman, who lived and worked on a farm in Burlington County, New Jersey. His parents were devout Quakers and members of the Philadelphia Yearly Meeting. Quaker religious training was integral to young John's daily life. This included regular reading of the Bible and "other religious books," as well as weekly participation in Quaker silent worship. After attending the village school for ten years, John worked on his father's farm until the age of twenty-one, when he left home to work in a retail store in nearby Mt. Holly, New Jersey. He eventually succeeded in setting up his own store. Over his lifetime he worked as a tailor, a surveyor, a lawyer, a teacher, and a farmer. He was also a husband and father of two children, one of whom died in infancy.

When he was twenty-three, two seemingly unrelated events changed the direction of John Woolman's life. The first event was his designation as a Quaker minister. Unlike many Christian denominations, the Quakers did not have official clergy set apart for leading the religious

---

[7] Frederick B. Tolles, Introduction to *Journal of John Woolman and A Plea for the* (New York: Corinth Books, 1961), viii.

services. All Friends were considered potential ministers in the broader sense of serving God and the world. However, when one was believed to have been granted a special "gift" of wisdom and insight to share with others, that person was "recorded" as a minister, thus recognizing this special giftedness. Thus in 1743 at the age of twenty-three, John Woolman was recorded as a Quaker minister, even though by his own admission after the designation he did not speak up in meetings for worship for nearly a year. However, having been so identified, he was allowed to go on "missionary journeys" on behalf of the wider Society of Friends to visit other Quaker gatherings. This freedom to travel and share with other Friends became critical, given the other significant experience that same year.

Around this same time Woolman was working in a store and was instructed by his employer to write a bill of sale for a Black slave woman, thereby transferring her as property from his employer to another man. He described the experience this way:

> My employer, having a Negro woman, sold her and desired me to write a bill of sale, the man being waiting who bought her. The thing was sudden; and though I felt uneasy at the thought of writing an instrument of slavery for one of my fellow creatures . . . through weakness I gave way and wrote it; but at the executing of it I was so afflicted in my mind that I said before my master and Friend that I believed slave-keeping to be a practice inconsistent with Christian religion.[8]

Woolman realized his complicity in this unjust practice and went on to write that speaking up "in some degree, abated my uneasiness; yet as often as I reflected seriously upon it I thought I should have been clearer if I had desired to be excused from it, as a thing against my conscience."[9] Eventually, Woolman's intent simply to avoid participation in slave transactions became a more active campaign to eliminate the slave trade altogether.

As he later wrote in his journal, he realized that there was deep conflict between his professed faith and values and his participation, even if indirectly, in the practice of slaveholding. Reflecting on the harsh

---

[8] John Woolman, *The Journal of John Woolman* (1774; Christian Classics Ethereal Library, 2007). See http://www.ccel.org.

[9] Ibid.

treatment of African slaves and the violence against Native Americans, Woolman wrote: "I was led into a close and laborious inquiry whether I, as an individual, kept clear from all things which tended to stir up or were connected with wars either in this land or in Africa; my heart was deeply concerned that in future I might . . . walk in the plainness and simplicity of a sincere follower of Christ."[10]

Campaign against Slavery

Using his newly appointed status as a recorded minister, Woolman began to visit other Quaker meetings and individuals to speak about the evils of slavery. Over the course of his life he traveled up and down the East Coast from New England to North Carolina. While he sometimes spoke at public gatherings, and on one occasion addressed a legislative body in Newport, Rhode Island, Woolman's most frequent and influential approach was visiting and talking face-to-face with individual slaveholding families. According to Moulton, "Over a period of 30 years he systematically visited leading slaveholders, urging them to consider seriously the unethical aspects of the [slaveholding] system in which they were involved."[11] Even though as a minister he was offered free room and board in the homes where he stayed, Woolman insisted on paying the slaves for the services they rendered him. Later in his life, when he began to link the slave trade to the economic benefits it provided, he refused to eat foods with sugar, molasses, and other goods specifically secured through the slave trade. He even went as far in his later years to wearing clothing without dyes as a call to simplicity and plain living.

The basis of John Woolman's stance against slavery issued from his belief in the sacredness of all life and the basic conviction that all human beings are created in the image of God and therefore equal. Woolman also advocated friendly relationships with Native Americans and deplored warfare, equally countercultural stances as his stance against slavery. He viewed the Black slaves as "children of God" and as the same blood and race as White people. Thus, to subordinate them and treat them as chattel was to dehumanize them. In one conversation a man from Virginia suggested that though slavery was onerous, he believed that the slaves were better off having been taken from

---

[10] Thomas S. Kepler, ed., *The Journal of John Woolman* (New York: World, 1954), 403.

[11] Moulton, "John Woolman's Approach," 404.

their native land than to have stayed in their original state. However, anticipating what today is called "internalized oppression," Woolman wrote, "Placing on men the ignominious title SLAVE, dressing them in uncomely garments, keeping them to servile labour, in which they are often dirty, tends to gradually fix a notion in the mind that they are a sort of people below us in nature."[12] Thus, in clear contrast to the prevailing belief in Africans as less than fully human, Woolman saw that it was not that Africans were inherently inferior to Whites, but rather that it was the oppression of slavery that caused people to live and act in less than fully human ways.

At the same time Woolman saw the negative impact slavery had on the slaveholders themselves in that it caused them to live in violation of their own ethical standards and gave them a false sense of superiority. Slaveholding caused an "'increase of inquietude' and the growth of 'a spirit opposite to that meekness and humility which is the sure resting place for the soul'"[13] and a rationale for greed and a love of comfort at odds with their higher nature. Woolman's larger concern was that as people of faith, Friends should seek to live their lives in accordance with God's will in all areas of life. Moreover, slaveholding provided a negative example to outsiders and inhibited those outside the Quaker faith from seeing the spiritual benefits of sincere religious faith.

Sometimes his interlocutors argued that in treating their slaves with kindness they were seeking the good of their slaves, even though they were being kept in servitude. Woolman replied that

> if compassion on the Africans in regard to their domestic troubles were the real motives of our purchasing them, that spirit of tenderness being attended to would incite us to use them kindly, that as strangers brought out of affliction their lives might be happy among us; and as they are human creatures, whose souls are as precious as ours and who may receive the same help and comfort from the Holy Scriptures as we do; we could not omit suitable endeavors to instruct them therein.[14]

In other words, Woolman accused the so-called kind slaveholders of being either dishonest or self-deceived.

---

[12] Moulton, *Journal,* 221.

[13] Moulton, "John Woolman's Approach," 400.

[14] Moulton, *Journal*, 61–62.

This last example shows the gentleness and wisdom with which Woolman made his antislavery argument. While remaining firm in his convictions, he usually did not confront his listeners head on, but rather sought to raise their awareness by pointing out the incongruity between their stated beliefs and their practice of slaveholding. Once this awareness was raised, Woolman left it to their consciences to make the changes in behavior that were required.

As he continued in his antislavery efforts, Woolman came to the conviction that the slave economy in its broadest sense was also against his basic ethical and religious principles. On a trip to Maryland in 1757, he became so vexed by the prevalence of slavery throughout the colonies, he decided he could no longer accept the hospitality of slave owners or their slaves. It was not enough for him to talk with the owners at the supper table or to pay for the services of slaves; he felt hypocritical to receive any kind of services as long as a landowner held slaves on his farm. Moreover, he got to the point where he would not accept transportation provided by slaves. Thus, on a trip in 1757 to the Southern colonies he walked most of the way to avoid indirectly benefiting from the work of slaves. He had come to the place where he could no longer participate in any activities that in any way supported the practice of slavery, and so he began refusing cakes and sweetened tea, since they too were made with sugar procured through the Caribbean slave trade.

While Woolman's words were powerful and convinced many Quakers to set their slaves free, he primarily sought to teach by example. Those who knew Woolman knew him to be a man of great integrity, who sought to embody ethical and spiritual purity in all his endeavors. He was also known to be emotionally balanced, not given to outbursts; he argued with reasonableness. Even those who disagreed with him felt regarded with sincere love and a spirit of gentleness. However, most evident was his humility. He routinely approached his Quaker elders with respect and was quick to point out how far short he fell from the standards of life and decency to which he called others. He did not exempt himself for the complicity with slavery of which he accused others, and he routinely submitted himself to others as one who needs to correct his own life of the evils he was battling. Moulton contends that it was these "distinct qualities of Woolman's character and personality which help account for his effectiveness."[15] In contemporary parlance, he was a man who "walked his talk."

---

[15] Moulton, "John Woolman's Approach," 410.

Words and Witness

Woolman also influenced others through his writing. Journal-keeping was a common Quaker practice and enabled people to relate their experiences and teachings after they passed on. Much of what we know about John Woolman today comes from his journals, which were published after his death. In these journals Woolman left a record of his experiences and reflections on his efforts at persuasion.

In addition to his journals Woolman wrote two specific pamphlets addressing the evils of the slave trade, *Considerations on the Keeping of Negroes* (1753) and *Considerations on Keeping Negroes, Part Second* (1762). Even though the Society of Friends offered to publish the tracts, Woolman insisted on financing the publication himself because he knew that there were still slaveholders among the Society of Friends who would not support their distribution. Self-publishing allowed him to maintain control of the content and distribution and enabled him to give the tracts away for free or sell them at cost.

In these tracts, his main arguments were as follows: all people are of the same human nature and are called to live in harmony with each other; and slavery introduced discord into that God-intended harmony. Furthermore, he stated that keeping others as slaves was patently wrong and that the slave economy would ultimately be detrimental to the good of the country because it was "carried on in the wrong Spirit."[16] In a particularly poignant section of *Part Second*, Woolman called on his readers to consider how they would feel if a child of a deceased parent was sold into slavery and how unjust they would consider such an action. Yet when such a thing happened to a Black person, Whites sought to justify the action. Woolman concluded by noting that "where false ideas are twisted in our minds, it is with difficulty we get fairly disentangled."[17] Woolman's words turned out to be painfully prophetic since more than two hundred years later, we are still seeking to undo the damage that slavery inflicted on our national spirit and the damage caused by the way in which racism has warped our ability to understand and relate to people of different races and ethnicities.

In 1772 Woolman traveled to England to convince the London Yearly Meeting to come out in opposition to the slave trade. The English found his manner confusing and his idiosyncratic dress to be peculiar.

---

[16] Ibid., 213.

[17] Moulton, *Journal*, 213, 225.

Even so, he was well received by his British hosts. While in London, he contracted smallpox and was confined to a bed, yet continued writing in his journal during what turned out to be the last weeks of life. Close associates attended to him and recorded his final sayings even after he lost his eyesight. John Woolman died in England on October 17, 1772. Long after his death, Woolman's writings were widely read and were credited with encouraging the abolitionist movement in England following the British defeat in the American Revolutionary War.[18]

His Enduring Legacy

On January 1, 1808, a Black pastor from New York named Peter Williams delivered an antislavery sermon in which he referred to John Woolman as one who had lived a "pattern of piety and brotherly kindness [adopted by] the humane of every denomination."[19] In 1847 John Greenleaf Whittier spoke of John Woolman as "God's voice against the desecration of His image."[20] Largely through the attributions of Whittier, John Woolman has been heralded as a great champion against slavery. Even though during his life he never ventured his arguments beyond the Society of Friends, his example has long since been an inspiration to many fighting the evils of racism.

Woolman's biographer Phillips Moulton points out that John Woolman "always identified himself with the oppressed,"[21] be they slaves, Native Americans, or impoverished Whites, while approaching slaveowners with a forthright conviction in the evils of slavery not only to the slave but also to the slave owner and the nation's economy as a whole. John Woolman's enduring legacy is that he did not succumb to the practices or attitudes of his time, but spoke openly and clearly even though it was over one hundred years before the nation in which he lived would abolish the practice of slavery, an evil whose rippling effects continue to haunt us even today.

---

[18] Geoffrey Plank, "The First Person in Antislavery Literature: John Woolman, His Clothes and His Journal," *Slavery and Abolition* 30, no. 1 (March 2009): 67–91; Walvin, "Slavery," 189–95.

[19] Plank, "First Person," 81.

[20] Ibid., 67.

[21] Phillips P. Moulton, *The Living Witness of John Woolman* (Wallingford, PA: Pendle Hill Publications, 1973).

Discussion Questions

1. John Woolman recognized a value conflict when he was asked to write a bill of sale for a slave. What experiences awakened you to the realities of racism and racial injustice?
2. John Woolman's primary means of persuasion was to speak one on one to slave owners about the injustices of slavery. How might you engage others in conversation about issues of racial injustice?
3. John Woolman drastically changed his lifestyle because of his sensitivity to the ways in which his life was supported by slavery. What lifestyle changes can be made by those concerned about racial justice today?

Bibliography

Aptheker, Herbert. "The Quakers and Negro Slavery." *Journal of Negro History* 25, no. 3 (July 1940): 331–62.

Bennet, Lerone. *Before the Mayflower: A History of Black America.* 6th rev. ed. New York: Penguin Books, 1987.

Birkel, Michael L. *A Near Sympathy: The Timeless Quaker Wisdom of John Woolman.* Richmond, IN: Friends United Press, 2003.

Cadbury, Henry. "An Early Quaker Anti-Slavery Statement." *Journal of Negro History* 22, no. 4 (October 1937): 488–93.

Du Bois, W. E. B. *The Philadelphia Negro: A Social Study.* 1899. Philadelphia: University of Pennsylvania Press, 1996.

Kepler, Thomas S., ed. *The Journal of John Woolman.* New York: World, 1954.

Moulton, Phillips P. "John Woolman's Approach to Social Action—As Exemplified in Relation to Slavery." Paper presented at the American Academy of Religion, 1965.

———, ed. *The Journal and Major Essays of John Woolman.* New York: Oxford University Press, 1971.

———. *The Living Witness of John Woolman.* Wallingford, PA: Pendle Hill, 1973.

Pendle Hill. *Introduction. A Plea for the Poor—John Woolman.* Pendle Hill Pamphlet 357. Wallingford, PA: Pendle Hill, 2001.

Plank, Geoffrey. "The First Person in Antislavery Literature: John Woolman, His Clothes and His Journal." *Slavery and Abolition* 30, no. 1 (March 2009): 67–91.

Reynolds, Reginald. *The Wisdom of John Woolman.* Westport, CT: Greenwood Press, 1981.

Tolles, Frederick B. Introduction to *John Woolman's Journal and A Plea for the Poor.* New York: Corinth Press, 1961.

Walvin, James. "Slavery, the Slave Trade and the Churches." *Quaker Studies* 12, no. 2 (2008): 189–95.

Woolman, J. *The Journal of John Woolman*. 1774. Christian Classics Ethereal Library, 2007. http://www.ccel.org.

2

Angelina Grimké
(1805–1879)

Sarah Grimké
(1792–1873)

*Turning the World Upside Down**

Speaking in the Midst of a Riot

On May 14, 1838, thirty-three-year-old Angelina Grimké married her friend and fellow abolitionist Theodore Weld in a simple Quaker-style service in Philadelphia. Though a native South Carolinian, for several years Angelina had made her home in Philadelphia. Three days later she joined a group of abolitionists in a three-day event held at Philadelphia's

* Images of Angelina Grimké and Sarah Grimké are reproduced from the Library of Congress *LOOK Magazine* photograph collection. Unless otherwise noted the primary sources for this chapter are Catherine Birney, *The Grimké Sisters: Sarah and Angelina Grimké: The First American Women Advocates of Abolition and Woman's Rights* (1885; New York: Haskell House, 1970); Gerda Lerner, *The Grimké Sisters from South Carolina: Rebels against Slavery* (Boston: Houghton Mifflin, 1967); Ellen Reid Gold, "The Grimké Sisters and the Emergence of the Woman's Rights Movement," *Southern Speech Communication Journal* 46, no. 4 (Summer 1981): 341–60.

newly constructed Pennsylvania Hall, a structure specifically designed to give antislavery speakers an uncontested venue in which to present their views. As on numerous other occasions, Angelina was invited to speak, and even though she had just gotten married, she eagerly agreed to do so, as did her new husband. Unbeknown to all involved, this occasion was to be her last public-speaking engagement, as well as the end of Pennsylvania Hall's brief existence.

Angelina had a reputation as an outstanding speaker with a captivating presence and adept use of words that usually drew large crowds of women and men alike. Despite her abilities as a speaker Angelina's presence on the platform was not without considerable controversy. Mid-nineteenth century women were not supposed to engage in public speaking on social and political issues, especially to "promiscuous audiences" of both men and women.[1] Despite her primary focus on the abolition of slavery, Angelina often found herself having to defend her very right to speak in such settings, and thus her presence that night was a double affront to many in Philadelphia. Not only was she speaking out against the long-established institution of slavery, but also as a woman speaking publicly she was stepping into a role traditionally reserved for men. Even some who agreed with her views on slavery objected to her taking the podium publicly to do so.

As she spoke in Pennsylvania Hall, the listeners before her were generally sympathetic, but outside the building a growing crowd of hecklers assembled. When she began to speak, stones came crashing through the glass windows. Angelina remained unfazed and even used the disruption to emphasize that a mob could not deter them from their task of ridding the country of its heinous "peculiar institution." Abolitionists such as Grimké were accustomed to angry mobs and had suffered their wrath on more than one occasion, and so despite the disruption she spoke for about an hour. Even though the catcalls and shouting continued outside, when she sat down, the applause was so loud it "drowned all the noise outside."[2]

However, the next night as the meetings continued and the mob became more violent, and as Philadelphia's mayor and police stood by passively

---

[1] On the origin of the phrase "promiscuous audiences" see Susan Zaeske, "The 'Promiscuous Audience' Controversy and the Emergence of the Early Woman's Rights Movement," *Quarterly Journal of Speech* 81, no. 2 (May 1995): 191–207.

[2] Birney, *Grimké Sisters*, 91.

watching a riot unfold, the hecklers stormed the building, beating the people inside, and burned Pennsylvania Hall to the ground. While she continued to work in various ways against slavery until it was outlawed, Angelina Grimké was never again seen or heard on a public stage.

Beginnings

Born on February 20, 1805, Angelina Grimké was the youngest of fourteen children born to Mary and John Grimké. They lived in Charleston, South Carolina. In the early 1800s Charleston was a major center of the slave trade, serving as a key port where newly arrived slaves were sold on the auction block in the town square before being sent inland. John Grimké was a plantation owner, a veteran of the Revolutionary War, and a Supreme Court judge for the state of South Carolina, which made him a well-respected man at the center of Charleston elite White society. His extensive wealth allowed his family to enjoy a life of luxury, including a full complement of African slaves at their beck and call for any and all things. Though they came to disagree vehemently with their father's slaveholding practices, both Angelina and her older sister Sarah loved and respected him.

Like her father, Angelina's mother came from an elite slaveholding family in Charleston, so that her marriage to John Grimké was something of a royal alliance as well as a marriage. Unlike her gregarious husband, Mary Grimké was reserved and even shy, not venturing much beyond the confines of their vast plantation. As the number of her children increased, Mary became increasingly overwhelmed and often treated the servants harshly in ways that disturbed her children. She became withdrawn, and neither showed nor received much affection from her children.

To truly understand the primary influences on Angelina's transformation from Southern belle to abolitionist, one has to start with Sarah, Angelina's older sister by twelve years. For it was through Sarah's influence that Angelina began to question the morality and legality of enslaving fellow human beings. Sarah was deeply religious and participated regularly in the activities of their family's Episcopal church. However, she found the Episcopalian approach to faith to be extremely formal and dry, and so against family tradition, she left the Episcopal Church and joined the Presbyterians, whose expression of faith was much more vibrant and heartfelt. As a child, Sarah used to play freely with the slave children on their estate, even teaching one girl to read and write against her father's explicit wishes. Yet her sensibilities were often shaken when she would witness her father, brothers, or White overseers whipping a slave for some infraction; she would run out of the house sobbing and wanting to run away. When she was a young child, her parents also gave her a slave girl to wait on her, but Sarah treated her more as a playmate than a servant and was deeply upset when the girl died a few years later. This experience among many others and her strong religious beliefs increasingly caused Sarah to question her father, who would have his slaves baptized in church but then not treat them as equals.

Sarah was close to the members of her family, and so when she was twelve years old her mother gave birth to a little sister, and Sarah developed a strong attachment to her "precious Nina," even being designated as her sister's godmother. Throughout her life, Angelina referred to Sarah as "mother," because Sarah's care nurtured Angelina through the early years of her life. Sarah had aspirations to study law like her older brother Thomas, who went away to Yale Law School. She would listen intently when he would share with her through letters and conversations on his trips home what he was learning. However, the patriarchal culture of their home and community did not allow Sarah to even consider pursuing such a career. So she grew up caring for members of her family with little opportunity for marrying and having a family of her own.

In 1819 when she was twenty-seven, Sarah accompanied her father to Philadelphia to seek medical treatments not available to him in South Carolina. He died shortly after arriving there, and Sarah stayed on and became involved with the Society of Friends (Quakers) in the city. In the Quakers she found a group of people who, like her, considered the institution of slavery to be abhorrent, immoral, and counter to basic Christian teachings. When she finally returned to Charleston, she quickly realized that she wanted to go back to Philadelphia and become a Quaker minister, which meant she would be able to travel as a representative of the Society of Friends around the region. Her devotion to her call was so strong that when a young widower and close friend proposed to her, she refused despite great affection for him. While in Philadelphia, she began a robust correspondence with her younger sister Angelina, who was now an adolescent, and had a profound influence on the younger one's development.

Whereas Sarah tended to be introspective and somewhat prone to self-doubt, Angelina came across as bright, cheerful, and self-assured. From an early age she was prone to speak her mind and respond decisively according to what she thought was right or wrong. Growing up, she did not question slavery. In fact in 1828 (at age twenty-three), she visited Sarah in Philadelphia, and her older sister bemoaned the fact that Angelina saw nothing wrong with the practice of slavery. Like Sarah, she had played with the slave children but did not question whether the slave system was morally justifiable.

However, shortly after returning to Charleston, Angelina came upon a slave woman who was being harassed and ridiculed by two White boys. Angelina attempted to intervene on the woman's behalf, but was threatened with arrest if she did not stop her intervention, and so walked on by. Later she wrote in her journal: "My heart sank within me. . . . My lips were sealed and my soul earnestly craved a willingness to bear the exercise which was laid on me. How long, O Lord, how long wilt thou suffer the foot of the oppressor to stand on the neck of the slave!"[3] This entry, when Angelina was twenty-four, is the first inkling historians have that she was questioning the institution of slavery like her older sister had done.

Another critical experience in Angelina's transformation involved a runaway slave named John. John belonged to Angelina's older brother Henry. She had witnessed her brother flogging John, and when John ran away, she saw it as quite logical that he would run away from such brutal treatment. She implored her brother not to beat John again if and when he was caught, arguing that such treatment could serve no good purpose. Henry listened to his sister and agreed, and when John was captured and returned, he received no further punishment.

As personally vexed as she was with the practice of slavery, at this point in her life Angelina was responding to it primarily on a personal case-by-case basis, but that soon changed. Following in her sister's footsteps, Angelina left her stodgy Episcopal church for the Presbyterians, because she too found the expression and practice of faith there more personally fulfilling. However, as her sensitivity to the horrors of slavery grew, she reasoned that the only way Christians could justify slavery was by "transgressing the laws of God."[4] She brought these concerns to the attention of her Presbyterian pastor, who told he shared her opposition to slavery but responded by saying, "All we can do is pray and wait." Angelina replied, "No, we must pray and work!" Disillusioned by her pastor's tepid response, she went to speak with the church's board of

---

[3] Ibid., 30.

[4] Ibid., 34.

elders, all of whom were slave owners. The elders listened and then told her that she was young and with time she would see the wisdom of their way of life.[5] Shortly thereafter, she stopped attending the church, and despite numerous attempts by the pastor and other members of the church to convince her to return, she eventually was dropped from membership for lack of participation. Like her sister, she then began to consider herself a Quaker, even though there was no active Quaker fellowship in Charleston.

Sarah urged Angelina to join her in Philadelphia, and at first Angelina insisted that she wanted to stay in Charleston and work against slavery so as "to act directly upon it."[6] For several months Angelina tried to convince her friends and family members to set their slaves free; she succeeded only in making everyone angry and uncomfortable with her. Though some agreed with her personal abhorrence about how slaves were treated, none were willing to take concrete steps to alleviate that suffering. During this time Sarah sent her several antislavery publications, including John Woolman's journal,[7] which strengthened her resolve but also increased her isolation from the people around her. Although Angelina was hesitant to leave her siblings and widowed mother, after several pleadings from her older sister she finally departed Charleston for Philadelphia in November 1829 and never returned to Charleston.

Philadelphia

Angelina immersed herself in the life and teachings of the Philadelphia Society of Friends in her first years in Philadelphia. At that time the Quakers were involved in an internal debate between what were called the Hicksite and Orthodox factions.[8] The Orthodox Quakers, which comprised most of the Philadelphia group, tended to focus on simple living, nonparticipation in civic affairs, and remaining separate from non-Quakers; they were also quite sensitive to any actions or statements by their members that they perceived reflected badly on the Quakers as a group. Although historically the Quakers had been on the

---

[5] Gerda Lerner, "The Grimké Sisters and the Struggle against Race Prejudice," *Journal of Negro History* 48, no. 4 (1963): 281–82.

[6] Ibid., 282.

[7] See chapter 1 on John Woolman.

[8] For a full treatment of the Orthodox-Hicksite Controversy, see Hugh Barbour, *Quaker Crosscurrents: Three Hundred Years of Friends in the New York Yearly Meetings* (Syracuse, NY: Syracuse University Press, 1995), 123–25.

forefront of the call for slavery's eradication, the Philadelphia Meeting tended to favor the gradualist views of the American Colonization Society, which called for slaves to be repatriated back to Africa or to be settled in a separate country from the United States; moreover, they tended to segregate the few free Blacks who attended their meetings for worship. This hypocrisy did not sit well with Angelina and Sarah, and they let their views on the issue be known. For a while Angelina taught in a children's school, but when she explored the possibility of attending a teacher training school in Hartford, Connecticut, she was warned against mixing with Presbyterians, many of whom were more outspokenly abolitionist in their speech and actions. Thus she stayed in Philadelphia with her sister within Quaker confines but soon felt stifled.

Meanwhile events and controversies around the issue of slavery heated up across the country. In 1831 a little-known Boston printer named William Lloyd Garrison began publishing *The Liberator*, a radical paper calling for the immediate abolition of slavery and full incorporation of former slaves into US society. That same year in Virginia, a slave named Nat Turner led a rebellion of enslaved and free Blacks that resulted in nearly sixty White people being killed before the rebellion itself was crushed. Simultaneously, the Virginia House Assembly was carrying on a debate on how to end slavery; they spoke of gradual emancipation and repatriation but never immediate release and incorporation, but they were so agitated by Nat Turner's insurrection that no clear decision toward freeing slaves was ever made. As Garrison's message of immediate emancipation spread, violent clashes erupted between pro- and antislavery groups, as well as White rioters terrorizing Black neighborhoods in Philadelphia, New York, and Boston.

The sisters' lives were also severely affected on the personal front. In 1832 a cholera epidemic swept the Eastern United States, killing thousands. Among those who died was a young man Angelina had been seeing and whom she expected to marry. In September 1834 Angelina and Sarah's brother, Thomas, who shared their abolitionist views and who was a leading advocate for peace, died suddenly while on a trip to Ohio. In the midst of all these events, Angelina felt herself internally breaking free from the cocoon her Quaker community was trying to create around her.

Though slavery was not something discussed among the Philadelphia Quakers, Angelina had begun reading *The Liberator* and other abolitionist literature and discovered that they were articulating beliefs she had held but never voiced. Angelina attended her first antislavery meeting in February 1835 at a lecture of the Philadelphia Female Antislavery Society. She officially joined the group a few months later. In July 1835 there was a White riot against a Negro community in Philadelphia, which prompted Garrison to write an appeal to the White citizens of the North to refrain from mob actions against Blacks in their cities. Angelina was so moved by Garrison's words she wrote a personal letter to him in which she expressed her full support for his work. She concluded the letter with these words: "The ground upon which you stand is holy ground; never—never surrender it. If you surrender it, the hope of the slave is extinguished."[9] Without asking her permission, Garrison reprinted the letter in the next issue of *The Liberator*. The letter was subsequently reprinted several times, and in a very brief period through no design of her own Angelina Grimké became a well-known name in abolitionist circles.

Public-Speaking Career

Angelina received condemnation for her public statement from her fellow Quakers and even initially from her protective sister, but she remained undaunted and decided to leave Philadelphia to become fully involved in the antislavery effort. Although Sarah at first resisted, attempting to reconcile her abolitionist views with her Quakerism, she eventually followed her sister. In 1836 Angelina was invited to speak to small groups of women organized in homes in New York by the American Anti-Slavery Society (only men spoke at and attended their larger gatherings). Around that same time she wrote a pamphlet titled *Appeal to the Christian Women of the Southern States*. This work has the distinction of being the only abolitionist tract written by a Southern woman to other Southern women. In it she argued on the basis of the Bible for the eradication of slavery and called on women of the South to free their slaves, to pay them for their work, and to convince their sons, husbands, and fathers to change the laws regarding slavery. Like her letter, this tract was reprinted several times and served to further spread her fame in abolitionist circles. However, when copies of the tract reached her native Charleston, they were burned, and her mother was informed by local authorities that if Angelina ever came home to visit, she would be arrested and held until she could be put on the first boat back north.

---

[9] Angelina Grimké, "Slavery and the Boston Riot," a letter to William L. Garrison (Philadelphia, 1835). Quoted in Lerner, *Grimké Sisters*, 123.

In preparation for a speaking tour in New York, Angelina and Sarah were invited to take part in a three-week "Agents Convention" in Rhode Island. They were the only women among seventy persons who were being trained to take the abolitionist message throughout the northern United States. For eight hours every day they listened to veterans of the abolitionist cause expound on the arguments against slavery, the likely objections they would encounter, and how to respond to the violence and other negative reactions they would most likely face. During this training Angelina heard and then met Theodore Weld, a leading abolitionist spokesman who had worked in the towns of Ohio. She also had a chance to meet Hicksite Quakers, who shared their desire to work in the abolitionist cause, much different than the Orthodox Friends she knew back in Philadelphia.

A few weeks after the training Angelina and Sarah embarked on a series of "parlor talks" in private homes in the Hudson Valley in New York. Sarah outlined the theological and moral arguments against slavery, and Angelina focused on political and organizational actions that the women at the gatherings could take. Although Sarah was considered a competent presenter, listeners were spellbound by Angelina's speaking abilities and her use of stories and metaphors; soon the sisters were much in demand, with Angelina doing the bulk of the speaking. The crowds got so large that they had to move the meetings from homes to local churches. Although this caused consternation among some who felt women should not speak from a pulpit, Weld and other abolitionist leaders prevailed upon them to allow it because of the practical need for larger spaces.

After the New York lectures the sisters did a similar series of lectures with women in New Jersey, and then in the spring of 1837 they were invited to be featured speakers at the Anti-Slavery Convention of Women in New York City. In preparation for that event Angelina made a special appeal for the convention to reach out to African American women in order to show true solidarity as sisters. One of the unique contributions the sisters made at that conference was to highlight the fact that racism needed to be fought in the North as well as the South. They further emphasized that White abolitionist women needed to show their convictions by treating their Black sisters equally. Although many Southerners referred to the Grimkés as "fanatical," their prominence in abolitionist circles continued to grow.

In the summer of 1837 the Grimké sisters traveled to the Boston area at the invitation of the Massachusetts Female Anti-Slavery Society.

They were escorted from town to town, usually speaking in churches or local town halls, and often to crowds of both men and women. Because pastors were afraid that debate over the issue of slavery would divide their congregations, churches often did not allow them to speak in their buildings. Even so, they carried on a rigorous schedule, often speaking to groups of up to a thousand people for several hours at a time. Sarah increasingly saw herself in more of a supportive role to Angelina, who had become the far more accomplished speaker; in that role Sarah attended to her sister's health, which was stressed due to the excessive demands of so much speaking.

Angelina's prominence as an outspoken abolitionist took a huge leap in Amesbury, Massachusetts, when two men interrupted her in the middle of her speech, challenging her description of the slaves' horrid estate. She countered their heckling by challenging the men to debate her in a subsequent meeting the next week. During the debate Angelina deftly dismantled the traditional biblical argument for slavery, by showing that the slave was considered as a person with dignity equal to the master. She then went on to describe the "un-Christian aspects of slavery: the separation of families, the destruction of marriages, the denial of the right to property and the denial of education." She even described what the editor of the *Amesbury Courier* called the "indelicate" issue of the White planters' sexual abuse of the slave women. Although the *Courier* censored her remarks because of this "indelicacy," abolitionist editors distributed her message and her reputation continued to grow.[10]

Even though both Sarah and Angelina focused their messages on the abolitionist cause, their mere public presence before "promiscuous audiences" of both men and women prompted increased opposition to their being women in such a public role. A group of Massachusetts Congregational Ministers passed a resolution denying them the right to speak in their churches. Some men, supportive of the abolitionist cause, wrote them private letters enjoining them to refrain from speaking to mixed audiences so as not to discredit or distract from the antislavery movement. Hecklers, as mentioned earlier, would sometimes harass them as they spoke. While privately and in letters the sisters defended their right as women to speak, they did not respond publicly to these accusations, even as they continued to speak to mixed audiences. Privately, Angelina admitted she was thankful that in their efforts they were "making a break in that wall of public opinion which lies in the

[10] Lerner, *Grimké Sisters*, 179–80.

way of woman's rights."[11] However, in public settings she allowed her eloquence to speak for itself. As one man later wrote after hearing her: "Never before or since have I seen an audience so held and so moved by any public speaker, man or woman, and never before or since have I seen a Christian pulpit so well filled, nor in the pews such absorbed hearers."[12]

The Grimkés' public stand on women's issues came in the form of written tracts. In the summer of 1837 Sarah wrote *Letters on the Equality of the Sexes*, and Angelina included an argument in favor of women's equality in her *Letters to Catherine Beecher,* which were published around the same time. Angelina's letters were written in response to an essay, written by the daughter of a prominent Congregational minister, in which the author criticized the radical stance of the abolitionists and called for a gradual approach to the eradication of slavery. Angelina offered an uncompromising attack on racism and any position that would seek to justify or tolerate slavery. Additionally, she pointed out that any consideration of rights for slaves should open the door for a discussion about the rights of women.

Because of controversy, the American Anti-Slavery Society became concerned that the women's issue might overshadow and dilute the antislavery cause. In a series of letters with Theodore Weld, Angelina argued that the deeper issue was that of free speech. She contended that if women were not restrained by male prejudice, they would be able to accomplish so much more for the abolitionist cause, and that in restraining them, Weld and others were undermining their own objectives. Although the two did not come to any meeting of the minds, they did agree that in public presentations Angelina and Sarah would not put an emphasis on the feminist cause but would remain focused on the antislavery message.

Marriage and a Change in Life

While the sisters continued to speak into the fall of 1837, Angelina came down with a lung disorder that she attributed to exhaustion from so much speaking and so had to refrain from public appearances. During that time she continued to correspond with Weld, whom, despite their prior disagreement, she considered to be a friend and an ally in the abolitionist cause. In the fall that friendship grew into something

[11] Angelina Grimké, letter to Catherine Beecher, July 25, 1837. Quoted in Lerner, *Grimké Sisters*, 183.

[12] Birney, *Grimké Sisters,* 73.

more, when he proposed marriage; she accepted. A wedding date for the spring of 1838 was set in Philadelphia.

The next several months were spent preparing for the wedding, which included purchasing a home and agreeing that Sarah would live with the newly married couple. On May 14, 1838, Angelina Grimké and Theodore Weld were married before a gathering of about fifty friends. The event was deliberately interracial, even being officiated by both a White and a Black pastor. To the Philadelphia public the gathering was considered a scandal because of "amalgamation" (the mixing of races) in a social setting. Because Angelina the Quaker agreed to adopt Weld's Presbyterianism, she was expelled from the Quakers for participating in a religiously mixed marriage. Sarah was excommunicated for merely attending the ceremony.

The newly married couple wanted to show that their marriage would not alter the nature of their abolitionist work, and so three days after the ceremony Angelina spoke at the meeting of the American Female Anti-Slavery Society in the newly constructed Pennsylvania Hall. She spoke on the first day of the three-day convention as was planned, and as described at the beginning of this chapter she did so amid catcalls, rocks, and breaking glass. Because of the combination of the abolitionist message, women speaking in public, and the mixing of races at the meetings, the crowd outside the hall quickly became frenzied. Also as described at the opening of this chapter, the next night the hall was burned down by an angry mob and the meetings canceled.

Married Life

The new couple and Sarah moved to a new home just across the river from New York City in Fort Lee, New Jersey. Sarah and Angelina assisted Weld in doing extensive research on the experiences of slaves in the South by clipping accounts found in Southern newspapers. The result was the publication of Weld's *American Slavery as It Is*, which until the publication of *Uncle Tom's Cabin* in 1852 was considered the most influential antislavery tract in the country. In December 1839, Angelina gave birth to baby boy, and though the baby was healthy, Angelina became quite ill following the birth. Shortly thereafter she became pregnant again and gave birth to a second son in January 1841. As it turned out this second son was born with some sort of physical disability or degenerative chronic disease that plagued him throughout his life and required constant attention and care.

At the same time that Angelina was adapting herself to motherhood and domestic life, the antislavery movement had begun to falter. A rift occurred between those loyal to the radical, absolutist rhetoric of William Lloyd Garrison and those who were more interested in pursuing a political course to reform through the newly formed, antislavery Liberty Party. Other women, who had been inspired by the example of the Grimké sisters, also began to speak out publicly, and the "woman question" further fractured the movement. Although there were petition drives and continued public meetings, the American Anti-Slavery Society experienced financial difficulties, and agents on the payroll had to be let go. Weld himself took a pay cut and had to seek loans from some of his wealthier colleagues in order to buy a farm he had begun purchasing after the birth of their first child.

Although neither the Grimké sisters nor Weld had expected marriage to end Angelina's public life, the strains of the double standard put on ordinary women in the early 1800s became a reality. As Gerder Lerner points out, Angelina and her husband were no longer debating the "woman question," they were living it.[13] Furthermore, Angelina experienced continued medical problems. Weld referred to these problems only in terms of his wife's "invalidism" and a statement that his wife was "twice severely injured" in a way that "[intensified] a lifelong weakness."[14] Sarah also referred several times to her sister's "accident." Lerner contends that this phrase was a euphemism for female-specific medical problems such as a prolapsed uterus or a hernia resulting from pregnancy or miscarriage. Today such problems are easily addressed, but in the mid-1800s these conditions were considered the "normal trials" of a married woman's life and contributed to the notion of their being considered the "weaker sex." Angelina suffered from occasional spells and bouts of weakness. Her condition may have been exacerbated by a strictly vegetarian diet that was popular at the time among educated woman and that which left her severely undernourished.

Much of Angelina's and Sarah's antislavery work took a more personal turn in that they sought to educate Angelina's children on the importance of the issue and to help former slaves, especially those previously owned by their family. Over time they convinced their mother to relinquish her slaves. These freed slaves came North and lived on the Grimké-Weld estate; Weld allowed one family to be tenants on their

---

[13] Lerner, *Grimké Sisters*, 293.

[14] Ibid., 289.

farm, and another one actually lived in the house with them for quite a while. In the midst of all these developments, Angelina also gave birth to a third child, a girl.

By 1844 years of public speaking had finally taken their toll on Theodore Weld's voice, and he too was forced to give up public speaking. Although he continued to write and support others in the antislavery effort, in 1851 they turned their home into a boarding school where Angelina taught history and Sarah taught French. Then in 1853 they were invited to join a utopian community in Raritan, New Jersey, where Weld was hired as the principal of the school and the sisters continued to teach. When the community folded in 1856, they continued the school as a private venture where they enrolled approximately fifty students, many of whom were children of fellow abolitionists.

As she had done throughout her life, Sarah dedicated herself to caring for her younger sister, even to the point of taking on a major portion of the child-rearing responsibilities. However, it appears that at some point the sisters had a falling out, and a long running conflict caused Sarah to move out of the household for a brief time in 1853. Eventually through a series of letters they were able to reconcile, and Sarah lived the rest of her life as part of their household.

The Civil War and Beyond

When the Civil War broke out in 1861, Angelina and Sarah put aside their lifelong pacifism and endorsed the war as "the final stand against the hated slavery system."[15] When Lincoln announced the Emancipation Proclamation freeing all slaves in the South, they wholeheartedly supported it. Angelina returned briefly to public life when she agreed to be the featured speaker at the Women's Loyal National League and spoke on behalf of the Constitutional Amendment to end slavery. The women's movement was divided between those who supported what became the Thirteenth Amendment and those who opposed it. Those who opposed the amendment wanted it to include equality and the vote for women as well as for Black men. During the war, Angelina also wrote *A Declaration of War on Slavery*, which unfortunately has not survived, but which Catherine Birney, a friend and biographer of Grimké's, considered to be her best work.

When the war ended in 1865, Angelina and Sarah reached out to their two sisters still living in Charleston by sending them supplies,

[15] Ibid., 341.

but both of them died shortly after. In 1866 they discovered that their brother Henry (who had died before the war's end) had fathered two sons by one of his female slaves, and had willed the two boys to his son. When they learned of their biracial nephews, the sisters convinced their nephew to release the former slaves and raised funds to enable the two boys to pursue a college education. The first, Archibald Grimké, attended Harvard University and became a lawyer and later ambassador to Haiti, and the second, Francis Grimké, went to Princeton Seminary and became a Presbyterian minister.

Eventually, the family moved to the Boston area, where Angelina and Sarah continued to teach and Theodore did public lecturing and ran a school. On March 7, 1870, the two sisters along with forty other women went to the town hall in Hyde Park, Massachusetts, to cast their vote in a local election. Although it was a small gesture, it was vindication of a life spent seeking to be treated as equals to men. Three years later in December 1873 Sarah died at the age of eighty-one. About that same time Angelina became paralyzed by a series of strokes, and spent six years bedridden until she died in October 1879 at the age of seventy-five. Weld lived another sixteen years until 1895.

Catherine Birney states that from her earliest years Angelina Grimké was "born a radical."[16] Angelina's life and legacy attest to the fact that she never ceased to be a person who pushed the limits of her age with eloquence, passion, and integrity. In April 1838 she was invited to speak before the Massachusetts legislature in historic Faneuil Hall. She spoke for three two-hour sessions before legislators and other onlookers on the topic of abolishing slavery. Later, when reporting on her experience, she commented to a friend: "What the effect of these meetings is to be, I know not. . . . This I do know, that the chairman was in tears almost the whole time I was speaking. We abolition women are turning the world upside down."[17] Like the prophets of old, through their words and actions Angelina and Sarah Grimké pointed to a future all people of all races were called to embrace, and today we are still trying to turn the racism of our society upside down.

---

[16] Birney, *Grimké Sisters*, 28.

[17] Ibid., 87.

Discussion Questions

1. Despite efforts to convince family and friends that slavery was inhumane, Angelina and Sarah Grimké eventually had to leave their home and community in Charleston to pursue their calling. What personal sacrifices might be necessary if we speak out openly and forcefully for racial justice?
2. Despite being an outstanding public speaker, Angelina was often dismissed and harassed because she was a woman. What are ways in which our work against racial injustice is hampered by other prejudices that people hold?

Bibliography

Barbour, Hugh. *Quaker Crosscurrents: Three Hundred Years of Friends in the New York Yearly Meetings*. Syracuse, NY: Syracuse University Press, 1995.

Birney, Catherine H. *The Grimké Sisters: Sarah and Angelina Grimké: The First American Women Advocates for Abolition and Woman's Rights*. 1885. New York: Haskell House, 1970.

Gold, Ellen Reid. "The Grimké Sisters and the Emergence of the Women's Rights Movement." *Southern Speech Communication Journal* 46, no. 4 (Summer 1981): 341–60.

Lerner, Gerda. "The Grimké Sisters and the Struggle against Race Prejudice." *Journal of Negro History* 48, no. 4 (1963): 277–91.

———. *The Grimké Sisters from South Carolina: Rebels against Slavery*. Boston: Houghton-Mifflin, 1967.

Zaeske, Susan. "The 'Promiscuous Audience' Controversy and the Emergence of the Early Women's Rights Movement. *Quarterly Journal of Speech*, 81, no. 2 (May 1995): 191–207.

3

John Rankin
(1793–1886)

*Prophet for Liberty**

The Final Ride Downriver

On a cold night in March 1886, six Black men stood on the wharf of the river town of Ripley, Ohio, and greeted a small boat that had come seventy miles downriver from Ironton. In the boat was the body of John Rankin, former resident of Ripley, who had died at the age of ninety-three after a long slow battle with cancer. After the Civil War, Rankin and his wife had left Ripley and even after all those years away, hundreds of people, both Black and White, traveled to Ripley to pay homage to the man who had changed their lives and their town in profound ways.

Rankin's fifty-one-year-old son, Rev. Arthur Tappan Rankin, presided over his father's service. Six Black men and six White men served as his pallbearers, and a large multiracial crowd followed the hearse as it took Rankin's body to its resting place. In the crowd that day were many people who owed their lives to the man who sixty-five years earlier had come to Ripley as a young Presbyterian preacher. At the time of his funeral, except among those who knew him directly, little was known about him. The complete story of John Rankin became known only after his death because much of his life was cloaked in

---

* Photo of John Rankin provided courtesy of the Ohio History Connection. Unless otherwise noted all information provided in this chapter is based on Ann Hagedorn, *Beyond the River: The Untold Story of the Heroes of the Underground Railroad* (New York: Simon and Schuster, 2002).

secrecy, intrigue, and shadows. Yet when asked who abolished slavery, the famous preacher and fellow abolitionist Henry Ward Beecher replied, "John Rankin and his sons."

Early Years

John Rankin was born on February 4, 1793, in East Tennessee, the fourth son of Jane and Richard Rankin. In that same year three events occurred that were to frame and shape the rest of his life. A few weeks after he was born, the US Congress passed the Fugitive Slave Act, which stated that anyone held in slavery in one state and escaped from his home state could and should be captured and returned to his or her original owner. John Rankin would spend most of his life challenging and breaking that law.

Also in 1793 Eli Whitney patented the cotton gin, a machine that made the processing of cotton much more efficient and therefore profitable. Whitney's invention revived the economy of the Old South and created conditions that exponentially increased the demand for slaves to pick the cotton to be processed.

The third portentous event of that year was a rebellion in Haiti in which slaves took over the island, burned plantations, and drove out the White slaveholders. In the minds of many White Americans, Haiti had been the image of harmony and peace between masters and slaves. The revolt exposed that image as a lie, and White plantation owners fled the island to reestablish their operations in the American South. Fears ran rampant through the slaveholding states as slave owners wondered if American slaves would take the same course as their Haitian counterparts. Thus laws were made stronger and penalties made more severe to protect White American slave owners and the cotton-based economy it was grounded on. Antislavery advocates like Rankin would be accused of undermining American interests and fomenting rebellion for their efforts.

The community in East Tennessee where Rankin spent his childhood was known for its antislavery sentiments, and so he grew up being taught that the holding of slaves was morally wrong. Groups like the Tennessee Society for the Manumission of Slaves called on citizens to set their slaves free and pressed for the gradual abolition of the practice of slavery.

Richard and Jane Rankin had moved their family to Tennessee in 1786 from Virginia. Richard was by trade a farmer, but in his personal life he was a devout Presbyterian who voraciously read any theological text he could get his hands on. Like her husband, Jane was a devout Calvinist who taught her children to live upright and moral lives and to refrain from "worldly" pursuits such as drinking, dancing, smoking, and slavery. Richard voiced his opposition to slavery only when asked, but Jane outspokenly pressed her antislavery views on her children, neighbors, church members, and anyone who would listen. At the same time both of young John's parents highly valued education, and taught him at home and then later sent him away to school, at personal sacrifice to themselves. Thus, John Rankin grew up in an environment "branded with the stern imprint of Calvinism,"[1] and a clear understanding that slavery was morally repugnant, and an affront to one's Christian faith.

Early Years of Ministry

In 1800 when John was seven years old, the religious revival known as the Second Great Awakening found its way to East Tennessee. Richard Rankin brought his whole family to the revival meetings taking place in nearby Dandridge, Tennessee. Although still young for a "conversion" experience, John recalled years later being moved by the outward expressions of spirituality he saw there. That same summer, a slave in Virginia named Gabriel Prosser recruited over a thousand slaves to march on the city of Richmond, killing White slave owners along the way. A torrential rainstorm washed out bridges and roads on their way, and two slaves who saw the weather as a warning from God revealed the plot to the authorities, so that the rebellion was crushed before it started. Prosser and twenty-seven others were executed, and the news spread throughout the South. However for young John Rankin the spiritual freedom he experienced at the tent revival became fused in his mind with the longing for material freedom pursued by Prosser and his followers. That fusion shaped Rankin's theology and his political commitment for the rest of his life.

Though their finances were limited, in 1812 John's parents were able to pay his tuition to go to Washington College in Jonesborough, Tennessee. While there he met Jean Lowry, whom he married in 1816. At the school John found himself at odds with the founder and president, Samuel Doak, who was a slave owner. Although he was a capable student, Rankin's challenge to his teacher's slave-owning practice earned him a critical note when he applied for ordination to the Presbyterian

---

[1] Ibid., 21.

Church, which said in part that he should be "accepted with suspicion and distrust because of his frequent expression of opposition to slavery."[2]

Rankin's early ministry involved traveling to various churches to fill vacant pulpits, where he sought to develop his speaking skills. One time in 1817 he was invited to preach at a church in Union, Tennessee, that was known to have antislavery sentiments. Thinking he was on safe ground to test out his still-developing preaching repertoire, Rankin delivered a strong antislavery sermon. Expecting the church leaders to praise him for his boldness, he was instead quietly advised to not speak about his views on slavery in public, and if he refused to relent, he would be asked to leave. So leave he did, with the intent to head to the free state of Ohio. To pay his way for his wife and children as they traveled, he preached in local churches. After delivering a sermon in the town of Carlisle, Kentucky, he was invited to become the full-time pastor and ended up staying for four years. The church in Carlisle had been a strong antislavery congregation and had joined with twelve other churches to form the Kentucky Abolition Society, in a state that itself was in the throes of a heated battle over whether or not to continue to consider slavery legal. This allowed Rankin to speak often and openly against slavery, and begin his work as an antislavery advocate.

While there he started a school for slave children, believing that if Blacks were educated they could be viewed as equals. For the first year the school operated without incident, but then local opposition developed and teachers and students were threatened. Rankin moved the school from the church building to a member's home, and the controversy died down for a while. However, one night while class was being a held, a mob broke into the house beating the slave children and teachers alike with clubs and guns. The harassment continued off and on for a period of weeks, and eventually slave owners refused to allow their slaves to attend the school, so it was closed.

On New Year's Eve, 1821, Rankin, his wife, and their four children packed up and headed north along the Ohio River. The next morning, New Year's Day, 1822, they pulled their little skiff onto the wharf of the small and rough river town of Ripley, Ohio. Located fifty miles up the Ohio River from Cincinnati, Ripley was founded in 1790 by a Revolutionary War veteran named James Poage who abhorred slavery. Poage's outspoken opposition to slavery attracted other antislavery activists to

---

[2] Ibid., 29.

the town, and a free Black community was established nearby. Nonetheless, the town to which the Rankin family moved was basically a mill town with several saloons that were the site of numerous shootouts and fistfights. Rankin entered the community with the idea of starting a Presbyterian church, but the locals harassed him, and few people dared to attend his church. Rankin's strong preaching against drunkenness, idleness, and slavery only fed the fires of hostility. The opposition got so bad that Rankin considered leaving, but his wife convinced him to stay and make a life.

Letters on Slavery

Although there was no organized system to help slaves escape to safety, runaway slaves regularly crossed from Kentucky into Ohio. Rankin witnessed runaway slaves being caught by slave catchers and returned to the masters; Rankin continued to speak out against the practice. In January 1824, Rankin received a letter from his brother, Thomas, who had come into substantial wealth and purchased a farm and several slaves. Rankin was horrified that his brother would turn his back on the clear antislavery teaching they had received from their parents, and for several months mulled over how he should respond. Proslavery sentiments were running high in the country because of the Missouri Compromise in 1820 and the crushing of a slave rebellion in South Carolina led by Denmark Vesey, a free Black. With these events fresh in his mind Rankin could be silent no longer. He wrote a series of letters to his brother, which were simultaneously printed under the title *Letters on American Slavery* in a local newspaper called *The Castigator*.[3]

In the letters, written and published over a period of six months, Rankin logically laid out a case against slavery that asserted the full humanity of Black people and described the moral deterioration of society by its continued practice of slavery. Although later his arguments would become standard in the abolitionist movement, in 1824 no one had so clearly and unabashedly exposed slavery for the evil that it was. Nearly two centuries later the words of these letters ring with an undeniable power of an Old Testament prophet.

---

[3] Later published as John Rankin, *Letters on American Slavery Addressed to Mr. Thomas Rankin* (1823). The letters are available at http://medicolegal.tripod.com.

He began the first letter in this manner:

> It gave me pleasure to hear of your health, and pain to hear of your purchasing slaves. I consider involuntary slavery a never failing fountain of the grossest immorality, and one of the deepest sources of human misery; it hangs like the mantle of night over our republic, and shrouds its rising glories.[4]

He went on to challenge the prevailing social and scientific theories about Africans' innate inferiority, asserting that Africans are as fully human as Whites and denouncing arguments that their skin color marked them to servitude. He challenged theories of Africans' lesser intelligence by pointing out that the conditions of privation, suffering, and brutality under which slaves lived prohibited them from pursuing and achieving their innate human potential. He attacked the slave industry itself as being tainted by a lust for unjust material gain, which in turn caused slave owners to concoct all sorts of devious and deceitful rationales to justify their evil behavior. He described in detail stories of beatings, whippings, rapes, and forced separations endured by slaves at the hands of their owners. He also showed the hypocrisy of those slave owners who contended they were kind and gracious with their slaves. He reinterpreted biblical passages used by proslavery preachers to legitimate slavery as an institution ordained and allowed by God. He then ended by addressing the various reasons politicians gave for opposing the abolition of slavery such as the fear that social chaos followed. He concluded the letters in words that proved to be prescient of things to come thirty-five years later. He wrote: "The storm is gathering fast—the dismal clouds already begin to darken our horizon. A few more years and the work of death will commence."[5]

On a personal level the *Letters* had their desired effect in that Thomas freed his slaves in 1827 and moved to Ohio. On a more public level the letters faded from view until 1830 when they were picked up by a publisher in New Jersey, and then again 1832 when they were published by the outspoken abolitionist leader William Lloyd Garrison in his newspaper *The Liberator*. They were subsequently republished several times and were widely distributed in abolitionist circles.

---

[4] Ibid., 5.

[5] Ibid., 108.

Light in the Window

The publication of the *Letters* marked Rankin as part of an "abolitionist radical fringe" that threatened to cause disruption in society. During his first years in Ripley, the Rankin family lived on Front Street on the river's shore. Although it is unclear whether at that time he had begun to harbor runaway slaves, slave catchers often pounded on his door at all hours of the night demanding that he hand over slaves in his care. For the safety of his family, Rankin decided to move off Front Street and bought a farm on the top of the bluff above and behind the town. The farm not only provided him the means to earn needed income but also enabled him to build a house with a false floor and a barn in which he could hide runaway slaves. Moreover, on a clear night slaves seeking to find a way to safety could see the house for miles because every night he put a lantern in the window. This vista also afforded him the ability to see slave catchers who might come looking for said runaways, so he could hide them safely and quickly. He constructed a staircase up the hill from the town, as well, to help slaves climb their way to safety. For the nearly forty years leading up to the Civil War, John Rankin and his family of thirteen children helped approximately two thousand slaves escape to freedom by providing them safe passage and shepherding them north to the next stop on the growing system of what came to be called the "Underground Railroad," a network of safe houses leading north through Ohio to Canada.[6]

However, it is important to note that the members of the Rankin family were not the only ones in Ripley participating in the effort to help runaways to freedom. Throughout the town there were people who opened their homes and guided people up the stairs to the Rankin house, who would then transport or guide them further north. Perhaps the most courageous citizen of Ripley was John Parker. Parker was a free Black who had been a slave in Virginia and Alabama and who had bought his own freedom by earning money as a craftsman. Parker moved to Cincinnati and eventually to Ripley where he worked as a blacksmith. However, Parker routinely went out on the river looking for runaways to ferry across the Ohio River from Kentucky to Ohio. He also occasionally traveled into Kentucky seeking ways to help runaways to and across the Ohio River. His exploits became so well known that

[6] See Wilbur Siebert, *The Underground Railroad in Ohio* (Columbus: Ohio Archeological and Historical Publications, 1993). This is a reprint of a pamphlet first written in 1895.

a bounty of $1,000 was placed on his life for either death or capture. Another Rankin associate, a White abolitionist named John Mahan, was arrested and imprisoned by officials in Kentucky for nine weeks because of his Underground Railroad activities. A high-profile trial was held, and he was acquitted with all charges dismissed. Thus although Rankin was the best known of the Underground Railroad conductors, he certainly was not alone in his efforts or in his infamy among slave owners and proslavery advocates.

Perhaps the most famous runaway slave incident occurred in February 1838, when a slave woman from Dover, Kentucky, just five miles from Ripley overheard her master talking about selling her two-year-old child. The next night she ran away with her child and found refuge in the home of an older White man at a place near the river called Stony Point. The woman knew that there were people in Ripley who would help her, and that the river had been frozen; thus she might be able to cross without incident. Though the old man warned her that the river was thawing, she decided that crossing the near-frozen river was her best chance.

As she started down the hill to the river she heard dogs chasing her and ran out onto the ice, only to have it break under her weight. She continued to cross in the frozen water, and collapsed from exhaustion on the Ohio shore. A recalcitrant slave catcher found her, had pity on her, and took her to the outskirts of Ripley. He was reported to have said: "Any woman who crossed that river carrying a baby has won her freedom."[7] Later that night, she made it to the Rankin home, where she was sheltered, warmed, and fed. She related her amazing account of crossing the icy river. When she was warm, they moved her on to the next house on her journey, never to see her again. A year later John Rankin shared the story of the brave mother with his friend Lyman Beecher and his daughter Harriet Beecher Stowe. Harriet was so moved by the story that it became the inspiration for the character Eliza, in her book *Uncle Tom's Cabin,* published in 1850. That book went on to call attention to the evils of slavery to the wider public, but Rankin's role as the source of the story was not revealed until after his death.

---

[7] Hagedorn, *Beyond*, 137.

Other Antislavery Efforts

Since his days of starting a school for slaves in Carlisle, Kentucky, Rankin had believed that education was a key to the abolition of slavery. So in 1828 he founded Ripley College and served as the chairman of the school's board. In 1832 Rankin also became the college president, after the former president died of cholera. By 1831 the school had nearly one hundred students primarily from Ohio and Kentucky. Not only did the sons of many abolitionists attend the school, but also the sons of proslavery Southern sympathizers. Most of the faculty were abolitionists and participated in the work of the Underground Railroad, as did some of the students.

Despite the apparent abolitionist leaning of the school's leaders, Rankin encountered strong opposition to his views on the equal status of Blacks and Whites. In 1831 Ripley College admitted its first Black student, a free Black by the name of Benjamin Franklin Templeton. The first few months following his arrival passed without incident, but one night Templeton was mugged on the main street of Ripley by a drunken man who happened to be the son of a prominent White citizen. A few months earlier in Virginia a runaway slave named Nat Turner had unsuccessfully tried to lead a slave rebellion. Many of the White citizens of Ripley saw Templeton's mugging as retribution for Nat Turner's rebellion. As a result of the mugging, Templeton's presence at the school became a matter of fierce debate. In a compromise move Rankin agreed to withdraw Templeton from Ripley College while simultaneously pledging to tutor him on his own. This became part of a practice in which in his home Rankin personally taught several young Black men seeking an education, even though it was not safe for them at Ripley College. Templeton went on to become an ordained minister in the Presbyterian Church, later pastoring churches in Pittsburgh and Philadelphia.

While Rankin had operated in relative obscurity and secrecy, others such as William Lloyd Garrison, Charles Finney, Lyman Beecher, and Theodore Dwight Weld became the faces and voices of the growing antislavery movement. However, as Hagedorn observes, "The despised abolitionist minority, which was barely a flickering ember in the 1820s was about to become a bonfire in the 1830s."[8] When Garrison published Rankin's *Letters on American Slavery* in *The Liberator*, Rankin became a nationally known figure and was able to make connections with these better-known abolitionists. So in December 1832 he was invited to

[8] Ibid., 67.

attend a meeting in Philadelphia to form a national antislavery society that had as its purpose "the entire abolition of Slavery in the United States."[9] Following the example of abolitionist leaders such as Weld and Garrison, Rankin embarked on a speaking tour throughout Ohio on behalf of the American Anti-Slavery Society. As a result of his efforts and the efforts of others, local affiliates of the society arose in communities throughout the state.

In April 1836 more than two hundred people gathered in Granville, Ohio, to form the Ohio Anti-Slavery Society. Local opposition to the gathering forced them to meet in a barn outside of town. Several resolutions were passed, after which Rankin addressed the gathering. He called upon every Christian church to take a public stand against slavery, to denounce proslavery biblical justifications, and to proclaim that those who supported slavery were committing a sin. Following the meeting the attendees marched into the city intending to demonstrate their views and were met by a mob throwing rotten eggs at them. Soon the violence became more physical, and people were pushed and shoved and even beaten; fortunately no firearms were used, and therefore no one was seriously injured. Later that same year Rankin and others founded the Ripley Anti-Slavery Society without incident. Rankin became part of a group called "The Seventy" and was commissioned to go on antislavery speaking tours, which were often confronted with similar incidences of mob violence.

Because Rankin's home received runaway slaves on a regular basis, the work of the Underground Railroad by necessity became the family business. Rankin's wife and thirteen children worked together to harbor and transport runaway slaves to safety. Some of his children eventually became leaders in the abolitionist movement in their own right. His oldest son, Adam Lowry Rankin (who went by Lowry), initially wanted to be a carpenter and not the clergyman his father desired. However, one day while doing a job on a steamer ship docked at Ripley, he stumbled upon fifty slaves chained together on the lower deck. He was particularly moved by the sight of a young light-skinned woman. He watched and listened as the men on the ship passed by making lewd remarks about her. Lowry became indignant and from that point committed himself to join the abolitionist cause with his father. He eventually attended Lane Seminary in Cincinnati where he was frequently called upon to escort runaway slaves to safe houses north of the city, assisting an estimated

[9] *Declaration of the Anti-Slavery Convention,* assembled in Philadelphia, December 4, 1833, available at https://archive.org/details/constitutionofan00amer.

three hundred slaves while working and studying to earn credentials to become a Presbyterian minister.

Two other sons, Samuel and John Jr., were often called upon to escort runaway slaves to houses further north, sometimes even taking them all the way to Canada. Then of course there was John's wife, Jean, who always provided food to the guests and often fashioned clothing that could be used as coverings and disguises as they moved north. Because Rankin traveled a great deal, the effort to hide and escort runaway slaves went on in his absence, and more than once his wife and children were accosted by slave catchers, even to the point of being threatened with legal prosecution. All in all, Rankin's work helping slaves get to safety was "always a family event . . . that often required members of the family to change their plans abruptly."[10]

Through the 1830s and 1840s Rankin continued his multifaceted work of local church ministry, college leadership, organizing and speaking for the abolitionist cause, while helping individuals escape through the underground network to safety in Canada. However, in the summer of 1850, the national pro- and antislavery tensions reached a climax when the US Congress renewed the Fugitive Slave Act as part of the Compromise of 1850. The act was designed to strengthen earlier fugitive slave laws and make it a federal crime to harbor or assist slaves from the South escaping north. White persons caught assisting a slave could be fined $1,000 and sentenced to up to six months in jail. Regional commissioners were appointed and earned $10 for every slave returned to his or her master. Persons who knew of efforts to assist runaways but did not report it, even if they did not actively participate, could be held liable. Moreover, the law encouraged the illegal detention of free Blacks who would be kidnapped and sold into slavery despite having been legally freed.

The Fugitive Slave Act outraged many in the North, forcing them to take a stand for or against slavery, and pushing more moderate abolitionists toward a more radical stance. At the same time, the law emboldened slave catchers and proslavery Northerners to not only aggressively pursue runaway slaves, but also to seek ways to snitch on and arrest their White abolitionist neighbors. Some of the slave catchers even posed as conductors on the Underground Railroad to capture slaves and identify safe houses along the network. The Kentucky legislature passed a bill establishing "slave patrols" of up to thirty people to patrol the banks of the Ohio River and instituted severe penalties for Whites assisting slaves

[10] Hagedorn, *Beyond*, 83.

of jail sentences up to nine years. All of these developments made the work of abolitionists like Rankin all the more dangerous, causing several of his allies to be arrested, fined, jailed, and even killed. Nonetheless, Rankin continued to speak out and write antislavery tracts, including one in which he called the Fugitive Slave Act "a standing monument of the most high handed wickedness ever a nation did."[11]

Ever the dedicated church leader Rankin sought unsuccessfully to persuade the Presbyterian Church to take a strong antislavery, pro-abolitionist stance. Despite the involvement of several leading Presbyterians in the abolitionist cause, the assembly failed to act fearing a denominational split. Eventually, Rankin's abolitionist activities led to controversy in his own local church in Ripley, and under false pretenses he was accused of unethical practices. So in 1846 after twenty-four years of ministry, Rankin resigned and started the Free Presbyterian Church, which eventually grew to a network of seventy-two congregations committed to the antislavery cause centered in Ohio spanning from Iowa to New York.

While most of Rankin's antislavery speaking was church based, as the national debate over slavery intensified, he was drawn into the political sphere. For a long time he supported the Whig Party, which had a lukewarm antislavery stance. However, as it became increasingly clear that the leaders of the Whigs did not intend to push the antislavery cause, Rankin followed his son Lowry and several of his fellow Ripley abolitionists to join the newly formed Liberty Party, which had as its primary goal the abolition of slavery. In 1857 he also joined the efforts of the National Compensation Emancipation Society, which sought to work for the extinction of slavery by compensating slaveholders for liberating their slaves.

By the late 1850s the country was heading toward civil war. In 1857 the Supreme Court ruled on the Dred Scott Case, which denied citizenship and the right to vote to all Black people, whether they were slave or free. In 1859 a group of Southern plantation owners began pushing for the reopening of the African slave trade, which had ceased decades earlier. That same year the antislavery radical John Brown led an unsuccessful raid on the arsenal at Harpers Ferry, Virginia, as a first step in leading a full-scale slave revolt. In 1860 South Carolina seceded from the United States after the election of Abraham Lincoln, and soon ten other states joined the Confederacy. Then in April 1861 Confederate

[11] Ibid., 264.

forces opened fire on Fort Sumter off the coast of Charleston, South Carolina, and the Civil War began.

While many Ripley citizens (including several of Rankin's sons) went off to fight in the war, Rankin and others continued to assist runaway slaves escape to safety. They also continued to press for a constitutional amendment abolishing slavery, and were greatly encouraged by Lincoln's Emancipation Proclamation, which took effect January 1, 1863. In December 1863 the American Anti-Slavery Society gathered in Philadelphia to celebrate Lincoln's proclamation. Now seventy-one years old and somewhat frail, Rankin did not attend, but he wrote a letter to be read to the delegates. In introducing the letter William Lloyd Garrison praised Rankin for working against slavery long before he and many other abolitionist leaders had even begun to think about the cause. In the letter Rankin wrote these words:

> From my boyhood to the present time, I have opposed the abominable system of American slavery. For the liberation of slaves I have labored long and suffered much reproach and persecution; but I regret none of the sacrifices I have made for the hapless millions that have been bought and sold as if beasts for the field and deprived of all that makes existence desirable.[12]

Rankin lived twenty-three more years. Too frail to care for himself after the war, he left Ripley to live with a daughter in Kansas and then with a granddaughter in Ironton, Ohio. He outlived his wife Jean, who died in 1878. The cancer that eventually took his life at the age of ninety-three not only ate away at his face but also infected his brain. By the time of his death, the country had abolished slavery and given Black men citizenship rights. However, after a brief period of Reconstruction, the government reneged on the promises of freedom and instead reinstituted a system of oppression and segregation that would be legalized in the 1896 Supreme Court decision of *Plessy v. Ferguson* and would enshrine a policy of "separate but equal" that was not equal at all.

Some, including John Rankin himself, might wonder if all the work and struggle had gained the victory he had dedicated his life to achieving. However, those Black men who gathered on the dock in 1886 to welcome the boat knew that John Rankin had been an ally and advocate for their

---

[12] Ibid., 274.

freedom. The White folks who gathered with the Blacks in the Ripley church for his funeral knew that he had been a prophet for freedom long before many of them were born, or had considered the rightness of the abolitionist cause. The work of securing civil rights for African Americans would continue well into the century after his death, but during his time John Rankin had worked so that others might breathe the air of liberty and pass along a passion for racial justice to the generations that would follow him.

Discussion Questions

1. Despite tremendous opposition and pressure, John Rankin never wavered, over a fifty-year period, from his commitment to the abolition of slavery. What current issues of racial justice should we address with equal commitment?
2. John Rankin unabashedly called slavery "wicked" and slave owners "evildoers," even though through most of his life, slave owning was a legal and accepted practice. What current legal practices have a similar ring of "evil" to them? How are we to speak of such issues in our day?

Bibliography

Hagedorn, Ann. *Beyond the River: The Untold Story of the Heroes of the Underground Railroad.* New York: Simon and Schuster, 2002.

Declaration of the Anti-Slavery Convention, assembled in Philadelphia, December 4, 1833, available at https://archive.org/details/constitutionofan00amer.

Rankin, John. *Letters on American Slavery Addressed to Mr.Thomas Rankin* (1823), available at http://medicolegal.tripod.com._

Siebert, Wilbur. *The Underground Railroad in Ohio.* Columbus: Ohio Archeological and Historical Publications, 1993.

4

Levi Coffin
(1798–1877)

*A Legacy Etched on Human Lives**

President of the Underground Railroad

Located nine miles north of the city of Richmond in eastern Indiana is the small town of Fountain City (population 796, in the 2010 census). Incorporated in 1834 the community was formerly known as Newport, and was established largely by Quakers who had migrated from North Carolina. On the main street running through the center of town stands a two-story, eight-room Federal-style brick house known as the Levi Coffin House, a registered National Historic Landmark. The house stands as a reminder that in the 1830s and 1840s Newport was a major hub of the Underground Railroad that helped enslaved Africans make their way from Kentucky and points further south to freedom in the North and Canada. The people of Newport were known to be welcoming and supportive to the runaways who often stayed days and weeks, and needed food, clothing, and medical care as they prepared

* Photo of Levi Coffin provided courtesy of the Levi Coffin House, Fountain City, IN. Unless otherwise noted the main sources for this chapter are Levi Coffin, *Reminiscences of Levi Coffin, the Reputed President of the Underground Railroad; Being Brief History of the Labors of a Lifetime in Behalf of the Slave, with the Stories of Numerous Fugitives, Who Gained Their Freedom through His Instrumentality, and Many Other Incidents* (Cincinnati: Robert Clarke and Co., 1880), http://www.unc.edu; Mary Ann Yannessa, *Levi Coffin, Quaker: Breaking the Bonds of Slavery in Ohio and Indiana* (Richmond, IN: Friends United Press, 2001).

to continue their journey to Canada out of the reach of slave catchers. At the center of this effort was a local businessman named Levi Coffin, who came to be known by friends and foes alike as the "President of the Underground Railroad."[1]

Early Influences

Levi Coffin Jr. was born on October 28, 1798, to Prudence and Levi Coffin Sr. in New Garden, North Carolina. As the only son in a family of seven children, young Levi was brought up to be a farmer like his father. The Coffins were Quakers who had moved south from Massachusetts in the 1760s. In 1767 John Woolman had come to New Garden to plead with his fellow Quakers to refrain from owning slaves, and calling for the release of any owned slaves. Ten years earlier Woolman had written to the Quakers in New Garden saying, "Where slaves are purchased to do our labour, numerous difficulties attend it."[2] The senior Levi had fully embraced Woolman's admonitions, as had many other members of his family and community. Moreover, Levi's older cousin, Vestal Coffin, became actively involved in helping slaves escape their bondage and was considered to be the main organizer of the Underground Railroad in that part of North Carolina. Thus, from a young age Levi learned that slavery was an evil that God-fearing Quakers abhorred and in some cases actively opposed.

Though Levi's family did not own slaves, they were surrounded by other White people who did, and so he was exposed to the harsh treatment that the slaves endured at the hands of their White masters. When Levi was seven years old he had an experience that he marked as his "conversion to Abolitionism."[3] One day as he was chopping wood by the side of the road, a group of Black slaves all handcuffed and chained together passed by and were being driven by a White man on horseback as if they were a herd of cattle. Levi's father addressed the group and asked why they were being chained. One of the slaves replied that they were being taken away from their wives and children, and were chained so they would not escape and return to them. The

---

[1] Waynet Levi Coffin House, Waynet, Fountain City, Indiana, http://www.waynet.org.

[2] Phillips P. Moulton, ed., *The Journal and Major Essays of John Woolman* (New York: Oxford University Press, 1971), 67.

[3] Coffin, *Reminiscences*, 12.

younger Levi listened in horror, and after they had passed by, he asked his father why anyone would do such a thing to another human being. In response his father explained what slavery was and how it was practiced in their region. Although he had certainly seen slaves before, on this day its meaning affected him like never before. As he listened, Levi thought, "How terribly we should feel if father were taken from us."[4] This comment reveals the human compassion and empathy that continued to grip Levi Coffin throughout his life. As one reads his *Reminiscences*, one quickly comes to see that the abolition of slavery was not primarily an issue to be debated, but rather the liberation of fellow human beings to be pursued.

During his childhood, another incident that left a strong impression on him involved an unnamed slave who sold Levi's father a fish from a local fishery owned by some slave owners. The next day, the man checked back to see if he enjoyed the fish and would be interested in buying any more that the man might catch. Seeing his slave talking with a White man in such a familiar way, the slave owner interrupted their conversation, picked up a burning log from the cook fire and beat and bloodied him, even setting his hair on fire. While the elder Levi protested, his son was sickened by the incident, so much so that he went off without breakfast and sobbed.

Coffin later wrote that "such instances of 'man's inhumanity to man' intensified my hatred of slavery and inspired me to devote myself to the cause of the helpless and oppressed."[5] By age fifteen he began assisting his cousin Vestal in aiding slaves to escape. His first effort involved a free Black named Stephen originally from Philadelphia, who had been kidnapped and brought south to be sold as a slave. The slave dealer, whose name was Holland, had stopped with his coffle of slaves in New Garden to take part in a local community gathering where it was customary for White people to bring their slaves along. As the White people went inside for supper, Levi remained outside talking with the enslaved Blacks. In conversation he learned that Stephen had once been free and was being taken further south where he would be sold as a slave. Levi brought his concern to his father's attention. The senior Levi then brought the matter before the local Quaker meeting, and they agreed to pursue Stephen's case. Since Holland had moved on and subsequently sold Stephen, Levi's father and others had to do some

[4] Ibid., 13.

[5] Coffin, *Reminiscences,* 14.

extensive investigation to locate him. They eventually found Stephen on a farm in Georgia and proved he was the victim of a kidnapping and should be released. After six months of legal haggling Stephen was released and allowed to come home.[6]

While most proabolition Quakers limited their antislavery work to cases such as Stephen's that could be accomplished within the law, the Coffins did not always operate within those confines. Because they were known to be staunchly antislavery, runaways would often hide in the woods near their farm seeking assistance. Under the guise of feeding the hogs that roamed in the woods, Levi would take supplies of bacon and cornbread to the fugitives. As they ate, he would listen to their stories. His kindness became so well known that sometimes the runaways would come right to his room seeking shelter and food for their journey north. Along with his cousin Vestal, Levi would often meet them in the woods and help them plan their escape, often writing sympathetic friends who could aid them along their journey. Coffin's *Reminiscences* of those early years recount several other such stories of slaves and their plight and the attempts to assist them.

In 1818 New Garden opened its own Sabbath school, which taught young people basic subjects with the purpose of increasing their religious knowledge and understanding of the Bible. In 1821 with the approval of some local slave owners Levi and Vestal also began a Sabbath school for the slaves. However, after several weeks some less lenient slave owners began to threaten legal action for bringing education to the slaves. These experiences gave Coffin the opportunity to teach, while deepening his commitment to help slaves, thus integrating two vocations he pursued for the next several years.

Although several decades earlier Quakers had taken a stand against owning slaves, generally speaking the Society of Friends sought to balance the opposition to slavery with a desire to not disrupt the local economy so dependent on slave labor. Furthermore, Quakers like Coffin who believed in immediate and full emancipation were in the minority, as most Quakers subscribed to the idea of gradual liberation and then colonization, sending slaves to colonize their own land in Africa. This practice promoted by the American Colonization Society assumed that

---

[6] There is historical evidence that the practice of kidnapping free Blacks and selling them as slaves was fairly common during this time. The most famous account was written by Solomon Northrup in the book *12 Years a Slave*, which was an Academy Award-winning movie in 2013.

Blacks had inherently inferior natures to Whites, and therefore it was not possible or desirable that Whites and Blacks live together. Coffin did not agree with this perspective. Although he did not object to a freed person going to Africa, he did not think that the proper response to slavery was repatriation but rather abolition.[7]

Move to Indiana

As the local and national debate about slavery continued to heat up, the slavery laws became increasingly restrictive and oppressive, causing thousands of Quakers in the Southern states to conclude that "slavery and Quakerism could not prosper together."[8] This realization caused thousands of Quakers to move from the South to the free territories of Indiana and Ohio. In the summer of 1822 Coffin assisted his brother-in-law and his family in their move to Indiana. He stayed in Indiana for about a year teaching and visiting friends and relatives. While there, he too became convinced that his family needed to leave North Carolina, and so he returned in November 1823 hoping to convince his family to follow the others north. Back in New Garden he continued to teach and continued his antislavery activities. In October 1824 he married his longtime friend, Catharine White, and together in 1826, the young couple moved to Newport, Indiana.

Indiana, along with Ohio, had originally been part of the Northwest Territory. Established in 1787, the original Northwest Territory charter outlawed slavery. However, as early as 1797 the territorial governor and future president of the United States, William Henry Harrison, had tried to overturn the antislavery provision so that slaveholding could be practiced there; however, his efforts were denied by the US Congress, and the territory remained "free."

Slowly legislative efforts began to chip away at the antislavery position. In 1805 the territorial legislature passed a law allowing slaveholders to move into the state and keep their slaves for ten years. In 1816 when Indiana became a state, a law was passed requiring all Blacks in the state to post a $500 bond stating they would not be "a nuisance or cause trouble"; no such requirement was imposed on White

---

[7] This was the same challenge faced by Angelina and Sarah Grimké, who like Coffin, fell out of favor with their fellow Quakers for their strong abolitionist stand.

[8] Yannessa, *Levi Coffin*, 11.

settlers.[9] Groups of Whites proposed that Blacks resettle in areas west of Indiana or relocate to Liberia. Thus, while Indiana was technically free of slavery, it was not necessarily a hospitable place for Blacks in general and runaways in particular. When Levi and Catharine Coffin arrived in Indiana they entered an environment that was hardly unified on its views or laws regarding slavery. Furthermore, the federal Fugitive Slave Law (which was first established in the Constitution and was renewed several times until its repeal in 1864) required that any person who had fled north to escape slavery was to be captured and returned to his or her master. Additionally, any White person found assisting runaways could face significant fines, prison, or both.

The Coffins moved to the rural community of Newport, which was home to many other Quakers as well a small community of free Blacks, many of whom were descendants of slaves who had been freed by their Quaker slave masters. Because of the presence of both Quaker and Black communities Newport soon became a major stopping place for runaway slaves seeking protection on their journey north. On the unofficial map of the Underground Railroad, three lines of travel converged on Newport—one from Cincinnati 80 miles to the southwest, the second from Madison, Indiana, on the border 120 miles to the south, and finally from Jeffersonville, Indiana. just north of Louisville, Kentucky. Although locally there was generally good support for antislavery efforts overall, active abolitionists like Coffin were in the minority. Even many of those who disapproved of slavery did not support the work of the Underground Railroad, because they saw it as aiding and abetting criminal activity. Also, as Coffin had found in North Carolina, there were many of his fellow Quakers who advocated gradual emancipation and colonization, rather than immediately and unreservedly granting Blacks full and free citizenship. Thus, in his community his efforts to assist runaways were not only illegal but also often quite dangerous.[10] Nonetheless, during the twenty years Coffin and his family lived in Newport they helped an estimated two thousand slaves on their way to freedom. Moreover, Coffin claimed that to his knowledge, none of the slaves he helped were ever caught. Although little is known of Coffin's children, his wife, Catharine, was an integral partner in the work with escaped slaves, and earned the name of "Aunt Katy" in the local Black community.

---

[9] State of Indiana, *The Underground Railroad in Indiana*, http://www.in.gov.

[10] Julia Conklin, "The Underground Railroad in Indiana," *Indiana Magazine of History* 6, no. 2 (1910): 63–74.

Antislavery Activities in Newport

In order to earn a living Coffin continued to farm, and he also pursued various business opportunities, including a mercantile business. In 1836 he built a mill to manufacture linseed oil. Often he would employ runaway slaves during the time they were with him. Because of his antislavery reputation there were periods when those opposed to his activities would boycott his business. Guided by his convictions rather than concerns for his success in business, Coffin trusted that God would provide for his family as long as he was faithful to his beliefs. Despite running several businesses and farming, Coffin writes, "I was never too busy to engage in Underground Railroad affairs,"[11] and he soon found that it was important that he always have a wagon with a team of horses available when fugitive slaves would come through seeking his help.

In his *Reminiscences* Coffin tells the stories of runaway slaves he helped to freedom in Canada, and it is obvious from those stories that other members of his community were also involved. For instance, whenever a runaway slave had a medical need, Coffin called on Dr. Way, whom he referred to as "a warm friend to the fugitive slave, and a hearty co-worker with me in anti-slavery matters."[12] If the fugitives needed clothing he would gather clothes from others in the community. If they needed rest, he would allow them to stay in his home.

Despite occasional boycotts by those who opposed his activities, Coffin became a leading political and business figure in the community. He was elected to the board of directors of the Richmond branch of the State Bank, which was the major source of loans for local merchants and farmers. Using his position as leverage, he was able to silence many of his proslavery critics, who needed his support if they were to get help from the bank. Though he received threatening letters, he did not let these attempts at intimidation deter him. Coffin wrote of one instance where a letter that had been mailed by a man from Kentucky warned him that he was bringing a whole band of armed men to burn his business and destroy the town. Coffin refused to be bullied and so went to bed at his usual time taking no special security precautions; the family woke the next morning to find everything as they had left it.

---

[11] Coffin, *Reminiscences*, 107.

[12] Ibid., 115.

What is striking about the stories Coffin relates in his writings is how often he focuses on the courage and ingenuity of the runaway slaves and how little his words highlight his activities to help them. For instance, he tells the story of Jim "The Cunning Slave" who escaped from Kentucky and made it all the way to Canada, but then a few months later returned to help fourteen of his fellow slaves escape with him. He writes about Robert Burrell, a runaway from Tennessee, who knocked on his door seeking employment so he could earn enough money to buy his wife's freedom. With the help of fellow abolitionist John Rankin[13] Coffin was eventually able to get Robert's wife out of Tennessee, and with the money he earned with Coffin Burrell bought a house and settled in Newport. Eliza Harris, whose story was made famous by Harriet Beecher Stowe's *Uncle Tom's Cabin*, also came through their house from Rankin's home in Ripley; Coffin and his wife were one of several abolitionist couples that served as the inspiration for the Quaker couple Simeon and Rachel Halliday in the book.

However, the most humorous story he told involved seventeen runaways who were brought to their house at one time. A free Black man escorted them to the house and knocked on the door. Coffin's wife asked, "What have you got there?

The man replied, "All of Kentucky."

She answered, "Well bring all of Kentucky in." The runaways were tired and had lost most of their clothing, and a few were badly injured. They were ushered into the dining room, served a meal, and given the medical help that was needed. Clothing was gathered, and arrangements were made to divide them into three smaller groups to the stations north of them. All of them eventually made it safely to Canada.

When Coffin was challenged for his antislavery work, he showed a creative ability to use his detractors' racism against them. A few weeks after he had helped the seventeen runaways to safety he was summoned to the county seat to appear before a grand jury deliberating over a possible indictment for harboring fugitive slaves. He was asked directly by the jury's foreman if he had harbored fugitive slaves in violation of Indiana and federal law. Coffin's response was perfect; he stated that the people he had helped had said they were slaves, but reminded the jury that Indiana law did not allow Black people to testify because it was presumed that such people could not tell the truth and that "the law

---

[13] See chapter 3 for John Rankin's story.

of our State did not admit colored evidence." He went on to say that the Bible instructs a Christian to feed the hungry and clothe the naked and that "no distinction in regard to color was mentioned in the good Book," so he had cared for the people who came to his door.[14] The case was dropped, and Coffin continued helping slaves.

Coffin showed an ability to use the law for his own purposes. A slaveholding family named Dawes was passing through Indiana on their way to Illinois. The wife in the family became ill, and so the family was required to stay in the state for a period of time while she recuperated. According to Indiana law, slaveholders were allowed to pass through the state, but if they stopped long enough to take up residence (that is, "locate" in the state), their slaves were to become legally free. Working with other abolitionists and a local lawyer, they determined that the Dawes family had "stopped to locate" and so moved quickly to have the slave girls freed and given their emancipation papers. Coffin helped the girls go to school and took care of them for several years until they were able to be on their own. One lived on in Newport, and another married and went to Canada.

While engaged in the efforts to help slaves to freedom, Coffin also supported efforts to spread the message of abolitionism more widely. When antislavery speakers such as Arnold Buffum and Frederick Douglass came to eastern Indiana, they usually made the Coffin house their headquarters. At the same time as the national debate on slavery heated up in the 1840s, divisions within the Society of Friends became more pronounced. In 1843 at a gathering of the Indiana Yearly Meeting of Friends, Coffin and his fellow Quaker abolitionists were ordered to cease their Underground Railroad activities and their support of abolitionist meetings. When Coffin refused to comply with their directive, he was put out of the meeting and considered disqualified as a Friend in good standing. In response, Coffin and his allies organized the Indiana Yearly Meeting of Anti-Slavery Friends and continued their work. As the Coffin biographer Mary Ann Yannessa points out, "Levi Coffin never put the law of the land or even the caution of his beloved Religious Society of Friends above his conscience."[15]

---

[14] Coffin, *Reminiscences*, 191.

[15] Yannessa, *Levi Coffin*, 17.

The Move to Cincinnati

By 1844 Coffin became convinced that helping runaway slaves was not sufficient; he also needed to refrain from buying or selling products that resulted from slave labor. The Free Labor Movement had been in existence ever since John Woolman raised the issue in the 1700s,[16] but as the concern about economic justification for slavery grew, free labor associations had been started to help import and distribute goods such as cotton and sugar from places where slavery did not exist. Coffin attempted to establish a free labor store in Newport but had difficulty making it profitable, and so in 1847 he moved to Cincinnati hoping that he could supply other general stores with the free labor goods, as he had in Newport. Having been in Newport for twenty years, neither Levi nor Catharine were eager to move, and initially they planned to live in Cincinnati for five years and then return to Newport. However five years turned into thirty, and they unwittingly had left Newport for good.

Like the rest of the country, and especially southern Ohio and Indiana, Cincinnati was a city in turmoil over the issue of slavery. As a city on the Ohio-Kentucky border, Cincinnati was a common crossing point for slaves seeking freedom and slave catchers seeking their runaway slaves. The city was the home of Lane Seminary, which had been established in the 1830s for the expressed purpose of training Presbyterian ministers toward the antislavery cause. James Birney, who eventually ran for president in the antislavery Freedom Party, started an abolitionist paper in Cincinnati called *The Philanthropist*, through which he propagated his views. However, in incidents similar to those suffered by fellow journalist Elijah Lovejoy,[17] Birney's printing presses were destroyed several times by angry mobs. Unlike Lovejoy, Birney survived and eventually moved his operation to the more abolition-friendly Buffalo, New York. So when the Coffins arrived in Cincinnati, they found a community caught up in all the controversies and contradictions around the issue of slavery throughout the country.

Coffin opened his store and began securing free labor goods through associations in New York and Philadelphia. He also made some trips to the Southern cotton-growing states, establishing accounts with small farmers who did not own slaves either because of economics or conviction. In Mississippi he met a farmer who had freed his slaves and was

---

[16] For information on John Woolman, see chapter 1.

[17] See chapter 5 on Elijah Lovejoy.

paying them as laborers. Coffin helped the man purchase a cotton gin (which he called the "Abolition Gin") that processed the cotton and then sent it to Coffin's store in Cincinnati. Unfortunately, the cost of finding free labor goods made his products more expensive than competitive products sold by other merchants, and in 1857 after ten years of trying to make it work, Coffin was forced to close the business.

When he moved to Cincinnati, Coffin had hoped that he would be able to concentrate on developing his new store and would not have to be as actively involved in Underground Railroad activity as he had been in Newport. However, he soon found himself again being sought out by runaway slaves, and those seeking to help them. Over their years in the city, the Coffins lived in several different houses, seeking structures that would accommodate their efforts to help the fugitive slaves. Eventually they bought a large house, which they operated as a boarding house for local educators and fellow Quakers. Because it was a boarding house there were always people coming and going, and so it became an ideal cover as a "depot" on the Underground Railroad heading north.

Because their location was not as secure as their old home in Newport, the Coffins had to employ more sophisticated methods of deception. Over the years the Coffins organized a network of persons to help in the efforts. They organized women's sewing circles and library associations, which focused on gathering and sewing clothes to be used as disguises for runaway slaves. Others—both men and women—served as conductors who accompanied the runaways all the way to Michigan or the Canadian border where they would be safe from slave catchers. Coffin himself developed contacts with antislavery persons in Southern states who could be called upon to help runaways even before they crossed into Ohio. One of the more ingenious methods of helping slaves escape was to dress them—men and women—in traditional Quaker dress with a gray dress or suit, a brimmed hat or veil and a downward tilt of the head. In this way runaways would be spirited to safety in broad daylight appearing to be Quakers simply going about their daily business in their carriages.

Although he was not a public speaker, Coffin often employed the Quaker practice of "gentle persuasion" to change the mind of his detractors. For example, Coffin tells the story of a man with whom he had frequent business dealings and who tried to taunt him by accusing him of "stealing niggers." In response, Coffin invited the man to his home to meet the runaway slaves who had come to the house seeking shelter the night before. The man accepted his offer and in Coffin's living room he heard the runaway, who was called "Sam," tell his story of suffering and the journey he had taken to get to Coffin's house. The man was moved by his story, and Coffin prevailed upon him to give Sam money to help him buy a train ticket north, which he did. Likewise on his travels south, Coffin often engaged the local proslavery farmers in discussions on the morality of enslaving another human being. Rather than creating increased hostility, Coffin was very adept at mollifying his detractors and in a few cases converting them to his views.

Although Coffin often was threatened, he never experienced any physical attacks for his antislavery work, unlike some of his fellow abolitionists.[18] He was a man who had a way with people and was known to be lighthearted and somewhat playful in his dealings with friends and foes alike.

During and After the Civil War

When the Civil War broke out in 1861, like many Quakers, Coffin found himself caught between his strong antislavery sentiments, and his commitment to nonviolence and nonparticipation in military affairs. Because Cincinnati was located on the Ohio-Kentucky border and was a major port, the city quickly became a major thoroughfare for soldiers coming from or going to the battlefield. In the fall of 1862 Confederates stationed in Kentucky launched an effort to capture the city. The mayor of Cincinnati responded by calling upon every able-bodied man, both Black and White, to report for military service in defense of the city. When Coffin did not report, one of the city officials came with a contingent of soldiers to forcibly enlist him into the army. Coffin informed the man that using a firearm against a fellow human being ran contrary to his religious beliefs and that he could not comply. When the official said regardless of his religious convictions the sixty-four-year-old had to enlist, Coffin responded by saying they would have to carry him and that would be a public embarrassment more for the mayor than him. Coffin prevailed, and local officials left him alone after that.

Though Coffin refused to take up arms, his house served as a makeshift hospital for soldiers injured in battle. At the same time he continued to assist runaway slaves. In 1862 he helped form the Contraband Relief Organization, a group of antislavery businessmen who helped secure

---

[18] For examples, see chapter 2 on Angelina Grimké and chapter 5 on Elijah Lovejoy.

goods for slaves who had either escaped behind Union lines or had been left by their masters fleeing further south. Coffin was put in charge of organizing efforts to secure blankets, clothing, food, and medical supplies for those coming into the city seeking shelter and refuge, and he also made trips to the South to visit camps where large groups of former slaves were being housed in often destitute and deplorable conditions. In 1863 he joined the Western Freedmen's Aid Commission, which had as its primary mission the establishment of schools for freed slaves. As a representative of the commission, he attended a meeting with President Lincoln in Washington, DC, designed to coordinate efforts to help newly freed slaves across the country. At that meeting he met not only the president but also the outspoken abolitionist William Lloyd Garrison. Coffin traveled throughout the North and eventually the South raising funds for the education effort, and helping to establish schools, shelters, and hospitals for freed slaves. In 1864 he made a fund-raising trip to England and was able to raise $100,000 in aid, which at the time was a sizable sum of money. Even after the war he continued to raise funds to assist in the commission efforts until it closed in 1870.

In 1870 Congress passed the Fifteenth Amendment which gave Black men the right to vote as full citizens. When this milestone was celebrated in Cincinnati, Levi Coffin was asked to give a speech. In his brief comments he noted that slave hunters had given him the title "President of the Underground Railroad" for his efforts at aiding runaway slaves. Noting that the government had granted Blacks full citizenship he said, "I resign my office and declare the operations of the Underground Railroad at an end."[19]

In September 1877 after being ill for nearly a year, Levi Coffin died one month shy of his seventy-ninth birthday. His funeral was attended by many people who had labored with him in the antislavery cause over the previous fifty years, as well as some of the former slaves he had helped find their way to freedom. While many kind words were spoken about him as both an abolitionist and a businessman, the service itself was very simple like the man and the Quaker faith he professed. As one of the speakers reflecting on a biblical passage said of Coffin: "He went about doing good, for God was with him."[20]

---

[19] Coffin, *Reminiscences*, 712.

[20] Ibid., 728.

Etched on the Lives He Saved

From his earliest days as a young boy in North Carolina, Levi Coffin's commitment to eradicating slavery had its roots in his personal relationships with slaves and former slaves, and his basic Quaker convictions that all people are human beings who should be treated with respect and human dignity. Levi Coffin lived and believed the adage that "there was no such thing as a slave to a Quaker."[21] Even those who opposed and threatened Coffin's antislavery work encountered him as a caring and compassionate person who used his powers of gentle persuasion to mollify his detractors and sometimes even win them over to his cause. As Yannessa writes: "His was a rare face that could smile at the slave hunters as well as the hunted, speak softly without a weapon, turn 'bloodhounds' away and still maintain a sense of humor, which only befuddled his enemies and confused the haughty."[22]

In 1864 while he was in London to raise money for the Western Freedmen's Association, he reflected on his life assisting runaway slaves to safety, and confessed that he felt inadequate, lacking the persuasive powers of such better-known abolitionists as William Lloyd Garrison, Theodore Weld, and Frederick Douglass; in fact, he had consciously avoided public speaking opportunities because he said he was "a worker and not a speaker in the anti-slavery cause." Often a person's greatness is measured largely by what they do visibly and publicly before others. Out of necessity most of Levi Coffin's work had been surreptitious and his accomplishments hidden. Yet Levi Coffin was a hero to the estimated two to three thousand people he helped escape to freedom; his quiet story was etched on their lives for all time.

---

[21] Yannessa, *Levi Coffin,* 34.

[22] Ibid., 37.

Discussion Questions

1. In both his personal life and his writings, Levi Coffin focused on the stories of slaves who came through his doors seeking freedom. How do stories personalize an issue in ways that data and figures cannot?
2. Coffin was often criticized by members of his own Quaker community for engaging in the illegal activity of helping runaway slaves, even though he himself saw his work as something that was required of him as a devout Christian and Quaker. How does religious faith inhibit people from seeking racial justice? In what ways does religious faith move people to work for racial justice?

Bibliography

Coffin, Levi. *Reminiscences of Levi Coffin, the Reputed President of the Underground Railroad; Being a Brief History of the Labors of a Lifetime in Behalf of the Slave, with the Stories of Numerous Fugitives, Who Gained Their Freedom through His Instrumentality, and Many Other Incidents.* Cincinnati: Robert Clarke and Co., 1880. http://www.unc.edu.

Conklin, Julia S. "The Underground Railroad in Indiana." *Indiana Magazine of History* 6, no. 2 (1910): 63–74.

Moulton, Phillips P., ed. *The Journal and Major Essays of John Woolman.* New York: Oxford University Press, 1971.

State of Indiana. *The Underground Railroad in Indiana.* http://www.in.gov.

Waynet. *Fountain City, Indiana.* http://www.waynet.org.

Waynet. *Levi Coffin House.* http://www.waynet.org.

Yannessa, Mary Ann. *Levi Coffin, Quaker: Breaking the Bonds of Slavery in Ohio and Indiana.* Richmond, IN: Friends United Press, 2001.

5

Elijah Lovejoy
(1802–1837)

*An Extremist for Justice**

Memorial to a Local "Hero"

Alton, Illinois, is a town of just under 28,000 people located on the banks of the Mississippi River approximately twenty-five miles north of St. Louis; Alton describes itself as "a great place to live, work, and prosper." Founded in 1837, it lays claim to being the final site of the Lincoln-Douglas debates, the birthplace of the jazz musician Miles Davis, and home to numerous cultural, educational, and recreational organizations."[1] One of the community's more notable monuments can be found in the Alton City Cemetery: the Elijah P. Lovejoy Memorial. Standing ninety-three feet tall, this granite column is topped by a seventeen-foot high statue of Lady Victory flanked by two eagles on separate columns. Established in 1897, the monument memorializes one of Alton's more notable citizens, Elijah P. Lovejoy.[2] His prominence is noted not only by the monument but also the presence of a Lovejoy school, a Lovejoy scholarship fund, and an annual Lovejoy week complete with a

* Woodcut image of Elijah Lovejoy provided by and used with permission of the Special Collections, Miller Library, Colby College, Waterville, ME. Unless otherwise noted the information reflected in this paper is from Merton L. Dillon, *Elijah P. Lovejoy: Abolitionist Editor* (Urbana: University of Illinois Press, 1961); and Paul Simon, *Freedom's Champion: Elijah Lovejoy* (Carbondale: Southern Illinois University Press, 1994).

[1] City of Alton, http://www.alton-il.com.

[2] Lysa Allman-Baldwin, "African-American History Runs Deep in the Alton Area," *New York Amsterdam News* 100, no. 36 (September 2, 2010): 24.

music festival, special lectures, and a community dinner.[3] Given the high honors paid him, one might be surprised to learn that on November 7, 1837, two days short of his thirty-fifth birthday, Elijah P. Lovejoy was killed by an angry mob while local officials passively looked on. For years after his brutal death, he was considered to be an agitator and a community menace, and his crime? Being a relentless and outspoken opponent of slavery.

Puritan Roots

Born on November 9, 1802, in Albion, Maine, Elijah Lovejoy was the oldest of Daniel and Elizabeth Lovejoy's nine children. Daniel Lovejoy was a minister and a farmer who had been mentored by the Rev. Elijah Parish, after whom Elijah was named. Although little is known of Elijah's early life, from an early age it was evident that he had a penchant for learning, and so in 1823 he attended the newly formed Waterville College (now Colby College), a Baptist-affiliated school where he excelled as a student and graduated in only three years. Despite his academic prowess and offers to remain on as a teacher, Elijah was restless and decided to first go to Boston, then New York City, and finally west to the burgeoning city of St. Louis.

The culture of New England in which Lovejoy was raised was highly religious, having been deeply influenced by Puritan Congregationalism. Puritans believed that society left to itself would turn toward immorality and evil, and so considered their calling to be the task of shaping society according to the principles and values of the Christian Bible. For the Puritans the kingdom of God as taught by Jesus was not merely a theological concept or spiritual ideal, but rather a blueprint as to how society ought to be shaped. Puritans in many ways saw themselves as eighteenth- and nineteenth-century descendants of the ancient Israelites who were called to establish a unique and special nation that would be a blessing to the whole world. For the descendants of Puritans like Lovejoy it was "the Christian's duty to aid [God] in the holy enterprise of sweeping away every man-made obstacle to pure religion, to virtue and to freedom."[4]

---

[3] "Lovejoy Week Set for Nov. 2–14," *Telegraph* (Alton, IL), October 29, 2008. EBSCOHost (AAT 2W6129522486).

[4] Dillon, *Lovejoy*, 173.

St. Louis and the Antislavery Cause

Lovejoy did not travel to St. Louis simply to see another part of the country, but rather he went with a sense of mission to bring about religious reform to this largely untamed part of the world. He found his new home to be a decidedly more secular and raucous environment than his New England home, and he even commented that the people there "were aggressively hostile toward organized religion of any kind."[5] Not knowing what else to do, he founded a private high school, but two years later he left teaching to become coeditor of the local newspaper, the *St. Louis Times*. Lovejoy soon found that he loved the opportunity to be involved in the political issues of the time and to share his views on the printed page. Newspaper editing was to consume the rest of his life and eventually led to his death. Yet Lovejoy's early years as a reporter and editor gave no indication that he would shortly become the ardent opponent of slavery he eventually became.

At the same time that he joined the *Times*, Lovejoy became actively involved in efforts through the Presbyterian Church to bring about moral reform on issues such as gambling, drinking, and Sabbath-breaking. Despite his interest in religious reform, Lovejoy ironically was deeply vexed by his own lack of the conversion experience expected of all genuine and authentic Puritan believers. This lack of a conversion so troubled him that on numerous occasions he sought the experience through attendance at evangelistic meetings; nonetheless, he always came away unmoved, until 1832 (at the age of thirty) when he finally had a conversion experience at a revival meeting under the preaching of David Nelson, a Presbyterian preacher from central Missouri. In addition to being Lovejoy's spiritual midwife, Rev. Nelson turned out to be a valuable mentor and companion for the rest of Lovejoy's short life.

Even though William Lloyd Garrison had begun publishing his abolitionist views as early as 1830, and Lovejoy's mother and brother Otis had become early allies in Garrison's cause, Elijah initially showed little interest in the antislavery cause. However, beginning with his conversion experience his views began to change. After his conversion, Lovejoy felt a call to the ministry, and he returned east to attend Princeton Seminary. Upon graduation in 1833 he returned to St. Louis, where he was persuaded by clergy and lay leaders to become editor of the *St. Louis Observer*, a Presbyterian newspaper dedicated to religious reform. At

---

[5] Ibid., 12.

the same time he was commissioned as a missionary of the American Missionary Society, which provided him numerous opportunities to preach in the areas in and around St. Louis.

Lovejoy began making his mark by writing about the common Puritan "evils" of Catholicism, as well as various moral issues such as gambling, drinking, Sabbath-breaking, and materialism. Eventually he also began to speak out against slavery, as there was an active abolitionist movement in the community, particularly in Presbyterian circles. Lovejoy's mentor, David Nelson, was an outspoken opponent of slavery and surely influenced him. At first Lovejoy subscribed to the more moderate views of the American Colonization Society, which advocated abolishing slavery and shipping slaves back to Africa in the belief that free Blacks were "a vile excrescence upon society" and thus had to be removed in order to preserve and build a racially homogenous and socially prosperous society.[6] Like many of the abolitionist religious reformers of his day, Lovejoy believed that through the application of reasonable moral argument Southern landowners could be persuaded to eventually give up slavery. Thus he had a gradualist view of abolition. However, as Lovejoy continued to share his views from the pulpit and in his newspaper, it became increasingly evident to him that slave owners had a deep economic interest in maintaining slavery, which meant that appealing solely to their moral and religious values had minimal effect. By 1835 he had adopted the views of the American Anti-Slavery Society, which called for immediate emancipation and the gradual integration of free Blacks into the fabric of American society.

An Outspoken Abolitionist

Lovejoy's abolitionist "coming out" was evidenced by a sermon he preached in Potosi, Missouri, during the summer of 1835 in which he condemned slavery along with drinking and gambling. The response to his sermon was pronounced and violent; a crowd sought to tar and feather him, but he was able to escape unscathed. As his views became more markedly abolitionist, a group of leading St. Louis citizens, including politicians, lawyers, clergy, and army officers, threatened to withdraw support for his newspaper. Threats of violence increased, and when

---

[6] For more on the views of the American Colonization Society, see David Streifford, "The American Colonization Society: An Application of Republican Ideology to Early Antebellum Reform," *Journal of Southern History* 45, no. 2 (1979): 207.

Lovejoy went out of town on preaching assignments, he had to hire guards to protect his offices and his home from violent mobs.

In response to Lovejoy's outspoken views, an assembly of St. Louis citizens passed a resolution calling Lovejoy and his abolitionist allies "misguided fanatics" and enjoined him to cease printing his abolitionist views, specifying that "freedom of speech does not give one the right to freely discuss the question of slavery" because it was "too nearly allied to the vital interests of the slaveholding states."[7] The resolution further accused Lovejoy of promoting amalgamation, that is, mixed-race marriages, which he in fact did not support. However, instead of being cowed into silence, Lovejoy responded by saying he would not give in. He wrote, "I am threatened with violence and death because I dare to advocate, in any way, the cause of the oppressed," and he indicated that "I am prepared to abide the consequences." Moreover, to the charge of amalgamation, he responded by alluding to the commonly known but publicly denied practice of White masters raping their Black slave women, and wrote that "the worst treatment of the Negro is not the public whipping . . . but what takes place 'in the cabins,'" and that several White slave masters were "practical amalgamationists." These examples illustrate the resolve, courage, and some would say, foolishness, with which he faced his accusers.[8]

Over time Lovejoy's antislavery views became increasingly clear. Like his mentor David Nelson, Lovejoy believed that "the slave was a human being with a soul, and that his master ought to treat him as a man and not property." Lovejoy wrote that "slavery is a sin—now, heretofore, hereafter and forever, a sin. . . . Consequently, it follows that whoever has participated or now participates, in that sin, ought to repent without a moment's delay." He therefore advocated immediate emancipation of slaves with the understanding that on release from slavery they could then could be educated and socialized gradually to take their place as full citizens. This view was captured in the motto he often stated: "immediate emancipation, gradually accomplished."[9]

Lovejoy's abolitionist views were not well received in the South or the North, among all socioeconomic classes. Some groups, like Southern slave owners, outright rejected the proposition that slavery ought to be eliminated, and feared that abolitionist rhetoric would give rise to

---

[7] Simon, *Freedom's Champion*, 38.

[8] Ibid., 390, 410.

[9] Dillon, *Lovejoy*, 54, 75, 56.

slave rebellions. More moderate citizens opposed what they saw as his strident rhetoric, believing that the elimination of slavery would happen naturally and gradually over time. Still others objected to his outspoken views because they stirred emotions to the point of causing groups of angry citizens to engage in mob violence.

The growing opposition to Lovejoy became abundantly clear in late 1835. He was attending a Presbyterian convention in Pittsburgh at a time when a free Black man was beaten and burned to death by an angry mob back in St. Louis. When the case came to trial, the judge (who ironically was named Lawless) dropped the charges against the murderers and instead blamed Lovejoy and the *St. Louis Observer* for "fomenting Negro Rebellion." After Judge Lawless's ruling, the offices of the *Observer* were vandalized. When Lovejoy returned to St. Louis, he decided that he could no longer operate safely there, and so he moved with his new wife twenty-five miles up the river to the small river town of Alton, Illinois. However, in the process of moving upriver, his printing press was captured by some vandals and dumped in the river before it ever got to its new home.

A New Home in Alton

The citizens of Alton were outraged that vandalism of this sort would occur in their community. So the leading citizens met with Lovejoy to discuss his presence in their city. Their concern was that the kind of violence experienced in St. Louis might be repeated in Alton. In order to quell their fears Lovejoy stressed that that the *Alton Observer* would be primarily a religious paper rather than an abolitionist paper. He stated that while he opposed slavery, he did not consider himself to be part of the abolitionist movement. Although many of his detractors would disagree with this characterization, for Lovejoy his opposition to slavery was primarily a religious position rather than a political one. He further indicated that because he now resided in a free rather than slaveholding state, he would need to devote less space in his paper to the slavery issue than in St. Louis. Those gathered at the meeting took this to mean that he would tone down, if not outright eliminate, his antislavery rhetoric; however, Lovejoy left with no such understanding and continued to write on slavery as well as other religiously oriented topics.

As his writings on slavery continued, and controversy continued to grow, Lovejoy started a Lyceum: a community forum where positions on issues of the day could be debated and decided. After a couple of months of discussing less controversial topics, Lovejoy initiated a discussion on slavery. However, after three sessions it became clear that no consensus could be reached, and a local group of citizens passed a resolution asking Lovejoy to cease from publishing and promoting his abolitionist views. Although they recognized his right to print his views by virtue of freedom of the press, they asked him to desist for the peace and stability of the Alton community.

Lovejoy's response was not only to refuse to abide by the resolution but also to join with others to establish a chapter of the American Anti-Slavery Society in Alton. Although Lovejoy's support continued to decline in Alton, Presbyterian and Congregationalist ministers in the area supported him and encouraged him for his strong and courageous stands against prevailing opinion. The stronger the opposition became, the stronger Lovejoy's rebuke of their proslavery and accommodationist views became. For him, the work against slavery was no longer simply an issue, but a personal crusade. In August 1836 he wrote his wife, "The cry of the oppressed has entered not only my ears, but into my soul, so that while I live I cannot hold peace."[10]

As Lovejoy persisted in his efforts to start a local antislavery society and his antislavery views continued to be published, violent opposition also grew. He was forced to hire guards to protect his home and on several occasions he moved his wife and newborn child out of the city to stay with friends or family members. As the tension around Lovejoy mounted, the debate centered not only on his opposition to slavery, but also on his right as a citizen to present his views. Both those who opposed him and those who chose a moderate stance believed that Lovejoy's outspoken condemnation of slavery was going to stir up the passions of the enslaved Blacks against their owners and generally cause division and conflict in the community. As in St. Louis, those who had originally offered financial and moral support for his newspaper began to withdraw their support, and a mob destroyed two of his printing presses: one when he moved and another before it was delivered.

Death by a Mob

All of these events eventually led to the fateful events of November 7, 1837, when by cover of night Lovejoy secretly had a fourth printing press delivered and stored in a local warehouse owned by a wealthy

[10] Ibid., 104.

supporter named Winthrop Gilman. Shortly after its delivery, a group of men gathered at a local tavern, marched to the warehouse, and started throwing stones at the building. Gilman and Lovejoy called on Alton's mayor, John Krum, to provide police protection against the growing mob. When the mayor refused to do so, Gilman hired a group of local militia to guard the warehouse and protect those inside. Eventually in the rising tension, one of the militiamen fired on the crowd and a man was killed. Although this temporarily caused the mob to pull back, eventually they called on Lovejoy and his supporters to turn over the printing press and threatened to burn the warehouse down if he did not comply with their demands. The mayor sought to be a mediator between the crowd and those in the warehouse, but to no avail.

Eventually, the warehouse was set on fire, and Lovejoy and the militiamen began firing on the crowd. A gun battle ensued, and Lovejoy was shot five times in the chest and died instantly while the warehouse continued to burn. In the chaos a group from the crowd climbed into the building and threw the printing press crashing to the ground out of a third-story window. Though a throng of more than two hundred people, including the mayor and other local officials, witnessed the entire event, no charges were ever brought against those who had participated in the violence that night.

A Martyr for the Antislavery Cause

While local opposition to his views remained strong, the news of his death energized the abolitionist movement across the North. Lovejoy's biographer Paul Simon contends that along with the publication of *Uncle Tom's Cabin*, Lovejoy's death "became one of the two great boosts to the anti-slavery movement."[11] Both his brother Owen and his close confidant Edward Beecher wrote moving tributes to him that were widely circulated. The American Anti-Slavery Society officially commemorated Lovejoy as a martyr, and his story became a poignant example of the "bloodthirstiness of slave power."[12] After Lovejoy's death it became abundantly clear to the antislavery advocates that moral suasion would not persuade the slave owners to release their slaves. They came to see that change would only come through political means, which eventually led to the Civil War. So although Lovejoy's views were not particularly

[11] Simon, *Freedom's Champion*, 155.

[12] Dillon, *Lovejoy*, 177.

unique among abolitionists, his death marked a turning point in the antislavery movement.

What is most striking in Lovejoy's story was his relationship with those who sought to silence him and avoid the unavoidable controversy produced by slavery. Although he expected slave owners and others invested in maintaining slavery to oppose him, what troubled him most were those individuals who professed to have no strong attachment to slavery, but who opposed him for voicing his opinions. Dillon puts it this way:

> In waging his reform campaign, Lovejoy was neither wise nor prudent in the sense ordinarily accorded those words. Such attributes belonged to his opponents—not the mob, of course—but to those moderates who sought to quell the discord in St. Louis and Alton by persuading him to be silent. Probably most of them shared Lovejoy's dislike of slavery in the abstract, but unlike him, they were willing to live with it in practice, whatever its enormities.[13]

In this sense Lovejoy's experience was similar to Martin Luther King Jr.'s opposition from White moderates in the South who accused him of causing disorder in the Black community. In his legendary "Letter from a Birmingham Jail" King responded to White clergy who had publicly called his nonviolent direct action in Birmingham "unwise and untimely." From his jail cell King criticized those who were "more devoted to 'order' than to justice" and who opted for "a negative peace which is the absence of tension to a positive peace which is the presence of justice." To those who called him an extremist King responded: "So the question is not whether we will be extremists, but what kind of extremists we will be. Will we be extremists for hate or love? Will we be extremists for the preservation of injustice or for the extension of justice?"[14]

Certainly, Elijah Lovejoy was an extremist for justice in his opposition to slavery. Although there is no indication that he had much personal interaction with either free or enslaved African Americans, he had taken on the cause of their freedom as if it were his own. Through his commitment to religious reform "he had become an abolitionist, perhaps without

---

[13] Ibid., 174.

[14] Martin Luther King Jr., *Why We Can't Wait* (1963; New York: Penguin Books, 2000), 73, 77.

realizing it."[15] However, once he embraced the abolitionist perspective, his imagination allowed him to vicariously identify with the slaves' degradation. He once wrote, "What is it to be a slave? . . . In one word it is to be degraded from a man to a brute—to become, instead of a free moral agent, a THING, a piece of property, and to be used as such."[16] For Lovejoy the slave was as much a child of God as the White person, and thus had a dignity worth defending even to the point of death.

Thus, it is ironic that sixty years after his death, the Lovejoy Memorial was erected in Alton, Illinois, in his honor. Time may have caused emotions to dissipate and memories to fade, but Elijah Lovejoy's lasting legacy is his unwavering defense of human dignity and his passionate pursuit of justice even at the cost of his life.

Discussion Questions

1. The call for Lovejoy to desist from publishing his abolitionist views was often couched in a concern for peace and order in a community. What are ways in which a concern for peace and order sometimes keeps people from speaking out on racial justice issues?
2. Lovejoy's gradual movement toward the abolitionist cause was initiated by his religious conversion. In what way can religious or spiritual experiences awaken people to racial justice issues?

Bibliography

Allman-Baldwin, Lysa. "African-American History Runs Deep in the Alton Area." *New York Amsterdam News* 100, no. 36 (September 2, 2010): 24.

City of Alton. http://www.alton-il.com.

Dillon, Merton L. *Elijah P. Lovejoy: Abolitionist Editor*. Urbana: University of Illinois Press, 1961.

King, Martin Luther, Jr. *Why We Can't Wait*. 1963. New York: Penguin Books, 2000.

Simon, Paul. *Freedom's Champion: Elijah Lovejoy*. Carbondale: Southern Illinois University Press, 1994.

Streifford, David. "The American Colonization Society: An Application of Republican Ideology to Early Antebellum Reform." *Journal of Southern History* 45, no. 2 (1979): 201–20.

Telegraph. "Lovejoy Week Set for Nov. 2–14." *The Telegraph* (Alton, IL), October 29, 2008. EBSCOHost (AAT 2W6129522486).

---

[15] Dillon, *Lovejoy*, 55.

[16] Ibid., 104.

Jim Crow and the Civil Rights Era

6

Mary White Ovington
(1865–1951)

*A Quiet Radical**

Motivated by a Race Riot

On the night of August 14, 1908, an angry mob of 5,000 to 10,000 White men gathered outside the Springfield, Illinois, city jail demanding that the sheriff hand over two Black prisoners being held in the jail. Earlier that summer one of the prisoners, Joe James, had been accused of breaking into the house of a local White resident and attempting to rape his daughter. The other prisoner, George Richardson, had also been accused of raping a White woman. In both cases the evidence against the men was spurious; they simply were Black and convenient scapegoats. However, in that racism-charged atmosphere facts were not important, and when the crowd was told that the prisoners had been transferred to a jail sixty miles away, they went on a rampage.

They moved into the predominantly Black neighborhood, destroying businesses and attacking anyone who was in their way; from there they proceeded to residential areas, throwing bricks and burning homes. As firefighters came to put out the fires, an estimated 12,000 Whites watched them burn. The next day thousands of Blacks fled the city, and the National Guard sent in 5,000 troops to restore order, but the mobs continued their path of destruction. When the riot was

* Photo of Mary White Ovington reproduced from the Library of Congress *LOOK Magazine* photograph collection. Unless otherwise noted, information reported in this chapter is based on Carolyn Wedin, *Inheritors of the Spirit: Mary White Ovington and the Founding of the NAACP* (New York: John Wiley and Sons, 1998).

over, forty homes had been burned, twenty-four businesses had been destroyed, seven people (two Black, five Whites) had died, and many more were injured. Indictments were brought against eighty individuals, but none were convicted. Although James was later executed for rape, Richardson was set free when his alleged victim admitted to making a false accusation.[1]

Unfortunately, the Springfield riots were only the latest in a series of such incidents during that same general period that affected major cities such as Atlanta, St. Louis, and Chicago. Violence against Black communities was a major problem throughout the nation; only some of the major incidents, like the one in Springfield, made the news. In response to the Springfield riots, a journalist named William Walling wrote an article titled "Race War in the North," in which he pleaded with White citizens of conscience to stop the ongoing violence. He asked: "Who realizes the seriousness of the situation, and what large and powerful body of citizens is ready to come to [the Negro's] aid?"[2] One of the people who read the article was a forty-three-year-old White settlement house worker named Mary White Ovington.

In the few years prior to 1908, Ms. Ovington had been conducting research on the status of Negroes in New York City. In the process of her research she had developed a friendship with the African American academic and civil rights leader, W. E. B. Du Bois. Ovington had been working among the poor immigrants of New York for over ten years and had been quietly advocating for equal access to services and justice for the Black citizens of New York. However, when she read Walling's article, she felt compelled to do more.

After reflecting on the events in Springfield, she contacted Walling and proposed that they convene a meeting to do exactly what he suggested. So a few days later Ovington, Walling, and a social worker named Henry Moskowitz issued a call to several prominent citizens, both Black and White, to come together for a meeting on February 12, 1909 (Abraham Lincoln's 100th birthday). From this first meeting, the organization that eventually became known as the National Association for the Advancement of Colored People (NAACP) was born. Mary White Ovington had been its midwife, and over the next forty years this quiet, determined White woman would come to be seen as the heart and soul of the organization.

---

[1] Wikipedia, Springfield Riots of 1908, http://en.wikipedia.org.

[2] Wedin, *Inheritors of the Spirit*, 105.

Who was Mary White Ovington, and how did she come to be such a powerful force for racial justice in the first half of the twentieth century?

Childhood

Mary White Ovington was born on April 11, 1865, two days after Robert E. Lee surrendered to Ulysses S. Grant, effectively ending the Civil War, and three days before President Abraham Lincoln was assassinated. She was born on a quiet street in Brooklyn, New York, but the national events surrounding her birth in many ways portended the direction her life would take. She was the third of four children born to Theodore and Ann Ketcham White. White's paternal grandfather had moved to the United States from England in 1798 and had helped to set up his two sons, Theodore and Edward, in a prominent china shop in Brooklyn. Until marrying Ann, Theodore and his family had attended Plymouth Congregational Church, where the famous abolitionist preacher, Henry Ward Beecher, held forth every Sunday. Mary's maternal grandmother, Emeline Ketcham, had been a close friend of William Lloyd Garrison, the great abolitionist leader, and had developed her antislavery views under the preaching of the Unitarian minister, Samuel May. Thus, Mary grew up in a family with a legacy of antislavery advocacy and activism.

She was raised in a relatively comfortable and privileged environment. Although her family was not rich by any means, and in fact suffered privation during the economic recessions of that period, as a child Mary was able to spend many summers outside the heat of the city in a summer home in Connecticut. Like other middle-class New Yorkers, she detested ugliness and the dirt of the city, but unlike many of her peers, early on she decided to be a person who would seek to transform the ugliness and suffering she witnessed. She also became aware at an early age of how hard her father worked to maintain his business and how much he had to sacrifice to provide for his family.

When Theodore White married Ann Ketcham, he transferred his church membership from the Presbyterians to the Unitarians, which was seen as somewhat scandalous at that time. Mary grew up frequenting both congregations, but eventually came under the influence of Second Unitarian's minister Henry Chadwick. Although his sermons were not particularly dynamic, she was impressed with the way he related his religion to the everyday affairs of life, and he influenced Mary to pursue a life of intellectual honesty and rigor. He also introduced her to the principles of socialism as a clear remedy to the exploitation of the working person. The struggle of laborers in the city that she observed and this teaching eventually led her to embrace socialism as her preferred economic perspective.

While still a teenager, Mary Ovington had the opportunity to hear an aging Frederick Douglass, the great Black abolitionist orator, speak in Plymouth Congregational Church. Douglass had recently prompted a scandal when he had chosen to marry a White woman after the death of his first wife. Although the young man who accompanied Mary that night was focused on the Douglass marriage, Ovington was more taken by the prominence of the man's features and the power of his voice. Although it was expected that a woman of her background and stature would marry in her early twenties, Mary chose to work instead. In 1887, at the age of twenty-two, Ovington began volunteering with a Unitarian Mission Sunday School that served working-class girls and their families. These experiences introduced her to what would eventually become her work among the poor in some of the city's settlement houses.

Formative Influences

While she was involved with the mission, she became interested in pursuing further education, and after attending a prep school, in 1890 she attended the Society for Collegiate Instruction for Women, commonly called the Harvard Annex, later to become Radcliffe College for Women in Cambridge, Massachusetts. Women in the program received instruction from Harvard professors and had access to most of the facilities on the Harvard campus even though they were not allowed to matriculate as Harvard students since Harvard admitted only men at that time. Ovington took a wide range of liberal arts subjects. She was particularly influenced by her economics professor, William Ashley, who helped her realize that history and economics were not just academic subjects focused on past events, but could be tools for shaping society. Not only did she earn her certificate, but she was able to work with Ashley in 1893 as his graduate assistant, being one of only a few women given that opportunity.

She returned to Brooklyn to help her father's struggling business. She also became interested in the settlement-house movement that that had been initiated in 1889 by Jane Addams and Hull House in Chicago. The vision behind settlement houses was that wealthy and middle-class persons should live in proximity to the poor by moving into low-income neighborhoods with the goal of sharing knowledge and providing essential services that would alleviate poverty. In low-income immigrant communities these services often took the form of childhood education and child care, and teaching the residents how to succeed in the culture with English classes, arts, and cultural activities.[3] In 1895, Ovington became the director of the Greenpoint Settlement in an immigrant working-class neighborhood of Brooklyn.

Despite having received a great deal of formal training, she said that her true education began during her seven years at Greenpoint. The experience at Greenpoint gave her a firsthand engagement with the economic and social struggles of working-class people in her community. She saw that young boys had few options besides working in the local factory and that girls were socialized toward domestic pursuits and motherhood. At the same time through her interaction with many families, she learned that the men who built the buildings and worked in the factories that fueled the burgeoning economy were not able to adequately provide for the families despite their hard work. She realized that the industrial system of that era was stacked against the workers and their families; it was rare that they could ever rise out of their desperate circumstances. These insights led her to the conviction that what she could offer the people of Greenpoint were the tools for their own advancement through education, union organizing, and helping them cope with stress in more constructive ways than simply drinking alcohol to drown their frustration. Moreover, she realized that as a middle-class person she could not honestly help the poor and remain untouched, but instead saw that persons like herself had to "renounce our most cherished possession, our attitude of superiority," if they were to ever effectively work among the poor.[4]

Most of her initial settlement work occurred with European immigrant families, and she noticed that these immigrant families quickly inherited the prejudices Whites across the county had toward Blacks. Once she took a group of Greenpoint children on a bus ride that required they drive through the Black community. As they rode through the community, little boys on the bus yelled "Nigger! Nigger! Nigger!" out the window, and when they were out of the neighborhood they sat down as if nothing significant had happened. Ovington later wrote: "They saw

---

[3] Louise Carroll Wade, "Settlement Houses," *Encyclopedia of Chicago* (Chicago: Chicago Historical Society, 2005), http://www.encyclopedia.chicagohistory.org.

[4] Wedin, *Inheritors of the Spirit*, 46

no harm in what they did. . . . As time went on I realized there was not personal animosity in their act. It was a custom."[5]

Ovington also became actively involved with the Socialist Party in New York. As part of her party activities she joined the Social Reform Club, a regular meeting of middle-class, educated persons like herself and some labor leaders, who met to discuss the pressing economic and social issues of their day. At one of their meetings, the prominent Black leader Booker T. Washington spoke to the group, and pointed out that the struggles faced by Blacks were not only in the South but that there was also "a Negro problem in [New York City]"; he emphasized that Blacks suffered more from segregation, poverty, and prejudice than any other group in the city. To that point in her life Ovington had not considered the unique challenges and struggles faced by the city's Black population.

She went home to Greenpoint that night with a new awareness and read James Russell Lowell's poem "A Present Crisis."[6] Though she had read them before the words of that poem grabbed her in a new way:

> Once to every man and nation comes the moment to decide,
> In the strife of Truth with Falsehood, for the good or evil side;
> Some great cause, God's new Messiah, offering each the bloom or blight,
> Parts the goats upon the left hand, and the sheep upon the right,
> And the choice goes by forever 'twixt that darkness and that light.

Within a year Ovington resigned her post at Greenpoint and began moving in a new direction that would consume her for the rest of her life.

A White Woman in a Black Power Struggle

Having been awakened to the unique plight of African Americans, Ovington was moved to start a settlement house in the Black community, but soon realized she knew few Black persons with whom she could consult. A friend and mentor suggested she make a study of the Black community in New York, and helped Ovington secure the funds to support her in doing so. Thus, in 1903 she wrote a letter to the

---

[5] Mary White Ovington, *Black and White Sat Down Together: The Reminiscences of an NAACP Founder* (New York: Feminist Press, 1995), 10.

[6] James Russell Lowell, "The Present Crisis," http://www.poets.org.

prominent African American sociologist, W. E. B. Du Bois, to seek his advice and counsel, as she wanted to use a methodology similar to the one Du Bois had used in his classic sociological study, *The Philadelphia Negro*. This correspondence began a forty-year relationship that would transform both of them.

Despite a full schedule Du Bois took a liking to Ovington and quickly responded to her inquiries. He encouraged her to talk directly with Negroes (as Blacks were then called) and learn from their experiences. He suggested readings for her and in 1905 invited her to make a presentation at a conference he sponsored in Atlanta. This was the first of many meetings they would have. All through this period, Ovington conducted research and published articles on various aspects of Negro life in New York. Then in August 1906 Ovington was invited to attend the second annual meeting of the Niagara Movement in Harpers Ferry, Virginia.

The Niagara Movement was a gathering of African American professional men founded by Du Bois in 1905 in response to Booker T. Washington's accommodationist and gradualist approach to racial justice outlined in the latter's famous speech, "The Atlanta Compromise." Washington's view was that Blacks must pull themselves up and earn the respect of the White population by diligence and hard work. In contrast, Du Bois and the Niagara Movement believed that Blacks should be granted full legal rights and economic access equal to that of Whites. Ovington was impressed by the eloquence and power of the speeches at the meeting, while recognizing that their work was crippled by a lack of funds. When she returned to New York, she reported on those meetings in a very positive light and sent a contribution.

Inadvertently by aligning herself with Du Bois, Ovington put herself in the middle of a struggle for prominence and power between the two greatest Black leaders in the United States at the time. Washington was widely popular with middle-class Blacks who saw him as their champion, as well as Northern Whites who saw him as a prophet. Despite his views that Blacks must gradually earn their place in US society, most Southern Whites still distrusted him. Nonetheless, Washington had a powerful organization, and many Blacks knew that an endorsement from Washington was an automatic "in" with White financial donors. Du Bois by contrast was uncompromising and demanding. Ovington wrote: "Du Bois and his followers wanted from the White man something more than money. They wanted a state of mind."[7] Du Bois's demands on behalf

[7] Ovington, *Black and White*, 22.

of Blacks were clear: the vote, an end to Jim Crow segregation, equal enforcement and justice under the law, education commensurate to that of Whites, and the right to gather freely when and where they pleased. Du Bois's directness was unnerving to many Blacks and intimidating to many Whites, and as a result he was less widely accepted even in the North. However, Mary White Ovington became one of his strongest advocates. Not only did she count Du Bois as a friend, but also she appreciated his radical perspective and approach, over against the often secretive and manipulative tactics used by Washington.

During the period between 1903 and 1909, Ovington carried on her research, even taking an extended trip to Atlanta and Alabama, observing the work in poor Black and White communities, and publishing many of her findings in the popular media. Also for seven months she lived in a section of Harlem named San Juan Hill, where she observed and participated in the life of that all-Black community. During this period she began participating in a monthly interracial discussion group called the Cosmopolitan Club. The group typically met in members' homes. However, in April 1908, they decided to hold their meeting in a local restaurant. To everyone's surprise, halfway through the dinner local reporters showed up unannounced. The next day a front-page article in the *New York Times* was headlined "Dinner Minus the Color Line: White Men of a Club Dine with Negro Women and Decry Caste." Soon the story was picked up by the national media and distorted, comparing the interracial meeting to interracial marriage, which was widely frowned upon by Whites, and outlawed in many states. Perhaps the most damning report for Ovington came from the *Savannah News*, which referred her as "the high priestess . . . [who] dined five nights a week with Negro men" and participated in a "Bacchanal feast" into which she would "take white girls into that den."[8] Following the dinner Ovington received a great deal of negative mail from angry readers. Circumstantial evidence suggests "that the whole thing had been set up by [Booker T.] Washington . . . who had arranged for the racially biased *New York American* to cover the event" for the purpose of discrediting Ovington and other allies (White and Black) of Du Bois."[9] However, Washington's tactics had the opposite effect on Ovington and strengthened her resolve to work more vigorously toward Du Bois's goals of racial justice.

---

[8] Wedin, *Inheritors of the Spirit*, 98.

[9] Ibid.

The Founding of the NAACP

Following the initial call to action in response to the Springfield, Illinois, riots, Ovington played a critical role in bringing the NAACP into being. The initial meeting was held on February 12, and sixty Black and White citizens signed on to form what was then called the National Negro Committee. A year later it would adopt its current name, the National Association for the Advancement of Colored People or NAACP. It is important to note that Du Bois was invited to join, but Washington was not. Although there was some risk in not including Washington, who was "unquestioningly the most influential and the most famous Negro living" at the time, Ovington felt that including Washington would undermine the organization's long-term goals and credibility. The rift with Washington became final when in 1909 the NAACP leadership issued a platform citing many of the same demands that Du Bois and the Niagara Movement had been advocating for the previous several years.

In the first ten years of the NAACP, Ovington played a key leadership role despite being one of the few women involved. She lobbied successfully for Du Bois to become the organization's director of publicity and research, which involved folding the Niagara Movement into the NAACP and making Du Bois editor of *Crisis*, the official NAACP journal. The iconoclastic Du Bois sometimes proved to be difficult to deal with and nearly impossible to manage; he had his own strong views and was resistant to taking direction from the NAACP leadership. As a result, Ovington often found herself mediating between Du Bois and the board members.

Ovington also launched several or the organization's early initiatives. She headed up efforts to conduct a campaign against the lynching of Blacks across the country and to pass federal legislation making it a federal crime. When the openly racist, but widely popular, film *Birth of the Nation* was circulated in 1915, she led the campaign to discredit the film and even have some of the more objectionable sections deleted. When the United States entered World War I in 1917, despite her pacifist views, she supported the formation of all-Black regiments to serve in the war. All the while serving as a member of the board of NAACP, Ovington dedicated herself to the task of building a viable organization for racial justice. She handled numerous administrative tasks as well as traveled widely to help start NAACP branches throughout the country, especially in the South. She also worked to increasingly diversify the staff and board membership to include more women as well as Persons of Color, since the initial board was predominantly made up of White men.

While engaged in these efforts, in 1911 Ovington completed her research study and published her first book, *Half a Man: The Status of the Negro in New York*. The title was taken from a comment made by a young man who had come North because he believed there he would be treated like a man and not a boy. However, in New York he discovered he was only "half a man. A Negro is wholly a man only in Europe."[10] In the study she compared the situations of the immigrant families she worked with at Greenpoint to the plight of the Black communities she studied. Although she decried the oppressive conditions faced by poor Whites, she showed how the pressures on Black families and individuals were much greater. Through her research she was able to show the direct relationship between structural racism and its disproportionate effect on family life, employment, educational attainment, and physical and emotional health in the Black community. Despite the emphasis on the male in the title of her book *Half a Man*, much of Ovington's study focused on the unique pressures and responsibilities placed on Black women to be supporters to their husbands, mothers, and breadwinners, and the toll it took. She concluded by stating that "it was not possible in 1911 to evaluate the capability of Negro Americans, since there had not been equal opportunity," and she challenged Whites to learn more about the struggles of their Black fellow citizens.

Her focus on and commitment to the Black struggle led her to reconsider her other social and political commitments when those commitments conflicted with the goal of racial justice. For instance, as the women's movement moved toward the passage of the Nineteenth Amendment that established that women had the right to vote, Ovington broke with the Women's Party when they refused to include the rights of Black women in their platform. Likewise, despite being a longtime member of the Socialist Party, she left the party when it refused to take up the cause of Black workers. Unions and workers' organizations were largely controlled by Whites and in many cases denied Black workers entrance to their ranks. Despite her deep commitments to economic and gender justice, when concrete political efforts did not include racial justice, Ovington chose to withdraw from those efforts.

---

[10] Mary White Ovington, *Half a Man: The Status of the Negro in New York* (New York: Hill and Wang, 1969), 1.

In 1919 she became chairperson of the NAACP board, a post she held until 1931. She worked closely with the new executive secretary, James Weldon Johnson, who took over the daily running of the organization. Weldon was an effective leader and organizer, and he helped build the NAACP into a powerful advocate for justice. He was a close personal friend of Ovington's, and she was devastated when he was killed in an auto accident in 1938. During her years as chairperson she continued to write books, articles, and short stories, largely highlighting the positive contributions Blacks had made and were making in society. She also authored a number of books intended for Black children. In 1931 at the age of sixty-six she stepped down as chair of the NAACP board and assumed the role of treasurer, a post she held until 1947. In that role she engaged in fund-raising and public speaking, something she had not previously done. However in that work she found great joy visiting local branches of the NAACP and encouraging their efforts.

In 1934 after a difficult relationship with the NAACP leadership, W. E. B. Du Bois resigned his post as director of publicity. Throughout its history, the NAACP had advocated that Whites and Blacks should work together. However, in an editorial in *Crisis*, Du Bois wrote that the failure to achieve racial parity meant that Blacks needed to separate themselves from Whites to promote their own social and political status, an idea echoed by radicals in the 1960s. Du Bois argued that "every Negro who has made a reputation [in the United States] has made it through segregation." Du Bois published the editorial without consulting the NAACP leadership and thus provoked a strong reaction among both the Black and White leaders in the organization. Ovington again found herself seeking to defend her bombastic colleague, and although she claimed to understand Du Bois's frustrations, she confessed that she wished he had not been so declarative in his stance. Like other Whites in the NAACP, Ovington had tried to work in concert with Black leaders, and she feared that actions such as the one that Du Bois advocated would usher in a new kind of segregation, where Blacks willingly separated from Whites. She argued for Blacks to "enlist the help of whites in sympathy with the [NAACP] goals" rather than push them aside. As a result of the editorial Du Bois was forced to resign and sever his ties with the organization. Du Bois's resignation strained Ovington's relationship with her former mentor, and they cut off all ties for a period.

Final Days

In 1947, at the age of eighty-two, Mary White Ovington resigned as treasurer and as a member of the board. In the years leading up to her resignation, her strength had diminished, her health had declined, and her ability to travel had lessened. She had lived with her mother until her death in 1927, and then had lived on her own; near the end of her life she moved in with her sister. In her final years even before she stepped down from the NAACP board, she had occasional difficulty with her eyesight, which in turn made it difficult for her to do many things she enjoyed. She became depressed, requiring brief periods in a psychiatric hospital. However, when she was able to do so, Ovington continued to publish, eventually writing her autobiography, which she titled *The Walls Came Tumbling Down* (1948). In 1944 Du Bois rejoined the NAACP, and Ovington and Du Bois were able to reconcile their differences. Eventually, Mary White Ovington's long life of advocacy came to an end on July 15, 1951, when she died at the age of eighty-six.

At the time of her death the NAACP had grown from a group of 60 signatories to an organization of more than 325,000 members and had fought hundreds of legal battles in courts throughout the South. Four years after her death, the NAACP won the landmark case, *Brown v. Board of Education* that forever outlawed segregated public schools, dealing a critical blow to the practice of Jim Crow segregation. Although she was rarely on the frontlines of that struggle, Mary White Ovington had played a pivotal role; she had been a radical ally working behind the scenes for racial justice. She had been a mediator not only between Du Bois and the NAACP board, but also between well-meaning Whites and frustrated Blacks. She had been an author who brought the Black struggle into public view and a tireless advocate for racial equality and healing. From not knowing any Black folks on a personal level in 1903, she had become a deep personal friend to some of the most prominent Black leaders of her day. Though she herself had come from a life of privilege that she never fully relinquished, she had constantly crossed barriers of culture, class, and race in pursuit of justice.

Carolyn Wedin sums up Ovington's life this way: "The clear theme of Mary White Ovington's life was the struggle for integration in all its senses. She is a force in U.S. history, in her NAACP work and in her personal life as she fought to remove legal and social barriers to Black people: integration in the racial sense. On a personal level, she integrated a happy, healthy childhood and youth with an active recognition of pain and suffering in the world."[11] She lived a life that spanned a history bringing a legal end to slavery to the legal end of segregation, and had actively participated in the progress between those points. At her death no one, least of all Mary White Ovington, believed that racial justice and equality had been achieved, or that White supremacist attitudes had vanished, but she died as she had lived working for those goals and for a society characterized truly by "liberty and justice for all."

[11] Carolyn Wedin, Afterword to *Black and White Sat Down Together*, by Mary White Ovington (New York: Feminist Press, 1995), 158.

Discussion Questions

1. Mary White Ovington combined her work in poor communities and in the NAACP with research and writing. What are ways that one's academic and scholarly work can contribute to the cause of racial justice today?
2. Although Ovington was instrumental in the formation and operation of the NAACP in its early years, she operated in a low-key, often behind-the-scenes manner. What are other ways that people quietly do the work of racial justice?
3. Ovington had a long-term but often difficult friendship with W. E. B. Du Bois, whom she admired but with whom she did not always agree. How do people of different races and cultures work together for racial justice amid divergent perspectives and strong emotions?

Bibliography

Lowell, James Russell. "The Present Crisis," http://www.poets.org.

Ovington, Mary White. *Black and White Sat Down Together: The Reminiscences of an NAACP Founder.* New York: Feminist Press, 1995.

———. *Half a Man: The Status of the Negro in New York*. New York: Hill and Wang, 1969.

Senghas, Dorothy, and Catherine Senghas. "Mary White Ovington." *Dictionary of Unitarian and Universalist Biography*, 2002. http://www25.uua.org.

"Springfield Race Riot of 1908." http://en.wikipedia.org.

Wade, Louise Carroll. "Settlement Houses." *Encyclopedia of Chicago*. Chicago: Chicago Historical Society, 2005. http://www.encyclopedia.chicagohistory.org.

Wedin, Carolyn. Afterword to *Black and White Sat Down Together: The Reminiscences of an NAACP Founder*, by Mary White Ovington. New York: Feminist Press, 1995.

———. *Inheritors of the Spirit: Mary White Ovington and the Founding of the NAACP*. New York: John Wiley and Sons, 1998.

7

J. Waties Waring (1880–1968)

*A Judge for Justice**

A Rock under the Sofa

On the evening of Monday, October 19, 1950, Federal District Judge J. Waties Waring of Charleston, South Carolina, and his wife, Elizabeth, were playing canasta in their living room. The months leading up to that night had been filled with controversy and tension, but that night was calm and peaceful. Nearly two years earlier the judge had ruled on a controversial case that required the previously all-White Democratic primary to allow Blacks to vote. From that point on the Warings had been the target of media criticism and various forms of harassment and intimidation. In January 1950, Mrs. Waring, at the invitation of the community leader Septima Clark, had given a speech at the Black YWCA in Charleston. In her speech Mrs. Waring had praised her husband's decision, criticized Charleston's White community as living a "selfish and savage white supremacy way of life," and praised the accomplishments of local Black citizens in the face of that overt racism. The speech had stirred up emotions in both the White and Black communities, so much so that people of both races were afraid to associate with them.

---

* Photo of J. Waties Waring is reproduced courtesy of Library of Congress. Unless otherwise noted the information in this chapter is from Carol Stokes Brown, *Refusing Racism: White Allies and the Struggle for Civil Rights* (New York: Teachers College Press, 2002); and Tinsley E. Yarbrough, *A Passion for Justice: J. Waties Waring and Civil Rights* (New York: Oxford University Press, 1987).

As the controversy and criticism of the judge and his wife continued to grow, they began to fear that like many of the Black citizens throughout the South, they might become targets for violence by the local Ku Klux Klan. That October night their fears were realized as their quiet living room calm was suddenly broken by the sound of three gunshots followed by the shattering of their living room windows as large stones came through. When the local police investigated, they told the Warings that the damage was caused by "nothing but a brick," but when the FBI investigated shortly after, they identified the stones as pieces of mortar. Although no bullets were ever found, the Warings knew for certain they were no longer safe in their hometown.

On the surface for a man of J. Waties Waring's position and lineage such an event might seem surprising. However, given the pilgrimage of thought and action that the seventy-year-old judge had gone through over the previous years, and the highly racialized nature of South Carolina political and social life at the time, the event was only the culmination of a long and arduous process of personal change.

Early Years

Julius Waties Waring was born in Charleston, South Carolina, on July 27, 1880, as the fourth child of Edward and Anne Waties Waring. The Warings' marriage had joined two aristocratic South Carolina families, who were long-time plantation owners. Furthermore, Edward Waring had served as an officer in the Confederate Army during the Civil War. After the war the family had experienced significant financial losses, but by 1880 they had begun to regain their fortune when the South Carolina economy rebounded. Although both of his parents were dedicated members of the Episcopal Church, young Waties inherited his questioning, challenging attitude from his mother, who was known to resist some of the stricter church doctrines.

As a young man and well into middle age, Waties shared the segregationist views of his family and other Whites in Charleston. As a child he had been cared for by a Black nurse named Hannah, whose last name he never knew or learned. He accepted the social mores of his day, later writing: "Most of the Negroes I knew were ex-slaves and you loved them, were good to them. We didn't give them any rights, but they never asked for any rights, and I didn't question it."[1] Even as

---

[1] J. Waties Waring, *The Reminiscences of J. Waties Waring* (New York: Columbia University Research Office, 1972, microfiche), 12.

a young attorney he seemed uncomfortable around Black people and often asked his law partner to work with the Black clients because he did not feel he understood their needs.

As one of the major ports of entry for slaves being brought from Africa, Charleston had a long history of racist practices that did not abate but only changed form after slavery was outlawed. The South Carolina of Waring's time was strictly segregationist and effectively barred African Americans from any significant influence in matters of public concern. Yet Waring lived very comfortably in this society and did not even begin to openly question such practices until he was in his sixties.

As a boy Waring attended private school and had hoped to attend college in the North like his older brother Thomas, but when his father's finances were depleted in 1896, he could only afford to attend the local College of Charleston. In college he studied the classics and graduated in 1900 with honors, ranked second in his class. By his senior year he had decided he wanted to become a lawyer, but again a lack of finances prohibited him from attending law school, so as was common at the time, he studied for the bar exam while working for no pay at the law firm of J. P. Kennedy Bryan, a friend of his father's. After about two years of study he was able to pass the bar and spent the next eleven years working with the Bryan firm.

In 1913 Waring married Annie Gammell, a Charleston socialite who had studied drama in New York City. Waring moved to New York to be with her, but a year after getting married, the couple moved from New York back to Charleston where they became prominent members of local society and devoted parishioners of the Episcopal Church. They had one child, Anne, who was born about three years after they had moved back to Charleston. Waring and his wife enjoyed all the benefits of elite White Charleston society, often entertaining at home or the summer cottage on the South Carolina coast. As was the custom, when their daughter Anne was of age she was presented as a debutante in high fashion.

In 1914 through some local political connections, the ambitious Waring was appointed assistant US attorney for South Carolina's eastern district, but after six years he returned to private practice. Waring established his own law firm with a friend and colleague, and they developed a thriving legal practice focused on maritime and real estate law. Although Waring treated the few African American clients he had with respect, he later confessed that he "accepted white supremacy without examining it."[2] He returned to government work in 1933, serving as the Charleston

[2] Brown, *Refusing Racism*, 55.

city attorney until 1942. As evidence of his White supremacist views at the time, he helped enforce a ruling making it illegal for Black soldiers from a nearby Army base to use public city parks. During his tenure as the city attorney, he aspired to higher political positions and made unsuccessful bids to become the South Carolina US attorney and a federal district judge.

Throughout his early career, Waring was an active and influential member of the Democratic Party in South Carolina. After leaving the attorney general's office, he maintained active involvement in local politics, which eventually opened up the opportunities to be the assistant attorney general, and later the Charleston city attorney. He also developed a relationship with US Senator Ed "Cotton" Smith and served as an adviser to his 1938 election campaign. Smith was well known locally and nationally for being an outspoken, race-baiting legislator, prone to go on public tirades against Black people and anti-lynching legislation.

Waring's relationship with Senator Smith was instrumental to his being appointed to the Federal District Court of the Eastern District of South Carolina in 1942, a post he was to hold for ten transformative years. According to Brown, "Waring outwardly seemed to have everything a Charlestonian could aspire to—achievement, wealth, status, pleasure,"[3] but this appointment was to mark a turning point in his life that would change his outlook and eventually his status in elite White Charleston society.

Divorce

Though it was well known that Waring was something of a ladies' man around Charleston, from all external appearances up until 1942 he and Annie were a devoted married couple. Although she did not share his interest in politics and law or his love of the ancient classics, she was known to be a devoted wife and mother. They often traveled together to exclusive resorts and were regular patrons of the theater both in Charleston and New York. Nonetheless, privately the Warings had a cold distant relationship that eventually led to divorce.

Sometime between 1942 and 1944 Waring became involved with Elizabeth Avery Hoffman, the wife of a Connecticut textile merchant who spent winters in Charleston. When Waring and Hoffman met, she was on her second marriage, having two children by the previous marriage. At some point in that period they began to carry on a discreet love affair, and in early 1945 Waring announced to his wife that he was

---

[3] Ibid., 57.

in love with another woman and wanted a divorce. Both Waring and Hoffman subsequently divorced their spouses and married each other. Because at the time divorce was not allowed in South Carolina, Annie Waring had to file for divorce in Florida at the request of her husband, and Hoffman filed for divorce in Nevada. Then on June 15, 1945, they were married in Greenwich, Connecticut.

Because Annie, Waring's first wife, was a well-respected member of Charleston society, and because the divorce had personally devastated her, the news of Waring's divorce and remarriage was met with strong disapproval from friends, colleagues, and even members of his family. Quickly the newly married couple became isolated from many of their former friends. In addition to the stigma around divorce, Elizabeth's history and the fact that she was from the North fueled distrust, animosity, and the desire to keep distance from them. Even though Waring had begun to change his views on racial segregation before his divorce and remarriage, many of Charleston's elite White socialites blamed his change of mind on his new Yankee wife.

A Segregationist Begins to Change

Waring referred to his transition from lawyer to judge as a "born again" experience in which he gained a new perspective where cases needed to be handled "justly and right."[4] Nonetheless, when he assumed his judgeship in 1942, he still held firmly to the Southern belief of White supremacy that had contributed to his rise to that position. However, he was also known to be eminently fair, insisting that both Whites and African Americans be addressed by their titles, stipulating that the seating in his courtroom be desegregated and requiring that Black jurors be treated to the same amenities as White jurors.

At the same time his racist ideas were being discreetly challenged. Waring later commented to the civil rights activist Septima Clark that in the early days of his judgeship, he noticed that there were "black men coming in that I knew were decent men, and they were considered bums and trash because they were black. And I would see white men that I knew were bums and they were considered gentlemen. I just couldn't take it anymore."[5] Thus began J. Waties Waring's transformation into a judicial advocate for civil rights.

---

[4] Ibid., 59.

[5] Carol Stokes Brown, *Septima Clark and the Civil Rights Movement* (Trenton, NJ: Africa World Press, 1990), 24.

The shift in Waring's judicial thinking first became publicly evident in 1943 and then again in 1944 during cases brought on behalf of Black schoolteachers who were being paid significantly less than their White counterparts. In both cases Judge Waring ruled that Black and White teachers should be paid according to the same pay scale and same standards. These rulings eventually led the South Carolina legislature to pass qualifying standards for all teachers and a common pay scale regardless of race. Thurgood Marshall, the lawyer for the NAACP who brought the cases, later commented that he was pleasantly surprised at Waring's commitment to fairness and order in those cases. Although the school cases did not get a strong reaction from White society, Waring later confessed these cases made him increasingly aware of the culture that created "two classes of citizens, and that Negroes were not treated as ordinary human beings" in many aspects of daily life.[6]

Even so, Waring did not think that change would or should come quickly; he advocated gradualism (which was common at the time in the South) as it related to eradicating laws supporting segregation and different treatment of Blacks and Whites. During this period Waring wrote:

> The old cliché that Rome was not built in a day, is applicable to this situation. The idea that emancipation of a race long enslaved and without political rights, without political or any other kind of education, and without training to assume citizenship, would bring about a satisfactory situation overnight could be held by only a few partisan, biased, persons motivated either by idealistic abstractions or by a spirit of political revenge and self-seeking aggrandizement. . . . These things have to be lived through and arrived at after generations of experience, before men will accept them, understand them, agree with them and work for their effect and efficacy.[7]

Although he objected to "the radical methods" of strong antisegregationists like First Lady Eleanor Roosevelt, he considered himself a "liberal-minded Southerner" who could pave the way for a "moderate, gradual and understanding action."[8]

---

[6] Ibid., 60.

[7] Yarbrough, *Passion for Justice*, 46.

[8] Ibid.

However, cases involving the unequal legal treatment of Blacks vis-à-vis Whites continued to come before him. In one particular case, Waring ruled in favor of a young Black boy who had been tricked into signing a work contract where he was paid one dollar a day and carried across state lines from Georgia to South Carolina. This case highlighted the ongoing abuse and manipulation that Blacks suffered in many of the rural areas of the South. Waring presided over another case in which the psychology of Southern racism was demonstrated. Black employees at a sawmill were being paid vastly lower wages than their White counterparts despite having the same jobs and doing the same work. The Black employees sued to have equal wages made mandatory, which by federal law they were entitled to have. The law was clear, and the evidence for the plaintiffs was overwhelming, but the jury acquitted the company of any wrongdoing. When Waring later interviewed one of the jurors, he was told that all of them knew the company was guilty, "but we can't send White men to jail for violating a federal law. We'll have Negroes all over the state rising up and demanding their rights."[9]

However, the case that affected Waring the most involved a Black soldier named Isaac Woodward who had recently returned from military service in World War II. In an act of overt racist violence Woodward was dragged off a bus, accused of public drunkenness, and beaten by the local police, although witnesses on the bus testified that he had not been drinking. The beatings resulted in Woodward's being permanently blinded. Judge Waring presided over the jury case. However, for fear of alienating its Southern constituency in a presidential election year, the US Department of Justice failed to prosecute the case aggressively. Despite Waring's attempt to bring out the obvious racist actions in the case, the jury acquitted the police chief on all charges. Unfortunately, similar cases can be seen in the twenty-first century. This case compelled Judge Waring to see clearly how violent and vicious racism was the norm in many South Carolina communities.

For Elizabeth Waring (who had watched the court proceedings), the Woodward case was her "baptism into racial prejudice."[10] During this time Elizabeth Waring had been reading about the history of Southern race relations, in books such as W. J. Cash's *Mind of the South* (1941) and Gunnar Myrdal's study of American race relations, *The American Dilemma* (1944). Elizabeth Waring also borrowed pamphlets from a

---

[9] Waring, *Reminiscences*, 205.

[10] Yarbrough, *Passion for Justice*, 53.

prominent local Black shoemaker, Samuel Fleming. At night in their home, Elizabeth would read to her husband from these sources, and eventually he began to read them on his own. He later commented that he found the readings "enlightening—and deeply disturbing." At first he resisted believing them and would spend evening hours driving in his car just to relieve his discomfort. But eventually like his wife, he "began to embrace what he read."[11]

A Completed Transformation

The court case that indelibly marked Waring as a pariah among White South Carolinians was his 1947 ruling abolishing the all-White South Carolina Democratic state primary. Later Waring wrote that when the case came before him, "I liked it because I felt it was an opportunity, and I felt that somebody in the country ought to take a stand. . . . I felt that my state was backward, that it had been blind to decency and right, and that somebody had at last to face the issue. I thought it was a fine opportunity."[12] He not only was taking on one of the most powerful institutions in the South, but he was also betraying the entity that had enabled him to be in his position of judge in the first place.

After Reconstruction, the Democratic Party was the only viable political party in the state, and in an attempt to maintain White supremacy in their political system, the South Carolina Democratic Party excluded African Americans from voting in political primaries. Because a Republican challenger had little chance of being elected, this effectively eliminated any influence African American voters could have on an election. Although the Supreme Court had outlawed White primaries in Texas in 1944, through a series of changes in state law, South Carolina Democrats were able to find a loophole in the law that allowed them to maintain their practice at the political primary level, and because of concerns not to alienate Southern Democrats, the Justice Department did little to challenge it.

In 1946 with the help of the NAACP a Black merchant named George Elmore challenged this practice, and the case eventually came before Judge Waring. Waring ruled in favor of Mr. Elmore's plea, writing: "It is time for South Carolina to join the Union. It is time to fall in step with the other states and to adopt the American way of conducting

[11] Ibid.
[12] Ibid., 60.

elections."[13] Eventually the case went all the way to the US Supreme Court, and Waring's decision was upheld. This decision won Waring the approval of most Blacks and even a few Whites, but the Democratic White political leaders still refused to abide by the decision and allow Blacks to vote in political primaries. As a result an NAACP legal team headed by Thurgood Marshall sought an injunction to allow Blacks to vote in the 1948 primary. Waring granted the injunction and threatened to send Democratic Party leaders to jail if they did not comply with his order. On the day of the primary, August 10, 1948, Waring made himself visibly present at polling places by driving throughout Charleston where large numbers of Black voters gathered to cast their vote. In all, approximately 35,000 Blacks voted in the primary without incident.

Prior to his decision on the Elmore case, Waring warned his wife that his actions might complete their isolation and alienation from White society in Charleston. Shortly after he issued the 1948 injunction, they started to be harassed by members of the White community, receiving threatening phone calls and being denied service in local stores. A South Carolina congressman even introduced a resolution in the US House of Representatives to have Judge Waring investigated, and other politicians called for his removal from the bench. The local newspaper, the *Charleston Courier*, of which Waring's nephew was the editor, ran numerous editorials denouncing Waring's decision and his character as a judge. Even so, they also received letters from Whites and Blacks throughout the South praising Waring for his courage. Nonetheless, the tension was so great that Waring and his wife left Charleston from August to October 1948 just to get some relief, and often stayed away from Charleston for extended periods of time whenever possible.

Outcasts in Charleston

Prior to the Elmore case, Waring had maintained the hope that the South would gradually become more open to Whites and Blacks being treated as equal members of society. However, during the proceedings of the case, he came to believe that action by the federal government would be necessary for substantive change ever to come to South Carolina's racist laws and practices. Though he thought improvement in relationships between the races was possible, he came to believe that "the windows would not be opened voluntarily."[14] The judge angered South

[13] Ibid., 64.

[14] Ibid., 96.

Carolinians further when he publicly stated that "my people have one outstanding fault—the terrible fault of racial prejudice."[15] Local media and even preachers criticized him for these and similar public statements. By contrast, the Democratic primary case received national attention with magazines such as *Time* and *The Nation* running feature articles on Waring and the case, which made him something of a national civil rights hero. He also received several opportunities to speak publicly on the need for the end of segregation, which he willingly accepted.

His actions and public statements made the Warings even greater social outcasts in Charleston, and they were sustained only by the support and encouragement they received from friends and colleagues outside the state.[16] With their social ties in White Charleston society all but eliminated, they began openly entertaining African American friends in their homes, including civil rights activist Septima Clark, who had become a close friend and confidant after the pay equity case, and Ruby and A. T. Cornwell, prominent Black Charlestonians. They also developed friendships with national African American leaders such as NAACP Chairperson Walter White, Morehouse College President Dr. Benjamin Mays, Thurgood Marshall, and UN Representative Dr. Ralph Bunche. They also developed relationships with White Southerners such as Virginia and Clifford Durr, Aubrey Williams and Jim Dombrowski,[17] who were long-time advocates for racial equality. Both Waring and Elizabeth openly spoke of their desire to see full equality for Blacks and Whites in the South, and encouraged their Black friends to take an aggressive approach to civil rights reform. Furthermore, he publicly criticized Southern and Northern moderates who urged a gradual process for civil rights reform.

By 1950, Waring had come to believe that it was the moment to ensure full equality for African Americans in all areas of South Carolina society, and so he sought a case to be brought to him that would reverse the 1896 *Plessy v. Ferguson* ruling that had established the practice of "separate but equal" and was the cornerstone of Southern Jim Crow segregationist policies. Eventually, a case was brought to his court by Thurgood Marshall and the NAACP against the Clarendon County

---

[15] Ibid.

[16] One of the most moving tributes came from Clifford Durr, lawyer and husband of Virginia Foster Durr, whose story is told in chapter 8.

[17] For more on the Durrs see chapter 8. For Williams and Dombrowski, see Appendix.

school district, which spent an average of $179 per White student compared to $43 per Black student. Because federal law required that a case such as this be heard by a three-judge panel, Waring had few illusions that he would be able to erase the practice of segregated and unequal schools, but "win or lose Waring wanted segregation attacked, then and in his court."[18] As was expected, in 1951 the three-judge panel ruled 2–1 in favor of the Clarendon County schools, with Waring the dissenting voice. In his dissent Judge Waring wrote: "If [Negroes] are entitled to any rights of American citizens, they are entitled to have these rights now and not in the future, and no excuse can be made to deny them these rights."[19]

Final Years in New York

Realizing that his usefulness as an activist judge had run its course, Waring retired shortly after in February 1952 at the age of seventy-two. The Warings moved to New York City where they had family and friends; they continued to speak out on issues of racism throughout the rest of their lives. He joined the National Urban League and worked with a number of civil rights organizations. Having become a staunch opponent of segregation of any kind, he was known to speak in harsh and uncompromising tones toward Whites and Blacks who did not share his views; friends and foes alike experienced him as sometimes difficult to relate to. At one point he even criticized the leaders of the NAACP for being too closely aligned with the Democratic Party, which had too often in his view compromised on its opposition to segregation. However, when in 1954 the Supreme Court permanently outlawed segregated education in the *Brown v. Board of Education*, Judge Waring's efforts three years before were validated. Although his dissent in the earlier case was not mentioned in the court's decision, the couple took the decision as a victory and quietly celebrated with friends in their apartment.

Waring had vowed not to return to Charleston until segregation was outlawed, so being true to his promise in November 1954 he returned on a visit to the city of his birth where he was met by several hundred cheering African Americans and a handful of Whites. He and Elizabeth continued to live in New York until he died on January 20, 1968, after which his body was returned to Charleston for burial where his funeral

---

[18] Brown, *Refusing Racism*, 72.

[19] Waring, *Reminiscences*, 360.

was attended by two hundred African Americans and twelve Whites. Six months later his wife passed away and was buried beside him; her funeral was attended by only six Blacks and three Whites. It took many years for the dislike of the Warings to dissipate in the people of Charleston, evidence being the vandalizing of their graves, but in 1981 the city of Charleston erected a monument in his honor.

Returning Home

The story of J. Waties Waring as an antiracist ally is significant in that he was able to use his position as a federal district judge to challenge existing laws and practices in the segregated South. Waring's shift in views came about gradually and were coupled with other significant changes in his life, most notably his controversial divorce and his reading of the history of Southern race relations. Moreover, it is significant that most of his work occurred after his sixtieth birthday and a long career living comfortably within a White supremacist society. The consequences of Waring's transformation into a strong voice against racist practices cost him friends and endangered his safety, while opening him up to a new set of friends and colleagues all committed to overturning legalized racism in the United States. So although the Warings were ostracized for their outspoken views and actions, they found new relationships that sustained and bolstered them for the work they felt called to perform.

J. Waties Waring's transformation is a testimony to the fact that when confronted with the reality of racial violence and discrimination, White allies can and must take a stand. Waring not only had to battle the values and beliefs of his White supremacist upbringing but also a culture and a political system designed to reinforce those values and beliefs. Although he was not alone among White Southerners in coming to see segregation as wrong, he was distinguished by his willingness to act in ways that dismantled the very system from which he had gained so much prominence and power. Although it took him nearly two-thirds of his life to realize and act on his antiracist convictions, when he did so, he acted with boldness and courage. Even after his change of perspective, he was not always an easy person to relate to; yet even his difficult personality can be viewed as a sign of the urgency with which he attacked the systemic racism of his time. For that boldness he is remembered and honored even today.

Discussion Questions

1. J. Waties Waring did not change his views and behavior until late in life. Discuss various experiences that have awakened different people to the realities of racial injustice.
2. Waring used his position as a federal judge to fight the racism of his day. What are some positions or opportunities that might allow people in the present to work for racial justice?

Bibliography

Brown, Carol Stokes. *Refusing Racism: White Allies and the Struggle for Civil Rights*. New York: Teachers College Press, 2002.

———. *Septima Clark and the Civil Rights Movement*. Trenton, NJ: Africa World Press, 1990.

Waring, J. Waties. *Reminiscences of Waties Waring*. New York: Columbia University Oral History Research Office, 1972, microfiche.

Yarbrough, Tinsley E. *A Passion for Justice: J. Waties Waring and Civil Rights*. New York: Oxford University Press, 1987.

8

Virginia Foster Durr
(1903–1999)

*Aristocratic Rebel**

"I Stand Mute"

In 1954, Senator James Eastland of Mississippi was campaigning for office on the platform that if the Supreme Court ruled that schools had to be racially desegregated, this would prove that the court was under the influence of a Communist plot. One of the judges ruling in the case was Justice Hugo Black, originally from Alabama and the brother-in-law of Virginia Foster Durr, a resident of Montgomery, Alabama. In an attempt to show that Justice Black was influenced by Communists, Senator Eastland convened a meeting of the Senate Internal Security Committee, whose mission it was to identify and root out Communists in the US government. The meeting was held in New Orleans in March 1954, and Virginia Durr was called to testify, along with several others, including Myles Horton[1] and Anne Braden.[2] After viewing the proceedings on the first day, Mrs. Durr decided that the whole thing was a sham. She was supposed to testify the next day.

* Photo of Virginia Foster Durr used by permission of the Schlesinger Library, Harvard University. Primary sources for this chapter are Cynthia Stokes Brown, *Refusing Racism: White Allies and the Struggle for Civil Rights* (New York: Teachers College Press, 2002); Virginia Foster Durr and Hollinger F. Barnard, *Outside the Magic Circle: The Autobiography of Virginia Foster Durr*, ed. Hollinger J. Barnard (Tuscaloosa: University of Alabama Press, 1985); James Smallwood, *Reform, Red Scare, and Ruin: Virginia Durr, Prophet of the New South* (Oklahoma: James Smallwood, 2008), Kindle edition.

[1] For more information on Myles Horton, see chapter 9.

[2] For more information on Anne Braden, see chapter 12.

That evening she could not sleep and drafted a statement that indicated that although she respected the investigative powers of Congress, what she witnessed the day before was a "kangaroo court." She ended the statement with the words, "I stand in utter and complete contempt of this committee." When she was called to testify, she refused to sit down and began to read her statement but was stopped by Senator Eastland, so she handed the statement to the press. All eyes and cameras were on her as she stood silently, saying quietly, "I stand mute" and powdering her nose as she stood there.

Senator Eastland had clearly miscalculated when he thought he could intimidate Virginia Durr into implicating her brother-in-law before his committee. Had he thought it through, he would have realized that he was dealing with a woman who had walked in the halls of the nation's capital as well on the streets of some of the South's poorest neighborhoods. He would have known that she came from aristocratic Southern roots and from that place challenged some of the nation's most virulent public racists like Senator Eastland. He would have known that though she had been raised to be a stereotypical Southern woman—silent and submissive to her husband—she had become an ardent defender of basic freedoms for all people, regardless of race, class, or gender. Eastland would have known that in many ways though she was an aristocrat, she was not a woman to be trifled with.

Growing Up an Aristocrat

Virginia Foster Durr was born on August 6, 1903, in the parsonage of the South Highland Presbyterian Church in Birmingham, Alabama, where her father, Sterling Johnson Foster, was the pastor. The youngest of three children, she was strong willed. She was nursed by her mother, Ann Patterson Foster, and if her mother was late with her milk, Virginia would howl and scream. This practice of demanding what she thought was right and necessary was a theme that ran through her entire life.

Both of Virginia's parents came from families deeply entrenched in the history and culture of the Old South. Her paternal grandfather had been a wealthy Alabama farmer who opposed going to war in defense of slavery, yet he continued to own slaves and through some shrewd financial dealings came out of the Civil War wealthier than before, unlike the vast majority of Southern farmers. Following the war he developed a huge plantation in Union Springs, Alabama, on which several ex-slaves lived and worked as tenant farmers. Virginia's father and his three siblings grew up in the midst of wealth, abundance, and servants at their beck and call, and were accustomed to the privileged life of the Southern elite. Virginia never knew her grandfather, but her grandmother lived until Virginia was eight years old, and left a strong impression on her. When Grandmother Foster died, her father took over management of the estate, but he was not a particularly good manager, and as the Southern economy declined, so did the estate.

Virginia's mother also grew up in Alabama but came from more modest means. Virginia's maternal grandfather, Josiah Patterson, fought with the Confederacy in the Civil War under Nathan Bedford Forrest and moved to Memphis after the war to be near Forrest and join in the organization he founded, the Ku Klux Klan. He served briefly in Congress, but after losing an election, he became the custodian of the battlefield at Shiloh, a Confederate war park. Although her maternal grandmother did not come from great wealth (something Virginia did not realize until much later in life), when she married Josiah Patterson she adopted the elitist Southern manner that accompanied his family and status.

Ann Patterson and Sterling Foster met at the Idlewild Presbyterian Church in Memphis where Sterling was the pastor. Shortly after they were married he took a position at the Highland Presbyterian Church in Birmingham, where Virginia was born. When she was about seven or eight, Sterling was removed from the pulpit for preaching "heresy" at the wealthy, fundamentalist church; the issue apparently centered on his belief that the story of Jonah and the whale was not a literal, historical event. After being removed from his pulpit and stripped of his clergy credentials, he had a nervous breakdown and went away for a while to a spa known to help people with such problems. With his mother's help he was able to purchase a home in Birmingham, and he worked as an insurance salesman but was generally unsuccessful in that role. Despite these underlying and largely hidden struggles and disruptions, Virginia's family continued to live a life that projected an air of wealth and privilege.

Virginia's parents taught her to believe that basically there were three groups of people in the world: the elite or aristocrats, the common folk (who were the poor Whites who worked in the fields and factories), and the Negroes. She was further taught that God had destined people to their station in life and that nothing could, would, or should change that. Moreover, she was told that poor Whites were poor because they did not work hard enough and Negroes were to be regarded as less than fully human.

Even so, Virginia grew up surrounded by Black adults who served her family. Her paternal grandmother had a Black servant named Easter who essentially ran the household and the plantation in Grandmother Foster's declining years. Virginia later described Easter as dignified and wise, "probably the smartest woman I ever knew." In her own home, Virginia was cared for on a daily basis by a woman named Alice whom she called "Nursie"; Nursie bathed her, dressed her, and put her to bed at night, acting as a second mother to her. Virginia played regularly with Nursie's daughter Sarah, as well as other Black children in the area. In a way that was typical of many White children growing up in the South during the pre–civil rights era, Virginia described her childhood this way: "I actually lived in two worlds until I was seven years old. I lived in a White world and Black world and was accepted in both."[3]

However, all of that changed on Virginia's seventh birthday. Because she had a summer birthday, she always celebrated it at the plantation in Union Springs with a barbecue in the backyard with all the Black children who lived on the estate where their parents worked. However, for this particular birthday her Grandmother Foster and Aunt May (who happened to be visiting from out of town) informed her that the Black children would not be allowed to attend her party; instead she was to have White children (who were strangers to her) attend, and the party would be held in the front yard. Virginia had a "temper fit," and so it was decided to have a party with the Black children in the morning followed by another party with the White children in the afternoon. During the afternoon party Virginia had another outburst and ran to Nursie to be consoled. Aunt May, said in a voice loud enough for all to hear: "The trouble with Virginia is that nurse. She spoils her. And besides I think it's terrible that you let her sit in her lap and sleep with her and kiss her and hug her. You know all those black women are diseased." Nursie put Virginia to bed that night, but the next morning she left, never to return. Virginia was so distraught that she never forgot the incident.[4]

When later in her life she reflected on that painful day, she wrote the following about her childhood: "You are given over to black people. They guard you and look after you and you love them devotedly . . .

---

[3] Durr, *Outside the Magic Circle*, 14.

[4] Ibid., 16–17.

and all of a sudden you are told . . . that they are inferior people and they should not be treated like other people. It makes you feel that there is something wrong with you."[5] This was the confusing world of race and privilege in which Virginia was raised.

She further learned that the rules of society applied differently to Whites and Blacks. When she asked why Black people who worked on their plantation were a variety of shades of black, brown, tan, and cream, her father informed her it was because of the Union soldiers who came to the South during the Civil War. She learned that one of her ancestors, Wilbur Foster, had been driven out of town because he was considered a "nigger lover" for donating the land for the building of Tuskegee Institute, the college started by Booker T. Washington. She witnessed a lynching, attended KKK parades, and like many Southerners of her era felt affirmed in their beliefs by the movie *Birth of a Nation*, a widely popular 1915 film that depicted Black people as ignorant and sexually aggressive toward White women.

Although Virginia loved school, from her parents' perspective the purpose of education was to groom her to a find a husband and become a dignified Southern lady. So when she was fifteen they sent her to New York to attend Miss Finch's Finishing School for Girls and to live with her Aunt Mamie; the expressed purpose of the school was to train young women to become cultured and well mannered, so they could attract a wealthy husband. After a year in New York she returned to Birmingham for her junior year of high school. Then during her senior year she was sent to the Cathedral School in Washington, DC, where she received further "finishing" as a Southern debutante.

When Virginia was sixteen, her older sister, Josephine, became involved with a young Birmingham attorney named Hugo Black. Black was a veteran of World War I, and a member of the local country club, even though he was not from a prominent Southern family. Furthermore, he was a Baptist and a labor lawyer, something frowned upon by Montgomery's elite. Virginia's parents were wary of Josephine's becoming involved with such a common man, but his prominence as a lawyer and professional success overcame their reticence. Josephine Foster and Hugo Black were married in 1921, and Virginia's brother-in-law became a lifelong inspiration, confidant, friend, and, paradoxically, a source of trouble to Virginia throughout her life.

---

[5] Smallwood, *Reform, Red Scare and Ruin*, Kindle loc. 494.

Young Adulthood

Despite his growing financial problems, in 1921 Sterling Foster found a way to pay for his daughter to attend Wellesley College in Massachusetts. Virginia loved the social life at Wellesley and joined the Southern Club, a social group in nearby Cambridge that catered to students from the South. There she got acquainted with Clark Foreman, a lifelong friend who eventually she reconnected with when he and her husband went to work in the Roosevelt administration during the New Deal of the 1930s.

On the first night of her sophomore year at Wellesley she had an experience that she later referred to as "the "origin of [her] doubt"[6] about the aristocratic Southern life in which she was raised. She lived on campus and was assigned by the headmistress to a seat in the dining hall across from a Black student. Having never talked with a Black person of equal status, Virginia felt insulted and complained to the headmistress that her father would be furious if she ate with a Negro. The headmistress explained that the college had rules that required students to rotate tables once a month, and it was now her turn to sit at the table where the Black girl happened to be seated. Furthermore, the headmistress explained that if she did not like the arrangement, she could leave the school. When Virginia explained that "[her] father would have a fit," the headmistress replied, "He's not our problem; he's your problem." This was the first time Virginia remembered her values being directly challenged, and she stayed up all night struggling with what she should do. The next morning she went to the headmistress and informed her that she would be staying and following the rules. She later wrote that she "realized it wasn't the Negro girl I was afraid of. It was my father's reaction."[7] This incident confronted her with the boundaries of her White supremacist upbringing and began a process by which Virginia continually and deliberately broke the rules of that upbringing step by step.

Because her father was not able to continue to afford the tuition at Wellesley and because he could not bear the embarrassment of having his daughter work on campus to pay for her tuition, Virginia was not allowed to return to Wellesley after her second year. Nonetheless, her Wellesley experience had freed her to use her mind and not bend to

[6] Durr, *Outside the Magic Circle*, 59.

[7] Ibid., 58.

the reaction when she did. She returned to Birmingham and, as was the custom in elite Southern society, began working the debutante circuit courting and being courted by potential husbands. Because of her father's struggles to pay for further schooling and other instances, Virginia became aware of her parents' financial difficulties, and so to help with the family finances she took a job at local law library. Despite their obvious need for support, Virginia's parents opposed their daughter's employment because it was an embarrassing public sign of their money problems and revealed to Birmingham's elite that the Foster family's outwardly aristocratic lifestyle was a mirage. This revelation in turn damaged Virginia's marriage "opportunities."

Despite these apparent social setbacks, in 1925 Virginia met Clifford Durr, a young attorney who had moved from Montgomery to Birmingham, and who had been a member of the same fraternity as her older brother. Like Virginia, Cliff had grown up in an aristocratic Southern family, and like her he had been surrounded by Black servants whom he was raised to think of as subordinate. Like her, he loved learning, graduating from college at age twenty. As a Rhodes Scholar, he then went to Oxford University in England, where he earned a law degree. Virginia and Cliff took an instant liking to each other, and after about a year for what was considered a formal Southern courtship, Virginia Foster and Clifford Durr were married before five hundred guests on Easter 1926.

By the time they returned from their honeymoon, she was pregnant with their first child, Ann. Cliff went to work for a corporate law firm in Birmingham, and Virginia stayed home with the baby. For the first few years of their marriage they lived with Virginia's parents, but in 1931 they moved to their own apartment.

As was customary for a young woman of her background, Virginia hired a cook and a nurse, and became part of the local Junior League, a service club for the city's elite women. During the 1930s Birmingham began to experience the impact of the Depression, and Virginia became increasingly aware of the impoverished people who had lost their jobs at the local steel mill and farmers who because of falling prices were not able to make a living on the crops they raised. Though Virginia and her family were relatively comfortable, she realized that huge disparities existed, that all around her people were starving, had no heat in their homes, and were visibly undernourished with rickets and pellagra.

From her limited perspective, Virginia sought to address these inequities. During that period, several Birmingham dairies were engaged in a price war, and instead of selling milk at reduced prices they were pouring it out in the local sewers. Along with some of her fellow Junior Leaguers, Virginia convinced the local dairy association to sell the milk to the Junior League at a reduced price, which they then turned around and made available to the White poor through the Red Cross. She also arranged for the local firemen's band to host free concerts in the park for local residents to enjoy.

This experience in the Junior League was the beginning of her political consciousness. Unlike many who shared her upbringing, which blamed people for their own poverty, she came to see that the greed of the Birmingham steel industry and the callousness of politicians all the way up to President Hoover were the real causes of people's suffering. As she later said, "The whole economic system had fallen flat on its face,"[8] and politicians and corporate leaders were profiting from others' poverty.

However, the reality of people's suffering became more personal when a difficult miscarriage landed Virginia in the hospital. In the hospital she met people who were suffering the worst effects of poverty. A person who had a particular impact on her was a woman who shared that she had been forced to turn to prostitution in order to make enough money to survive. After this point Virginia could not ignore the harsh circumstances of people's lives and so entered into a process of transformation that forever altered her life and consciousness. She publicly expressed anger at local corporations for their profit-first policies, and she expressed open disgust with local preachers who blamed the poor for their own poverty, offering them hellfire damnation sermons instead of material assistance. She also began to appreciate why unions were so important for the dignity and livelihood of working people. As she later wrote, "I began little by little to wake up to the world."[9]

As she awakened to the reality of poverty, the stability of her privileged world continued to crumble. Virginia's mother had a nervous breakdown, was diagnosed with melancholia, and was sent to a sanitarium for treatment; she never fully recovered, and her husband had to care for her for the rest of her life. During that same period Cliff had a falling out with his boss over ethical issues and left his secure position with the law firm. While he was still trying to figure out how he would make a living, Cliff received a call from his brother-in-law Hugo Black, now a US senator from Alabama. The newly elected president, Franklin Delano Roosevelt, was putting together a social and economic plan called the New Deal, and Black had recommended Cliff for a job

[8] Smallwood, *Reform, Red Scare and Ruin*, Kindle loc. 819.

[9] Durr, *Outside the Magic Circle*, 77.

in FDR's administration. So in 1933 the Durrs moved to Washington, DC, where he became a lawyer for the Reconstruction Finance Corporation (RFC), a program designed to help banks resolve their financial problems and remain operational.

Washington Years

For the next fifteen years, while Cliff worked in a variety of roles for the Roosevelt and Truman administrations, Virginia discovered and then vigorously engaged in the world of politics. Primarily through her husband's work, Virginia became acquainted with members of the liberal, largely Democratic, elite who were working in Washington during the New Deal years. She also renewed her relationship with her sister and Hugo Black, with whom both Cliff and Virginia would meet regularly and have vigorous debates over supper. Over the course of several conversations, the Durrs' Southern conservatism shifted toward Black's more progressive views. They bought a house in Northern Virginia that became their home for their time there. During the first six years in Washington, Virginia gave birth to three more children, but even so was able to be engaged in political volunteer work since she was able to afford to hire servants to take care of her children and attend to other domestic responsibilities.

One of her first forays into political life involved serving with Eleanor Roosevelt in the Women's Division of the Democratic Party; one of the major goals of this group was to abolish poll taxes in the Southern states. Poll taxes, levied by state and local governments, required people to pay a tax in order to vote. Although poll taxes were often justified as a way of funding public schools, in effect their real function was to keep low-income people too poor to pay the tax from voting. The political leaders who designed such taxes specifically structured them to keep poor Whites and Blacks from voting so that the elite Whites could maintain control over local affairs. In order to vote, individuals not only had to pay the tax, they had to present their receipts when they came to vote on Election Day. Although single women were allowed to pay their own poll taxes, married women could only vote if their husbands paid the tax for them. Through such means the Southern political establishment had effectively disenfranchised poor Whites, all Blacks, and many women from voting.[10] Virginia began her work against the poll tax primarily

[10] J. Morgan Kousser, "Poll Tax," *International Encyclopedia of Elections* (Washington, DC: Congressional Quarterly, 1999), http://www.hss.caltech.edu.

on behalf of Southern women, but over time she began to see the need to expand her vision of the poll tax's implications.

She also had occasion to reconnect with her college friend, Clark Foreman, who had been hired as an adviser on Negro affairs in the office of the secretary of the interior. Foreman created a minor controversy when he hired a Black woman to be his secretary, and Virginia was among those criticizing him for betraying his Southern heritage by hiring a Black woman in such a responsible position. Her criticism led to a heated argument, and finally Foreman confronted her saying: "You are just a white, Southern, bigoted, prejudiced provincial girl." As she later said, "He just laid me out."[11] Despite what seemed like a relationship-ending fight, they met for dinner the next week and continued the friendship for years to come. She credits Foreman with challenging her bigoted views, and eventually he convinced her to host a tea in honor of an African American opera singer named Mattiwilda; this seemingly innocent event turned out to be Virginia's first public act of public integration and solidarity with African Americans.

Virginia also broadened her knowledge of the labor movement by listening to the Senate hearings headed by Robert La Follette, who was investigating the union-busting practices of large corporations, including TCI Steel, the largest employer in Virginia's hometown of Birmingham. She became acquainted with the labor leader and founder of the Congress of Industrial Organizations, John Lewis, who was actively attempting to organize workers throughout the South. She heard stories of company men being hired to shoot people organizing miners in Kentucky and of organizers for the International Ladies' Garment Workers' Union being run out of Mississippi by a mob. She met Joe Gelders, a physics teacher at the University of Alabama, who was so moved by the plight of poor workers in Alabama that he left his university position to organize workers and farmers in Alabama only to be beaten, harassed, and eventually killed for his efforts by company police headed by Bull Connor, whose brutality would later become widely known during the Birmingham campaign in 1963.

During this period she also became acquainted with a young senator from Texas named Lyndon Baines Johnson. She often consulted Johnson at critical moments during her efforts to abolish the poll tax. Virginia and Johnson had a close but stormy relationship. Many years later when he became president she vigorously opposed his position on the Vietnam

---

[11] Durr, *Outside the Magic Circle*, 104.

War, yet publicly applauded his sponsorship of the Voting Rights Act of 1964. Through it all, she remained a good friend to both him and his wife, Lady Bird, who also was a native Alabaman.

In 1938 Cliff Durr served on a task force that issued the *Report on the Economic Conditions of the South*, which focused on the poverty-stricken conditions created by the restrictive politics and oligarchic leadership of the South. It was meant to be a direct challenge to members of Congress who were undermining Roosevelt's New Deal programs in the South. The report dealt with all aspects of the economy and demonstrated how the practices of tariffs, absentee land ownership, monopolies, and discrimination against minority groups needed to be changed or outright eliminated. The report also highlighted the exploitation and political disenfranchisement of the sharecroppers and laborers—Black and White. The report highlighted the fact that the few were profiting on the backs of the many and the culture and practice of such things needed to be changed.

As a way of publicizing and advocating the report's recommendations, the Southern Conference on Human Welfare (SCHW) was formed and convened its first meeting in Birmingham, Alabama, in November 1938. Virginia attended as a delegate from the Women's Division of the Democratic National Committee, representing the state of Virginia. Attending the meeting were a number of Southern activists who had long been working for the changes advocated in the report. Among those were Myles Horton and Jim Dombrowski of Highlander Folk School, and the African American educator Mary McLeod Bethune. Featured guests included First Lady Eleanor Roosevelt and Virginia's brother-in-law, Hugo Black. About three hundred of the fifteen hundred people in attendance were African American, and on the first night of the conference the group defied Southern custom by encouraging Blacks and Whites to sit intermingled together. However, when the delegates came to the city auditorium the next day, they were met by Birmingham Police Commissioner Bull Connor, who insisted that the state's segregation laws had to be obeyed and that Blacks and Whites had to sit on opposite sides of the center aisle. When Mrs. Roosevelt arrived, in defiance she took a folding chair and sat in the middle aisle, thereby challenging Bull Connor's segregation order.

Although Virginia referred to the SCHW gathering as a "love feast" for economic and racial justice, she also learned how far she had come and how far she still needed to go in her understanding of racism in the South. She took the occasion of the trip to visit some old high school friends, and over a lunch conversation realized that she no longer embraced the segregationist views of her former friends. Later she learned that following the SCHW convention, J. Edgar Hoover, director of the FBI, initiated surveillance of Virginia, an investigation that continued for decades. However, in talking about her efforts to abolish the poll tax, she was challenged by African American educator Mary McLeod Bethune, who told her that for her efforts to prevail, she needed to broaden her campaign beyond women to include Blacks and poor Whites as well. As Bethune pointed out, the poll tax was not simply a women's issue or a racial issue but a human issue—"the exploitation of human beings by other human beings"[12]— and had to be portrayed as such.

The reaction among the Southern power elite to SCHW's initial meeting was swift, strong, and uniformly negative. Conservative critics in the media accused SCHW of being infiltrated by Communists. Although it was true that members of the Communist Party had been in attendance, this media smear overlooked the fact that at the time the Communist Party was one of the few groups actively seeking to organize poor Whites and Blacks to work together. Almost immediately SCHW came under the scrutiny of the newly formed House Un-American Activities Committee (HUAC) created to investigate "subversive" individuals and organizations that supposedly were a threat to the US government. As it evolved, HUAC became a vehicle for defaming anyone who was challenging the racial status quo in the South, among other things.[13]

Through SCHW and a group that grew out of it named the National Committee to Abolish the Poll Tax (NCAPT), Virginia continued to work to abolish the poll tax. However, when World War II erupted in Europe, it became difficult to interest political leaders in the issue. Even FDR, who had been initially supportive, backed away from the poll tax issue because he needed Southern political leaders' support for his effort to involve the United States in the war. Owing to disagreements within SCHW on the role the United States should play in the war, and the ongoing "red scare" tactics used by SCHW's opponents, the organization lost many members. However, Virginia along with others continued to push forward on the poll tax issue. Because of her singular focus on repealing the poll tax, she accepted the support and involvement of people of many different political persuasions, even Communists; this

---

[12] Ibid., 131.

[13] For another example of the "red scare" tactics see chapter 12 on Anne Braden and her struggles with being labeled a Communist.

position invited continued anti-Communist criticism. As she continued the campaign, she increasingly realized that the dynamics of race, class, and gender intersected on the issue. Eventually, the continued anti-Communist rhetoric caused SCHW to fold, although out of SCHW, the Southern Conference Education Fund (SCEF) was born and continued the focus on racial desegregation for twenty more years.[14]

Shortly before the end of the war FDR died in office, and the New Deal reforms were quickly undermined or dismantled. Cliff had since moved into a position within the Federal Communications Commission (FCC), but in 1947 when President Truman issued an order that all persons working for the federal government had to take an anti-Communist "loyalty oath," Cliff objected. In response to this anti-Communist political swing, Virginia supported the Progressive Party candidate, Henry Wallace, in the 1948 presidential election. In addition, she ran for senator of Virginia on the Progressive Party ticket. In the end Virginia felt Wallace was too aloof as a candidate, but she was impressed that he was the only candidate who purposely addressed integrated audiences, even if it violated local ordinances in certain Southern communities.

When Truman narrowly won the 1948 election, he asked Cliff to accept reappointment to the FCC, but Cliff refused because of his opposition to the loyalty oath policy, and the way in which the policy allowed anonymous persons to accuse others of being a Communist; so Cliff resigned. To a certain degree the pressure on Cliff to sign the loyalty oath was a result of Virginia's political work with the Progressive Party, NCAPT, and SCHW, and so to a degree she was indirectly responsible for his resignation. Her impact on his career and well-being continued to be a theme throughout their marriage.

Cliff's resignation was a turning point in the Durrs' lives. They were both in their mid-foties and had four children at home, and no source of income. To help with finances Virginia worked part-time as an English teacher. After turning down several offers from large corporations, Cliff opened a law practice in Washington, DC, defending persons who had lost their jobs after being labeled as Communists. Cliff's first client was a man named Roy Patterson, a former employee at the Department of Labor, who was known to be a member of various peace groups and who also had interacted with African Americans to help them overcome challenges in the labor market. In a high-profile hearing Cliff proved that Patterson had been wrongly accused of sedition, and Patterson was

[14] For further discussion of SCEF see chapter 12 on Anne Braden.

reinstated in his job. However (with the help of FBI propaganda), the victory earned Cliff a reputation as a radical, and soon potential clients were avoiding him for fear of simply being accused of guilt by association.

Thus, after struggling financially for two years, the Durrs decided to leave Washington. Cliff wanted to return to his hometown of Montgomery, but Virginia was not ready return to the South after working so hard to undo the racist practices there. So instead Cliff took a job in Denver, Colorado, with the Farmers' Union. The year was 1950. Cliff was emotionally and physically stressed by his ordeals in Washington and had suffered severe back problems for a several years; so he asked Virginia to refrain from political involvements for a while just to relieve the stress in their lives. Virginia sincerely intended to comply with her husband's wishes. However, during their first year in Denver, Virginia signed a public petition opposing the bombing of China during the Korean War, naïve to the public effect of her action. Patriotism and anti-Communist sentiment during the Korean War were very high, and so signing the petition action was viewed as unsupportive of the war effort and therefore unpatriotic. Although in itself her action was small, because of the Durrs' previous political involvements, the seemingly insignificant act became a matter of public controversy. When a local news outlet noted her name on the petition and made her action public, Cliff's superior at the Farmers' Union insisted that he force his wife to retract her name from the petition. However, Cliff refused to back down, voicing his support for Virginia's action and her refusal to retract her public stance.

As a result, Cliff was fired, and the stress of the incident triggered his severe back problems, and he landed in a Denver hospital for several weeks. When he was finally able to travel, the family returned to Montgomery, where they moved in with Cliff's mother.

Montgomery and the Eastland Hearing

Because Cliff needed time to heal from his back-related problems, because Cliff's family did not share the Durrs' integrationist views, and because Montgomery was highly segregated community, Virginia agreed to "lay low" in her social and political activities and "to avoid controversy in the interest of family peace."[15] Eventually in 1952 Cliff was able to open a law practice, and Virginia served as his secretary, even though

[15] Smallwood, *Reform, Red Scare and Ruin*, Kindle loc. 3389.

he was hesitant to hire her for fear she would get too involved in his cases (which she did). Many of Cliff's early cases involved Blacks who had been defrauded by White businesspeople, many of whom he knew personally. E. D. Nixon, president of the local chapter of the NAACP, regularly brought cases to Cliff. Even so, Cliff avoided high-profile or national cases to not call attention to himself in the local community.

For her part Virginia also remained relatively quiet, though it was admittedly not easy for her. At one point she told Hugo Black: "We live among and with people who don't agree with us on any single thing or even on the basic premises of our thought."[16] She resigned from several national organizations of which she had been a part, although she did agree to serve on the board of SCEF. Through her church she got involved with United Church Women, a local ecumenical organization that had both Black and White contingents. When the two groups began holding integrated prayer meetings (some of which were held in Virginia's home), a local KKK leader took down the women's license plate numbers and publicized their names in a local KKK publication. Perhaps because of that incident, when she applied to join the local Business and Professional Women's Club, her application was denied, even though many of the members had been her friends from earlier days.

Despite their efforts to remain apolitical and noncontroversial, all of that changed in March 1954 when Senator James Eastland summoned Virginia to appear before his Senate Subcommittee on Internal Security. Many other former SCHW members were also summoned, including Myles Horton, James Dombrowski, and Aubrey Williams. Eastland had no particular interest in Virginia except that her brother-in-law Hugo Black was ruling on the *Brown v. Board of Education* Supreme Court case, and, by smearing Black, Eastland sought to enhance his political stature. Also, as previously indicated, Virginia refused to testify and expressed her contempt for the whole proceedings. Cliff was there supporting his wife and served as an attorney for one of the other defendants. On the last day of the hearings, an FBI informant (who as it turned out had been released from prison in exchange for being a paid informant) accused Virginia of being involved in a Communist espionage ring. Cliff got so enraged that he lunged at the man, triggering a heart attack that required him go to the hospital for treatment. Although Eastland threatened to have Virginia and the others jailed, he never followed through on his threat.

---

[16] Ibid.

When they returned to Montgomery after the hearings, the Durrs faced all sorts of threats and negative responses to their stand. Because they feared that the local KKK might burn crosses on Cliff's mother's lawn, they decided to move to an apartment. Their children were harassed at school for being part of a family that supported integration, and their six-year-old daughter was disinvited from a birthday party. On the first Sunday after the hearings, Cliff went to teach the adult Sunday School he had taught for years at the First Presbyterian Church, but no one came to the class that day or ever again. The message was clear: the Durrs were pariahs in Montgomery White society.

Yet for Virginia the controversy turned out to be a form of liberation. During the hearings, Virginia received a telegram of support from an Alabama State University English professor named JoAnn Robinson, who was also the founder of a Black women's activist group in Montgomery. Virginia and Professor Robinson had never met, so on returning home Virginia went to meet her and the group she represented. After thanking them for their support, the group explained: "We knew if Jim Eastland was after you, you were pretty good."[17] Thus began the next phase of Virginia's civil rights career.

Montgomery and the Civil Rights Movement

As soon as the Durrs had moved into their new apartment, Virginia joined the Council on Human Relations, the only officially sanctioned interracial group in the city. There she met other like-minded people, including a young African American minister named Martin Luther King Jr., who had recently arrived in town. She became acquainted with King's wife, Coretta, when she conducted an alumna interview with the Durrs' daughter who was applying to Antioch College in Ohio, which Mrs. King had attended. Virginia also became acquainted with a local activist named Johnnie Carr. Following the *Brown v. Board of Education* decision, some Blacks immediately sought to enroll their children in previously all-White schools. The first to do so was Mrs. Carr, who enrolled her son Arlam in the local White high school. Virginia had met Mrs. Carr at the integrated prayer group, and because the Durrs lived right across the street from the school where Arlam attended, Virginia offered to let him come over to the house if Mrs. Carr was ever late in picking him up. As it turned out Arlam only came over a few times, especially when he was feeling

---

[17] Durr, *Outside the Magic Circle*, 272.

harassed, but generally the school integrated without violence. Nonetheless, her willingness to support the school integration effort cemented Virginia's relationship as an ally of Montgomery's Black community.

In the summer of 1955 Virginia received a call from Myles Horton, who indicated he had a scholarship for a two-week workshop at Highlander for a local Black leader from Montgomery. Virginia immediately thought of Rosa Parks, who had done some seamstress work repairing some of the Durr children's clothes. Virginia knew that Rosa had been an active member of the local NAACP for several years, and despite Rosa's initial hesitation, Virginia convinced her to attend the workshop. Virginia helped her make the arrangements; this was the first time Rosa Parks had been in an integrated setting where race was not a contentious issue. Although Virginia never knew if the time at Highlander motivated Rosa Parks to take the courageous move of refusing to give up her seat on the bus to a White man, she did feel that it gave her a sense of inspiration and support.[18]

After Rosa Parks was arrested for her action, E. D. Nixon called on Cliff Durr to help pay her bail. Although Nixon had the money, the police would not accept it unless a White man delivered it. So Cliff and Virginia headed down to the jail to deliver the bail money and then returned with Parks to her home. Cliff advised Parks that she could probably get the charges dropped because she had not actually broken bus policy.[19] However, he continued, if she wanted to contest the constitutionality of the segregated bus system, she could do so, but it would be a much longer, involved case. She opted to do the latter. Soon local leaders called for a boycott of the buses, which initially was to last only one day but ended up lasting a year, while Parks's case went all the way to the Supreme Court. As arrests for the boycott mounted, most of the Black defendants, like Rosa Parks, were represented by Fred Gray, a prominent African American lawyer, while Cliff defended the White clients.

On the Monday night following the first day of the boycott, Virginia tried to attend the mass meeting held at the Holt St. Baptist Church, but

---

[18] For more on Rosa Parks's relationship with Highlander, see chapter 9.

[19] Rosa sat down in an area of the bus that was not designated either Black or White. Although bus drivers typically ordered Black passengers in this middle section to give up their seat to a White person, by law they could not do so unless there was a seat further back in the so-called Black section. See Durr, *Outside the Magic Circle*, 280.

the crowd was so large, she was not able to get inside.[20] Virginia subsequently attended many of the mass meetings held during the boycott, and participated in the car pools that helped women get to their jobs in the wealthier neighborhoods where many of them worked as domestics. Virginia was not the only White woman offering rides, as many of the wealthy housewives themselves drove their servants so they would not miss their jobs. The situation got to the point where the mayor of Montgomery publicly pleaded with White women to stop providing rides to their servants and ordered the police to issue them tickets when they did so. In defiance of the mayor's plea the women persisted, since, as they stated, the mayor was not about to come and do the housework and other domestic chores the Black servants were hired to do.

In a letter to Eleanor Roosevelt Virginia expressed her frustration and depression over the slow progress in Montgomery and throughout the South because in her view the boycott had stirred up even more White resistance instead of moving toward integration. In the letter she noted that in response to the boycott, several Southern congressmen, including Harry Byrd of Virginia and Strom Thurmond of South Carolina, had drawn up a "Southern Manifesto," which condemned the Supreme Court's use of "naked judicial power" and publicly declared their intention to use all the legal means at their disposal to resist efforts to integrate the South. Also White Citizens' Councils were being organized in many communities, which Virginia simply regarded as uptown versions of the KKK.

After the Supreme Court outlawed Montgomery's segregated bus policy, Black leaders pushed to expand integration to all public areas such as parks, swimming pools, and libraries. However, the decision precipitated a violent response from members of the White community. Less than a month after the bus boycott ended in December 1956, the homes of Rev. Ralph Abernathy and Rev. Robert Graetz were bombed as well as First Baptist Church where Rev. Abernathy was pastor. Virginia offered to take in the Graetz family for their safety, but they decided to stay in their home.[21] Furthermore the city closed the zoo, all the parks and swimming pools, and even took chairs out of the public library in an effort to forestall integration. In these and other ways race relations

---

[20] Other than White media persons, Robert Graetz, pastor of the local Lutheran church was the only White leader who attended that first mass meeting. See chapter 14.

[21] For the full story of Robert Graetz and the Montgomery bus boycott, see chapter 14.

remained tense in the city.

These tensions continued to strongly affect the Durr family. When their oldest daughter Lucy got married in 1957, the leaders of the Highland Presbyterian Church insisted that any Black guests would have to be segregated in the balcony from the Whites. In the end the one invited Black guest, attorney Fred Gray, chose not to attend, and so a confrontation was avoided. Also because of his role in the *Brown* decision, Hugo Black and his wife, Virginia's sister, had chosen not to attend so as not to draw attention away from the bride and groom. Meanwhile, the Durrs' two youngest daughters, Tillah and Lulah, continued to be harassed in school with children taunting them by saying their parents were "nigger lovers" and Communists. When the family began receiving direct threats, the Durrs decided to send the girls to boarding schools in Massachusetts, paying for the tuition with the help of some friends. Virginia suffered another loss when her friend Juliette Morgan committed suicide. Juliette had been one of the few other Whites willing to speak out on the racism in the city, and had killed herself after being fired from her job and receiving numerous death threats. She left a note which simply read: "I can't go on. I am not going to cause any more trouble to anybody."[22]

These assaults on her family and personal friends left deep scars on Virginia. In a letter to Anne Braden (whom she had met through her involvement with SCEF)[23] in the spring of 1960, Virginia revealed the dilemma faced by so many women like Juliette. She wrote: "Just as Negroes have been barred from life or they have tried to bar them, so have [Southern women] been barred from life so often, the life they have been offered has been nothing but cotton candy. Even women like us who have been saved by events (and our own efforts). . . . We too suffer from a sense of guilt, as we have caused so many people pain, and also we have suffered so much hostility from our family and early friends, so we too have problems."[24] Even with these setbacks and rejections, the Durrs continued to support integration efforts and fight efforts to harass and punish those who challenged segregated ways.

Despite all that they had witnessed and experienced during the boycott and the years that followed, the most horrific event for Virginia

---

[22] Smallwood, *Reform, Red Scare and Ruin*, Kindle loc. 4423–93.

[23] See chapter 12 on Anne Braden.

[24] Patricia Sullivan, ed., *Freedom Writer: Virginia Foster Durr, Letters from the Civil Rights Years* (New York: Routledge, 2003), 203.

occurred on May 20, 1961, when the Freedom Riders arrived at the Montgomery Bus Station. Originally organized by the Congress of Racial Equality (CORE), seven Blacks and six Whites boarded public buses in Washington, DC, with the intention of riding them to New Orleans. Their purpose was to test a recent Supreme Court decision that had outlawed segregation in interstate train and bus stations by sitting together on the bus and by defying the practice of segregated waiting rooms and restrooms. On May 14 one of the buses was attacked and burned in nearby Anniston, Alabama, which temporarily halted the ride. After students from Nashville volunteered to continue the Freedom Ride and received the promise of protection from the Alabama State Police, the buses continued to Montgomery.

On the morning of May 20, the buses pulled into the Montgomery bus station. The state police pulled back because they had agreed that once inside the city limits the protection would be carried on by local law enforcement. However, the Montgomery police chief had secretly informed the angry crowd of mostly White men gathered to meet the bus that he would give them thirty minutes to have their way with the riders before law enforcement stepped in. Virginia and a friend, Jessica Mitford, had gone to Cliff's office on the second floor of a building directly across from the station. As they arrived, they were able to witness the entire horrible ordeal. They saw the Black and White bus riders beaten by the violent mob, and White mothers laughing as they told their children, "See the nigger run." Any hope Virginia had of the White Southerners peacefully changing their ways vanished that day as she watched the brutal scene. The next night Mitford and a male companion attended a rally at First Baptist Church where Martin Luther King Jr. had come into speak in support of the riders. The church was soon surrounded by an angry mob, and the people inside, including Virginia's friend, were saved only when President Kennedy sent in five hundred US marshals to escort them out.[25]

Out of the Freedom Rides, the Student Nonviolent Coordinating Committee (SNCC) was born and Virginia served as a mentor and supporter to many of the young activists, both Black and White. As they were passing through on their way to work in Mississippi, they would often stay at the Durr home. Virginia was particularly close to

---

[25] For a full account of the experience in Montgomery and the Freedom Riders' experience, see Raymond Arsenault, *Freedom Riders: 1961 and the Struggle for Justice* (New York: Oxford University Press, 2006).

Bob Zellner, who was one of the first White staff members of SNCC, and Ella Baker, mentor and adviser to the many young leaders of SNCC.

Retirement

In January 1964, the Twenty-fourth Amendment to the Constitution was ratified, outlawing poll taxes in federal elections. Despite the apparent victory, Southern governors vowed to fight the ruling, and Virginia despaired of the South ever changing. The Durrs chose not to attend the 1963 March on Washington but watched it on the television, and followed the tragic aftermath in Birmingham when four little girls were killed in the bombing of Birmingham's Sixteenth St. Baptist Church. In November 1963, as they were mourning the assassination of President Kennedy, their grief was intensified as they heard crowds of White Montgomery citizens cheering and blaring horns in celebration of his death on the streets outside their home.

In 1965, when Martin Luther King Jr. called upon people from across the country to come to Selma, Alabama, to participate in a fifty-mile march for voting rights from Selma to Montgomery, the Durrs opened their home to friends from across the country, including the Yale historian C. Vann Woodward, the SCEF activist Carl Braden, the singer Pete Seeger, and the author Studs Terkel. After the march the Durrs faced a great deal of hostility from many of Montgomery's White citizens. One woman accused them of letting "scum [stay] at your house." To which Virginia replied: "I hardly think the Dean of the Yale Law School and the Sterling Professor of History from Yale are exactly scum."

On the evening following the march Virginia, Cliff, and several of their guests were sitting in the living room when they received a call from a reporter friend informing them that Viola Liuzzo had been killed shuttling marchers back from Montgomery to Selma. The news stunned the Durrs; however, in a tragic but hopeful turn of events the next evening an emotional President Johnson (whom Virginia had befriended during her days in Washington), called for passage of the Voting Rights Act, which in the aftermath of Selma quickly became law. Even despite this victory, as she followed the trial of the men arrested in the Liuzzo murder, Virginia further despaired of the South changing, and she sincerely desired to leave the South.[26]

[26] To learn more of Viola Liuzzo's story, see chapter 13, including details of the corruption and deceit involved in the trial of the men accused of her murder.

Virginia continued her activism supporting the SNCC activists and opposing the Vietnam War. She became quite disillusioned with SNCC, however, when they rejected Martin Luther King Jr.'s nonviolent approach and became increasingly militant, eventually becoming an all-Black organization after having begun as a place where Blacks and Whites worked together. Despite her disapproval of their shift in emphasis, she maintained her relationships with several Black SNCC leaders. Cliff persisted in his struggling law practice until the couple retired in 1969 to Wetumpka, the Durr family homestead about twenty miles outside of Montgomery.

In the 1970s Virginia had a sobering experience with some Black students that left her further confused and disillusioned. Two longtime friends who were sociology professors at Tuskegee College invited her and Cliff to speak to their classes about their civil rights work over the years. As Virginia spoke she felt hostility, coldness, and nonresponsiveness coming from the African American students. She asked them if they had studied some of the key cases in the struggle for voting rights and if they had read books like *The Souls of Black Folk* by W. E. B. Du Bois. One of the students spoke up and accused Virginia of being "an old lady just trying to take us down." Other students started flapping books and making other kinds of noises just to distract her. One student shouted that they hated her because she was White. She continued to speak until the students' resistance made it impossible to continue. Later, the two professors who had invited her, both of whom were civil rights veterans, expressed their frustration with the students because they felt they had no appreciation of their right to vote or the struggles that had gotten them there, or for politics in general. Like many of the early civil rights generation, they bemoaned the rise of the Black Power movement, which had chosen to separate itself from the White community rather than working with those Whites who sought to be allies in the struggle. Like her Black counterparts, Virginia had difficulty accepting the attitudes of the students. In reflecting on that experience she wrote: "The things I believe in, the law and the vote, have not brought about the change the young people are demanding. I don't know how to bring about those changes. I certainly don't believe in revolution. I don't think that people know what they want."[27] She had hoped the civil rights movement would usher in an era of racial reconciliation, but she realized that despite the efforts of so many like

[27] Durr, *Outside the Magic Circle*, 331.

herself, hostility among Whites and Blacks still ran high, and that the hope of people of both races living together in harmony was still a distant dream.

Cliff died in 1975, and Virginia was deeply affected by the loss, as she and Cliff had been together for nearly fifty years. Friends and family gathered around her and paid tribute to the man who had been her husband and greatest supporter. At his funeral Justice Black described Cliff as "the personification of gentleness, kindness and toleration." Her partner in marriage, who, like her, had dedicated his life to serving others and who himself had willingly suffered in support of his wife's outspoken ways, was no longer by her side; she now would have to carry on alone.

For the next two decades Virginia continued to be an advocate for racial justice and women's rights. In 1976 she agreed to serve on the Alabama Advisory Committee to the US Civil Rights Commission. She taught courses on Southern women's history at the University of Alabama. In 1980 she helped organize the twenty-fifth anniversary of Rosa Parks's arrest. She received a number of awards and honorary degrees for her work, and collaborated with the oral historian Hollinger Barnard to write her autobiography, *Outside the Magic Circle*. In 1989 she helped organize Rosa Parks's seventy-sixth birthday celebration in Montgomery.

After a long, slow physical decline, Virginia Durr died in 1999 at the age of ninety-five. Smallwood writes, "Despite honors and awards, Virginia was in some ways disappointed about her career as a reformer—or, rather, she was disappointed when noting Southern political developments from the 1970s to the 1990s."[28] In her autobiography, Virginia wrote, "Life has a strange irony. You fight for something—like the right to vote in the South. Give Negroes and poor folks the right to vote. And you win. And they elect George Wallace. You fight for women to get representation, and they elect Lurleen Wallace."[29] However, despite her misgivings, her efforts were not in vain. The poll tax was abolished. The Civil Rights Act and the Voting Rights Act became law. The violently segregated South that she once referred to as a "cesspool" did eventually accept desegregation, and Black leaders achieved positions of political leadership.

Virginia Foster Durr was an iconoclastic and complex person. She was a woman of the Southern aristocracy who attacked some of the

---

[28] Smallwood, *Reform, Red Scare, and Ruin*, Kindle loc. 5471.

[29] Durr, *Outside the Magic Circle*, 333.

South's most sacred institutions, namely racial segregation and Southern patriarchy. Yet throughout her life she maintained an aristocratic air about her. Sue Thrasher, who interviewed Durr for an oral history project of veteran Southern progressives, teased Virginia for her "aristocratic need to keep up with everybody's bloodlines."[30] Indeed as one reads *Outside the Magic Circle*, one is struck by how often Durr introduces people by giving their ancestral pedigree. Moreover, Durr enjoyed the company of powerful political people from her days in Washington and saw herself as operating in the realm of the ruling elite. She admitted as much when she wrote: "I've been a fortunate person. In spite of the hard times we've had, I've always felt like I was part of the group that ran the country. It's very difficult to explain without sounding snobbish, but I've always felt I belonged to the ruling class."[31]

In addition, although she is remembered here because of her work against racial injustice, she did not come to a full awareness of racism's extensive reach until middle age. She engaged in the campaign against the poll tax first as a Southern woman, second as a person of privilege concerned for the desperate White poor, and only after a slow process did she become an advocate of justice for African Americans; it took a challenge from Mary McLeod Bethune for Virginia to see that including Blacks in the poll tax fight was not only politically savvy but the right thing to do. Thrasher observes that Virginia "never fully overcame a tendency towards racial paternalism."[32] That being said, she repeatedly put herself in difficult and dangerous situations in order to advocate for the full rights of all people. Moreover, her willingness to stand up to virulent racists like James Eastland earned her the respect of civil rights leaders from JoAnn Robinson to Rosa Parks to Martin Luther King Jr.

She also was not always an easy person to be around. Those who knew her felt at times she was bossy, pushy, and excessively opinionated. Her husband, Cliff, probably suffered the most because of her bullishness, and yet he always publicly supported her, even when it cost him his job or his health. She did not mince words when talking about her adversaries. She denounced James Eastland as someone from the hill country, "poor White trash," "as common as pig tracks," and not

---

[30] M. Sue Thrasher, et al. "Learning from the Long Civil Rights Movement's First Generation: Virginia Foster Durr," compiled by Sarah Thuesen, *Southern Cultures* 16, no. 2 (Summer 2010): 75.

[31] Durr, *Outside the Magic Circle*, 334.

[32] Thrasher, "Learning," 76.

an aristocrat like her.[33] She was "disgusted" with George Wallace; she was appalled at the "freeness of the sixties generation" and the revolutionary bent that SNCC adopted in its later years. She had "complete disgust" for Stokely Carmichael.[34] Yet she was a loyal friend who sacrificed significantly for the people and the causes she believed in, often putting herself and her family in danger and under duress because of her convictions. Speaking of her children, she regretted the difficulties they experienced because of her outspokenness. Yet she defended her actions saying: "There were no choices to be made."[35] Durr explained it this way: "What good [was staying home to bake brownies] in a society that tolerated poverty and denied people the education to enable them to get out of poverty? What good were brownies in a society that denied people the right to vote?"[36]

In the end Virginia Durr was a person who used her position and power to challenge structures and practices that denied basic rights to Black people. She was person of conviction who operated as best she could through, and sometimes in spite of, her personality. Although she came to resent the Southern aristocracy that raised her, she never fully left that aristocracy. Instead she rebelled from within and helped bring justice to many.

---

[33] Durr, *Outside the Magic Circle*, 172, 254.

[34] Smallwood, *Reform, Red Scare and Ruin*, Kindle loc. 5080

[35] Anne Colby and William Damon, *Some Do Care: Contemporary Lives of Moral Commitment* (New York: Free Press, 1992), 127.

[36] Durr, *Outside the Magic Circle*, 336–37.

Discussion Questions

1. Virginia Foster Durr came from a background of immense privilege, yet she used her position to help the civil rights causes. What are ways that people of privilege can ally themselves with those who suffer under the oppression of racial injustice?
2. Many of Virginia Durr's actions and statements caused her discomfort and difficulty, as well as for her husband and children. How does one stay true to one's convictions for racial justice, when living out those convictions may cause pain or suffering for those closest to one?

Bibliography

Brown, Cynthia Stokes. *Refusing Racism: White Allies and the Struggle for Civil Rights*. New York: Teacher's College Press, 2002.

Colby, Anne, and William Damon. *Some Do Care: Contemporary Lives of Moral Comm*itment. New York: Free Press, 1992.

Durr, Virginia Foster. *Outside the Magic Circle*. Edited by Hollinger F. Barnard. Tuscaloosa: University of Alabama Press, 1985.

Kousser, J. Morgan. "Poll Tax." *The International Encyclopedia of Elections*. Washington, DC: Congressional Quarterly (1999). http://www.hss.caltech.edu.

Smallwood, James. *Reform, Red Scare, and Ruin: Virginia Durr, Prophet of the New South*. James Smallwood, Xlibris (Kindle Edition), 2008.

Sullivan, Patricia, ed. *Freedom Writer: Virginia Foster Durr, Letters from the Civil Rights Years*. New York: Routledge, 2003.

Thrasher, M. Sue, Jacqueline Dowd Hall, and Bob Hall, "Learning from the Long Civil Rights Movement's First Generation: Virginia Foster Durr," compiled by Sarah Thuesen, *Southern Cultures* 16, no. 2 (Summer 2010), 72–89.]

9

Myles Horton
(1905–1990)

*Radical Hillbilly**

Prelude to a Revolution

On December 1, 1955, forty-four-year-old Rosa Parks boarded a bus in Montgomery, Alabama, on her way home from her work as a seamstress at a local department store. The bus was filled with commuters, two-thirds of whom were Black and sitting in the "colored section," as the law required. As the bus continued to fill, the driver came back to the front of the "colored section" and instructed the Black riders to give up their seats to White commuters. Parks refused to get up. She later explained that her action was in no way prearranged, but she did not feel like complying with the driver's demand. As she later said: "This is what I wanted to know; when and how would we ever determine our rights as human beings?"[1] Local civil rights leaders had long been waiting for

* Photo of Myles Horton used by permission of the Wisconsin Historical Society, Image Number Whi-3500. Unless otherwise noted, the major sources of information for this chapter are Frank Adams and Myles Horton, *Unearthing the Seeds of Fire: The Idea of Highlander* (Winston-Salem, NC: John F. Blair, 1975); Frank Durham, "Ethos in Action: Public Relations at the Highlander Folk School, 1955–1956" (paper presented at the Annual Meeting of the Association for Education in Journalism and Mass Communication, Kansas City, Missouri, August 11–14, 1993); John M. Glen, *Highlander: No Ordinary School, 1932–1962* (Knoxville: University of Tennessee Press, 1996); Myles Horton, Judith Kohl, and Herb Kohl, *The Long Haul: An Autobiography* (New York: Teachers College Press, 1998); and Myles Horton and Dale Jacobs, *The Myles Horton Reader: Education for Social Change* (Knoxville: University of Tennessee Press, 2003).

[1] Letter from Rosa Parks to Myles Horton, February 25, 1956. Highlander

a test case with which to challenge the racist bus-riding policy. Parks's good standing in the community and impeccable character made her the perfect candidate. Out of her action the Montgomery bus boycott was spawned and the modern civil rights movement was ignited under the leadership of Martin Luther King Jr.[2]

Five months earlier, Rosa Parks had attended a workshop on school integration at a place called the Highlander Folk School, founded and run by a man named Myles Horton. Parks had come to Highlander on a scholarship provided by local White civil rights activist Virginia Durr.[3] E. D. Nixon, a local union organizer from Montgomery who had worked with Horton to organize farm laborers in Alabama, encouraged Parks to attend the event. So in late July and early August she went to the workshop at Highlander. People who were there remembered her as being shy and quiet when she arrived, but through the course of the two weeks she opened up about her struggles in Montgomery to bring about integration reform.

Although Parks's attendance at the workshop did not directly lead to her action five months later, it did give her a new perspective. Prior to her arrest Parks had been involved in local NAACP efforts for nearly ten years,[4] but she held little optimism for the success of these efforts to bring about racial justice for the African American community of Montgomery and throughout the South. She had seen and suffered too much to believe that there was a reason for hope. However, at Highlander she met African Americans such as Septima Clark and Whites such as Horton who were committed to work together to bring about a racially just society. Reflecting on her Highlander experience, Parks later said, "I found out for the first time in my adult life that this could be a unified society, that there was such a thing as people of all races and backgrounds meeting and having workshops and living together in peace and harmony."[5] Virginia Durr later wrote that when Parks returned

---

Folk School Paper, Box 22, folder 22. Quoted in Frank Durham, "Ethos in Action," 10.

[2] For background on the Montgomery bus boycott, see chapter 14 on Robert Graetz.

3 For more on Virginia Foster Durr, see chapter 8.

[4] For the pre–bus boycott activism of Rosa Parks, see Danielle McGuire, *At the Dark End of the Street: Black Women, Rape and Resistance—A New History from Rosa Parks to the Rise of Black Power* (New York: Alfred E. Knopf, 2010); and Herb Boyd, "Rosa Parks, 1913–2005," *New York Amsterdam News* 96, no. 44 (October 27–November 2, 2005): 1, 30.

[5] Excerpted quote of Rosa Parks at Loop College Community Workshop

to Montgomery from the workshop at Highlander, she "was so happy and felt so elated and then as time went on she said the discrimination got worse and worse to bear after having, for the first time in her life, been free of it at Highlander. I am sure that had a lot to do with her daring to risk arrest."[6] Parks returned to Highlander the following year to share her story with other workshop participants, despite the tremendous economic and emotional stress the arrest and subsequent public attention placed on her life. As she told the people gathered at a workshop in March 1956, "[Highlander] was the place for me to stop being pushed around."[7]

What was this place in the mountains of East Tennessee that had played such a significant role in the early civil rights movement? Who was this White hillbilly named Myles Horton of whom Rosa Parks said, "[He] was the first white man I ever trusted."[8] Who was the man whose vision and efforts brought into being a place where Whites and Blacks in the South could come together as equals at a time when such gatherings were considered illegal and subversive by state and local authorities? Who was this man whose educational efforts grew out of the conviction that given the right set of circumstances, poor and oppressed people could come up with solutions to the problems that beset their communities?

An Early Respect for People and a Love of Learning

Myles Horton was born on July 9, 1905, to Elsie and Perry Horton in Savannah, Tennessee, in the southwestern corner of the state. Horton's parents both served as schoolteachers until the state government required teachers to be certified, after which they served in a variety of odd jobs. However, their commitment to learning instilled a love of learning in Myles at an early age. His grandfather had been born before the Civil War and never had a chance to go to school and learn how to read; however, Myles said that through his grandfather he learned to respect the inherent wisdom of common people and came to believe that poor

directed by Mrs. C. T. Vivian, May 13, 1970, Chicago; also Rosa Parks and Jim Haskins, *Rosa Parks: My Story* (New York: Dial Books, 1992), 105. Quoted in Frank Durham, "Ethos in Action," 9.

[6] Letter from Virginia Durr to Zilphia Horton, January 30, 1956. Highlander Folks School Papers, Box 79, folder 1. Quoted in Durham, "Ethos in Action," 11.

[7] Durham, "Ethos in Action," 14.

[8] Horton and Jacobs, *Myles Horton Reader*, 151.

people had inherent value equal to or greater than those who were well-off. His parents also instilled in him the value of service and the idea that one did not learn simply for personal gain but also to serve others. From his mother he further learned that the essence of religion was to love one's neighbor, and from his father, who was a union worker, he gained an appreciation for the value of workers joining together for the improvement of job conditions.

His parents' commitment to lifelong learning was evidenced by their decision to move to a county that had a high school for Miles to attend, since there was none where they were living at the time. In high school Myles nurtured his love of learning, while also playing on the football team. He worked a variety of jobs at a local store, a sawmill, and a tomato crate factory. These experiences opened his eyes to the harsh and often demeaning conditions that workers faced, and the demeaning attitudes factory owners held toward their employees. He wrote: "My people were farmers, sharecroppers, factory workers, clerks—anything to make a living. When I heard my people insulted by the factory owners, it hurt me personally. I didn't feel a bit inferior to the guy who owned the factory. I felt just as smart; in fact I knew I was smarter than he was. Who was he to talk about people like me and my family?"[9]

At the age of nineteen Horton enrolled at Cumberland University. He had already begun to develop an appreciation for the inherent intelligence of common people and possessed a commitment to organizing people as a way to bring about positive changes in their communities. However, Horton caused frustration among the faculty and administrators of the school because instead of following the prescribed curriculum, he insisted on learning how and what he wanted to learn. As he later wrote (somewhat tongue in cheek, I suspect): "I probably profited by going to a small college where I didn't have many good teachers. The college had a fairly good library, so I learned to educate myself. If I'd had to spend time with good teachers, I probably wouldn't have come out as well educated as I did."[10] When it came time for Horton to graduate, although he had earned more than enough credits, he had not satisfied any particular major. Nonetheless, he was allowed to graduate despite the reservations (and probably to the relief) of the faculty and school administrators.

---

[9] Horton, Kohl, and Kohl, *Long Haul*, 8.

[10] Ibid., 13.

Pieces of the Picture

More significantly, Horton's college years enabled him to broaden his horizons through his summer work with mountain communities and his involvement in the statewide Student YMCA/YWCA. As part of a summer missions emphasis (Cumberland was a Presbyterian school), Horton ran children's daily vacation Bible schools in several Appalachian communities. Through these efforts he met local clergy who were focusing their ministry on improving the daily lives of people in their communities. He also met a county agent named Bob Lyons who was interested in setting up local cooperatives. Through these contacts Horton used his role as the local Bible teacher to work with children during the day and then at night to bring parents and other adults together. In these nighttime meetings, community residents would share their struggles with one another, and then talk together about how cooperatively they might address those problems. Through those experiences Horton began to develop a philosophy of learning that later informed his educational work. He wrote: "I made a very valuable discovery. You don't have to know the answers. The answers come from the people, and when they don't have answers, then you have another role, and you find resources."[11] This was later to become the foundation of the educational approach used at Highlander.

Horton first became involved in racial justice issues when he worked with the student YMCA. At that time the YMCA had interracial commissions throughout the South that brought Black and White students together to discuss racial reconciliation. However, in accordance with the customs and laws of the Jim Crow South, Black and White students never actually ate a meal or even drank coffee together. In his senior year Horton became the secretary of the Tennessee Student YMCA, and he decided to involve the students in an action that directly challenged segregationist policies. Somewhat deceptively, he organized a convention where the students were to meet and eat together. He knew that such an event was technically illegal, and so he invited both Whites and Blacks to the banquet without telling either group that they would be attending an integrated event. When the students came through the doors, and the Black waiters realized they were being asked to serve Blacks and Whites eating *together*, they initially balked, but after some persuasion the waiters were enticed to serve the whole group. As Horton later explained: "I was committed to breaking the pattern of segregation

[11] Ibid., 23.

and to practicing social equality. I wanted action to be the main thrust, instead of just talking about future action that you don't practice. . . . I took the gamble of doing something about a moral problem instead of simply talking about it . . . and over 120 people learned that they could change things if they wanted to."[12]

After graduation from Cumberland in 1929, Horton attended Union Theological Seminary in New York City at the urging of one of his Appalachian clergy friends. Still informed by the Christian faith of "love thy neighbor" inherited from his mother, Horton went to Union "to try to find out how to get social justice and love together."[13] At this time Union Seminary was the center of Christian social gospel thinking, and Horton came under the influence of Reinhold Niebuhr, the renowned public theologian and social commentator. Moreover, he visited a wide variety of gatherings from Catholic churches to Muslim meetings to Socialist and Communist rallies to union halls. At one point he took part in a demonstration on May Day and was beaten by a police officer who accused him of being a "Goddam Bolshevik" for wearing a red Cumberland University football sweater. While at Union he also studied the works of Marx, Lenin, and John Dewey. As he had at Cumberland, he went to Union with the attitude of learning what he felt he needed to learn, rather than pursuing a particular degree program.

After only one year at Union he moved to the University of Chicago in the fall of 1930 to study theories and methods of social change. Under the renowned sociologist Robert Park he learned the value of conflict for precipitating learning. He also had numerous opportunities to interact with Jane Addams, the founder of Hull House, a settlement house in Chicago established in the late 1880s for recent immigrants. While in Chicago Horton began to formulate a vision of starting a school for the rural poor in the South and he talked with Addams extensively about what he needed to do to start such a school. From Addams he learned about the Danish Folk School Movement started by Bishop N. F. S. Grundtvig in the mid 1800s. After working to save money, he traveled to Denmark to learn firsthand about the Danish folk school movement and their contribution to the development of social and cultural democracy among the Danish people. His ideas for his rural Southern school crystalized while he was in Denmark. On Christmas night 1931 he woke from a dream with a clear conviction that he was ready to turn his dream into reality and start an American-style folk school in the rural South.

[12] Ibid., 16, 18.

[13] Ibid., 32.

The Beginnings of Highlander

Horton returned to Tennessee in the fall of 1932 and looked for land on which to build his school. His former professor and mentor Reinhold Niebuhr wrote a fund-raising letter on behalf of the project, which helped generate needed funds. Horton was joined by several of his old Union Seminary classmates who shared his concern for rural poverty and who, like him, were driven by the opportunity to translate their ideals into reality. Through an acquaintance, he was introduced to Don West, a theology student from Vanderbilt. The search for a location eventually led to a farm owned by Dr. Lilian Johnson, a former teacher, who had unsuccessfully attempted to start a farmers' co-op on her place in Monteagle, Tennessee. She offered to let them use the farm for a one-year trial, and if their venture seemed to be successful, she promised to grant them the land for free. After some debate they named their new venture Highlander Folk School. When they passed the one-year trial, Dr. Johnson granted them the title, and Highlander became a permanent venture.

Horton, West, and another Union alumnus, Jim Dombrowski, began the work by offering courses for local residents. Many volunteers came and went in the first couple of years, one of whom was Zilphia Johnson, an award-winning musician, who later became Horton's wife and shared the work with him until her accidental death in 1956. Zilphia introduced music into the work of Highlander and among other things is credited with popularizing the union song "We Shall Overcome," as a song that became the anthem of the civil rights movement. However, in the early years there were many stops and starts, as the young educators sought to practice their experience-based, grassroots approach to education. Their first big break came one night in the first year when a group of woodcutters met in their building to discuss some deplorable conditions in which they worked. Coming out of the meeting some of the men suggested that the woodcutters get together and go on strike. Right there in front of the school that night the Cumberland Mountain Workers' League was born, and Highlander and Myles Horton serendipitously entered the work of union organizing. As time went on Highlander became a significant facilitator of the early industrial union movement in the South.

As the Great Depression spread across the country and more workers found themselves being exploited or fired by employers, the Congress of Industrial Organizations (CIO) began using Highlander as an official training center for educating leaders in the union movement. At that time most unions shared the segregationist attitude at large in the country, and so kept their Black and White workers separated, with the Blacks typically getting paid significantly less than their White counterparts. Horton pointed out to CIO leaders that employers would often use their segregationist practice to play Blacks and Whites against each other in order to weaken union efforts to bring actions against them. By contrast, from the beginning Horton insisted that all union trainings at Highlander were to be integrated and that all members were to be treated equally and be given equal opportunity to succeed. He emphasized that a unified front was not only just but effective.

In this vein Horton tells a particular story of organizing textile workers in McColl, South Carolina, in 1937. As was common throughout the South, the workers were not treated equally across racial lines. Nearly 20 percent of the mill workers were Black, yet they generally were given the dirtiest and lowest-paying jobs. Horton began by working with the White leaders, and after a concerted effort he was able to convince them that the Blacks and Whites should work together to form a union. However, after watching Horton talk to the White leaders, none of the Blacks would even talk to him. From past experience they suspected that this White Southerner was just going to use them to improve the lot of the White workers, and that if the Blacks were given raises, they would be fired before they could enjoy them. However, Horton persisted in bringing the two sides together and eventually was able to talk with the leader of the Black workers, who hesitatingly agreed to sign up the Black workers for the union. Throughout his conversations Horton stressed that both Blacks and Whites were to be part of one union, and as a union they needed to work together and advocate equally for each other. When they sat down to negotiate, as expected the factory owner sought to divide the Blacks from the Whites, but the Black and White negotiators resisted his attempt to pit them against each other, and the workers not only got their union but also won a significant pay increase not determined by race, but by position. Despite this positive outcome many of the White workers received a negative reaction from their neighbors, church leaders, and members of the local Ku Klux Klan. Horton himself was vilified, but he maintained his principles and over time developed a philosophy for changing people's behavior by pushing them to examine the negative impact of their racist attitudes. His strategy was to help Blacks and Whites realize their common stake by putting them in situations where their efforts were strengthened when they united across race rather than remaining divided. He helped the White workers see that their racism actually weakened their cause, and in this very practical way he confronted them with the fallacy of racist attitudes.

Citizenship Schools

In the early 1950s as the United States and the Soviet Union entered into the Cold War, the CIO began to insist that Highlander incorporate anti-Communist language in its charter. Horton believed Communists had been essential to the labor struggle, and he did not want to give in to the "red scare" tactics sweeping the country at the time, and so he broke his ties with the CIO. In 1955 after exploring a variety of different issues, the board of Highlander decided to focus on addressing racism in its workshops. Through one of the workshops, Horton became acquainted with a man named Esau Jenkins. Jenkins was a businessman who lived on the Sea Islands just off the coast of Charleston, South Carolina, where the Black residents spoke a mixture of an African dialect and English known as Gullah. Jenkins was concerned about the Gullah people's inability to vote due to literacy tests that prohibited them from being able to even register. Jenkins drove a bus for domestic workers going back and forth to Charleston, and on the thirty-minute trips in and out of town attempted to teach his riders how to read. Jenkins shared his frustrations with Horton, and together they agreed that Highlander would try to help the Gullah people start what came to be known as Citizenship Schools. Horton went to the islands and spent several weeks working alongside of and living with the people, seeking to understand their work and the struggles they faced. Out of his familiarity with the people he hoped to develop an approach to literacy training relevant to their culture and needs.

Another Highlander workshop participant, Septima Clark, got interested in Jenkins's program. Clark was a former schoolteacher in nearby Charleston who had been fired from her job by the all-White school board for being a member of the local NAACP chapter. Clark and Jenkins came up with the idea that a local beautician named Bernice Robinson should run the reading program. Horton, Jenkins, and Clark had agreed that whoever was the teacher had to be someone who was familiar with the ways and daily lives of the people. Despite having no formal teaching credentials, as a local beautician Robinson daily interacted with people and understood the intricacies of their lives. Under

Bernice Robinson's leadership, Horton, Jenkins, and Clark developed a reading program based on writing personal stories. As the students learned to write their stories, they simultaneously learned reading skills rudimentary enough to enable them to pass the literacy test. The first Citizenship School graduated thirty students, and 80 percent of them passed the voting literacy test.

Soon the idea of Citizenship Schools spread to other communities in South Carolina and throughout the South, so Horton hired Septima Clark to develop the schools. Highlander became a center for training teachers to run Citizenship Schools in their local communities. Though Horton had a different teaching philosophy from that of Clark (she was more teacher-centered and didactic than he), he chose not to interfere and instead gave her the freedom to develop and direct the program as she thought best. Clark traveled through the Southern states setting up programs and training teachers. In 1961 Horton convinced Dr. Martin Luther King Jr. to make the Citizenship Schools a program in the Southern Christian Leadership Conference (SCLC). So in 1961 Septima Clark and a young theology student named Andrew Young, who had just come to work with Clark at Highlander, went to work for the SCLC. Young later became a valuable assistant to King, and later a representative to the US House of Representatives, a mayor of Atlanta, and an ambassador to the United Nations.

A Center for the Civil Rights Movement

Although Highlander was best known for its work on the Citizenship Schools during this time, Horton and his associates also sought to make Highlander a place where Blacks and Whites could meet together as equals. As such, they held many workshops, such as the one attended by Rosa Parks, that addressed a variety of issues related to racial segregation and injustice. Because in the South anyone advocating racial justice was characterized by the White power structure as a Communist, Highlander soon got the reputation for being a Communist Training School. In 1957 when Highlander celebrated its twenty-fifth anniversary, Dr. Martin Luther King Jr. was the featured speaker. Someone attending the event under false pretenses took a picture of the event, which shortly thereafter began to appear on huge billboards all over the South reading: "Martin Luther King at Communist Training School."[14]

---

[14] On a trip to Highlander in September 2005, I saw a replica of this sign prominently displayed as a reminder of Highlander's history.

In 1961 the attorney general of Arkansas, Bruce Bennett, held hearings investigating organizations that were working for racial reconciliation. *The Nashville Tennessean* published photos of the hearings that showed Bennett at a chalkboard analyzing the subversive influences in racial reconciliation organizations. At the center of his diagram was the name "Horton," indicating that he saw Horton as the centerpiece of a Communist network throughout the South. Eventually the state of Tennessee held hearings at which Horton was asked to explain the purpose of his school. Horton never denied that they, or the others he was allegedly connected to, were against racial segregation and injustice, but at the same he consistently denied being Communist. In his wry and biting way Horton often answered his interrogators in ways that left people in the gallery laughing. As a result the state was never able to prove Highlander to be a Communist training school. However, when the hearings failed to get the desired result, in 1961 (while Horton was conveniently out of the country) the state closed the school on the trumped-up charge that alcohol was being served to minors. Within two months of the closing, all the buildings were burned.

When asked about Highlander's forced closing Horton said: "You can padlock a building. But you can't padlock an idea. Highlander is an idea. You can't kill it and you can't close it in. . . . It will grow wherever people take it."[15] Shortly thereafter, Horton and his staff moved to a house in the Black community of Knoxville where they had support from both workers and local residents. Nonetheless, the harassment continued and their building was firebombed, the tires on their cars punctured and their windows shot out. Horton applied for and received a new charter under a new name, Highlander Research and Education Center, and continued to operate for ten years in Knoxville, until it opened its current facility in 1972 in New Market, Tennessee, about twenty miles east of Knoxville.

While still in Knoxville, Highlander became the target of a large protest sponsored by the KKK. When asked about his response to the threatened rally, Horton replied that he did not object to their rally, citing their right to freedom of speech, as long as they stayed on the public streets. However, to counter the threat Horton invited all his Black neighbors and White friends to attend a picnic at Highlander to watch the KKK parade. Black off-duty policemen agreed to serve as security. As a result, what the KKK had planned to be a march of

[15] Adams and Horton, *Unearthing*, 133.

intimidation became more of a circus, and the KKK participants went away humiliated. This is just one example of how Horton was able to orchestrate events in such a way that people felt empowered even in the face of serious threats.

Throughout the 1950s and 1960s Horton made the space and staff at Highlander available to leaders of various civil rights organizations. Highlander hosted or coordinated workshops for the Student Nonviolent Coordinating Committee (SNCC), the Mississippi Freedom Democratic Party, and the SCLC under Dr. Martin Luther King Jr. Horton's approach was not to run workshops himself but to identify local civil rights leaders and turn the leadership over to them. He provided logistical support and necessary resources, be they finances or people with expertise, but he believed that people in the midst of a situation were the best suited to come up with strategies to address that situation. Furthermore, when programs like the Citizenship Schools got to a certain size and scope, Horton chose to spin them off to work on their own, so his workshops could stay small and on the cutting edge.

At the core of Horton's approach was a commitment to use education as a means to extend people's participation in democracy. Horton understood democracy to be when "people are really free and empowered to make collectively the decisions that affect their lives."[16] Although democracy certainly involves voting, more importantly it involves helping low-income and working people see that although the power structure often sought to silence them or discriminate against them, they had inherent wisdom from the experience they shared collectively with others. In this way he enabled otherwise disempowered people to band together to make positive changes in their communities.

Between 1964 and 1968 the Highlander staff shifted their focus from civil rights to developing a multiracial poor people's coalition. The shift toward Black leadership and Black control in the civil rights movement, especially in SNCC under Stokely Carmichael, reduced the need for Whites to be directly involved. Horton agreed with Carmichael that White allies could assist the civil rights movement best by organizing poor Whites, who, like their Black counterparts, were manipulated and marginalized by the Southern White oligarchy. With other civil rights organizations, such as SCLC, Highlander participated in the Poor People's Campaign and March on Washington in June 1968. Horton and other Highlander staff lived in the makeshift Resurrection City on the Washington Mall

[16] Horton, Kohl, and Kohl, *Long Haul*, 169.

and ran cultural workshops for a variety of racial and ethnic groups. However, like many who participated in the event, Horton was disappointed with the lack of attention paid by the politicians and the lack of true multiracial unity in the event. Despite the disappointing failure of the campaign, the experience led Horton and Highlander into the next phase of their work, which was to address the many needs of poor Whites living in the Appalachian region.

The Dream Lives On

By 1970 Highlander had reduced its role in the civil rights movement because significant gains had been made and the leadership was strong. Horton resigned as Highlander's director in 1973, and became a senior consultant, speaking and traveling around the world running workshops, while still remaining active in many local issues. Highlander continued to work on issues endemic to the Southern United States such as environmental pollution, mountaintop removal, and more recently the rights of undocumented immigrants and African American youth empowerment.

Despite his strong record of supporting the efforts toward racial justice in the South, Horton never forgot that, like all Whites, he grew up with racist tendencies. In an interview conducted in the early 1970s Horton confessed, "I grew up knowing that Negroes were different and different meant inferior." He often cautioned liberal Whites against "unconscious racism," the assumption that well-meaning, social justice–oriented White people always know the right thing to do. As he always had insisted, Horton emphasized to liberal Whites that the answers to any issues of social justice must originate from the people most directly affected by that injustice. When asked to explain his place and role in the civil rights movement, he said, "I am part of the civil rights movement because I am not free," and "the role of concerned Whites is to help strengthen Negro leadership, not seek to share leadership. Whites who have had their time and failed should play second fiddle and let the Negroes call the tune."[17]

The paradox and challenge that was Myles Horton is illustrated by two unconnected but related events that occurred in 1983. In that year Rep. Ronald Dellums of California and Mayor Andrew Young of Atlanta, both African American leaders, nominated Myles Horton as a

---

[17] Horton and Jacobs, *Myles Horton Reader*, 180, 181, 166.

candidate for the Nobel Peace Prize. That same year Sen. Jesse Helms, a longtime White conservative from North Carolina, spoke out on the US Senate floor against a bill seeking to establish the Martin Luther King Jr. federal holiday. As evidence for his objection, Helms noted that King had been associated with the "Communist training school," Horton's Highlander Folk School. Until the end Horton lived out his principles being honored by some and vilified by others.

Myles Horton died in 1990 after a long struggle with brain cancer. Until his death he continued to work and speak wherever he was needed. In 1982, TV journalist Bill Moyers interviewed Horton on the porch of the main house at Highlander overlooking the east Tennessee hills. In his wry Southern drawl Horton relayed story after story of his work at Highlander; the two-hour PBS program that aired was called "Adventures of a Radical Hillbilly."[18] Today Highlander continues to work and advocate for the poor, particularly focusing on the rights of undocumented immigrants and African American youth empowerment. In 2012 Highlander celebrated its eightieth anniversary and serves various social justice concerns throughout the South. Moreover, Highlander has been an inspiration and model for similar centers in different parts of the country.[19]

John Glen, a historian, writes: "Horton . . . tried to educate by the example of his life. For both his friends and his enemies, Horton symbolized a challenge to the South's traditional beliefs and practices. . . . Most of all Horton imparted a belief that a time would come when there would be greater human dignity and justice." In his later years as he struggled with failing health, Horton expressed disappointment that his dreams had not been realized. However, Glen continues: "Southerners may not have understood or agreed with him, but they knew he was on the side of the oppressed. That reputation sustained both Horton and Highlander."[20] The dream that woke Horton up on a Danish Christmas night over eight decades ago continues to live on.

---

[18] Transcripts of the program can be found at Bill Moyers, "The Adventures of a Radical Hillbilly: An Interview with Myles Horton," *Appalachian Journal* 9, no. 4 (1982): 248–85.

[19] Drick Boyd, "Under the Radar: Popular Education in North America," unpublished paper, 2011.

[20] Glen, *Highlander*, 223.

Discussion Questions

1. Horton said that growing up in relative poverty gave him a way of relating to poor people and understanding their problems. Have you had a similar experience?
2. Even though he worked for racial justice all of his life, Horton recognized that as a White person he had been socialized to think of African Americans as inferior. If you are White, have you experienced this? If you are a Person of Color, how has this socialization of Whites affected you?
3. Horton insisted that the role of Whites in racial justice work was to support the leadership of People of Color. What is your reaction to this perspective?

Bibliography

Adams, Frank, and Myles Horton. *Unearthing Seeds of Fire: The Idea of Highlander.* Winston-Salem, NC: John F. Blair, 1975.

Boyd, Drick. "Under the Radar: Popular Education in North America." Unpublished paper, 2011.

Boyd, Herb. "Rosa Parks, 1913–2005." *New York Amsterdam News* 96, no. 44 (October 27–November 2, 2005): 1, 30.

Durham, Frank. "Ethos in Action: Public Relations at the Highlander Folk School, 1955–1956." Paper presented at the Annual Meeting of the Association for Education in Journalism and Mass Communication, Kansas City, Missouri, August 11–14, 1993.

Glen, John M. *Highlander: No Ordinary School, 1932–1962*. Knoxville: University of Tennessee Press, 1996.

Horton, Myles, and Dale Jacobs. *The Myles Horton Reader: Education for Social Change*. Knoxville: University of Tennessee Press, 2003.

Horton, Myles, Judith Kohl, and Herb Kohl. *The Long Haul: An Autobiography*. New York: Teacher's College Press, 1998.

McGuire, Danielle L. *At the Dark End of the Street: Black Women, Rape and Resistance—A New History from Rosa Parks to the Rise of Black Power*. New York: Alfred E. Knopf, 2010.

Moyers, Bill. "The Adventures of a Radical Hillbilly: An Interview with Myles Horton." *Appalachian Journal* 9, no. 4 (1982): 248–85.

Parks, Rosa, and Jim Haskins. *Rosa Parks: My Story.* New York: Dial Books, 1992.

10

Abraham Joshua Heschel

(1907–1972)

*Prophet and Friend**

Called to Selma

On Sunday, March 21, 1963, Dr. Martin Luther King Jr. led a group of several thousand people across the Edmund Pettus Bridge in Selma, Alabama, initiating a fifty-mile march to the state capital, Montgomery, advocating for the rights of African Americans to vote. Three weeks earlier, a smaller group under the leadership of John Lewis, chairman of the Student Nonviolent Coordinating Committee (SNCC), and Hosea Williams from the Southern Christian Leadership Conference (SCLC), had attempted the same march, but it had ended violently. As the group crossed over the bridge leading out of Selma, they were met by police in riot gear and on horseback. The marchers knelt to pray and with little warning the police moved forward wielding clubs and spraying tear gas. People panicked and ran back across the bridge with the police in pursuit. Over fifty of the marchers were injured on the day that became known as "Bloody Sunday." It was televised nationally.

* Photo of Abraham Joshua Heschel used courtesy of Joel Orent. Unless otherwise noted the information in this chapter is taken from the two-volume biography of his life: Edward K. Kaplan and Stuart Dresner, *Abraham Joshua Heschel: Prophetic Witness* (New Haven, CT: Yale University Press, 1998); and Edward K. Kaplan, *Spiritual Radical: Abraham Joshua Heschel in America, 1940–1972* (New Haven, CT: Yale University Press, 2007). Input and interpretation of events also provided by Dr. Susannah Heschel, daughter of Abraham Joshua Heschel.

Dr. Martin Luther King Jr. was invited to join the cause. He issued a call for people sympathetic to the civil rights cause to come to Selma to continue the aborted march; thousands from across the country had responded. As King led the marchers across the bridge this second time, a UPI photograph showed Dr. King in the center with his close friend Rev. Ralph Abernathy to his right and to his left a bearded man with white hair, glasses, and a yarmulke, "the perfect media symbol of a Hebrew prophet,"[1] Abraham Joshua Heschel.

How is it that this renowned Jewish scholar and teacher found his way to Selma? Who was he and why was he there?

From Poland to the United States

Abraham Joshua Heschel was born in Poland in 1907 to a prominent Jewish family. He was named after his grandfather, who himself was named after an earlier ancestor who had been one of the early founders of Hasidic Judaism. Hasidism is a pietistic movement led by rabbis whose positions were passed down from father to son. His mother was also descended from a prominent Polish rabbinical family. So by virtue of his lineage and his name young Abraham was destined to become a great "rebbe" himself, and from a young age he was tutored in traditional rabbinical texts and Hasidic spiritual formation. Moreover, the little apartment in Warsaw he shared with his parents and four siblings was also the place where his father received a constant flow of visitors seeking spiritual counsel. Thus, by tradition, observation, and direct tutelage, Heschel was raised in the essentials of the Hasidic Jewish faith.

Heschel's father chose to carry out his rabbinical duties in a low-income neighborhood. In his ministry he emphasized the importance of prayer, observance of Jewish law, and study of the Torah. He received only small fees for his counsel, and in accordance with his family religious heritage, he never kept money in his house overnight. So what money was available had to be gathered and spent that day on the needs of the family. Thus despite their rich family history and local prominence, the Heschel family lived in constant poverty dependent on the beneficence of the rabbi's followers. However, in 1916 when young Abraham was nine years old his father died suddenly at the age of forty-three due to a citywide typhoid epidemic during the German occupation of Warsaw in World War I. As a result the family was plunged into even deeper

[1] Kaplan, *Spiritual Radical*, 223.

poverty. Later in life Heschel remembered that period of his life for the terribly frigid winters that caused his fingers to become permanently swollen from the cold.

However, as Heschel's daughter, Susannah, notes, "What transcended their poverty was the religious atmosphere." He frequently recalled his great grandfather Apt Rev, whose teachings were known to be infused with empathy and generosity, bringing hope and healing to those stressed by the sufferings of life. Thus, even in his childhood poverty, Heschel believed he was the object of God's compassionate concern. This awareness stayed with him throughout his life.[2]

After a time he came under the tutelage of an uncle who continued his rabbinical training. Susannah Heschel notes that her father "grew up surrounded by 'people of religious nobility' that gave him inspiration and strength in the midst of his privation."[3] Thus, he came of age in an environment of study, warmth, ritual, and deep respect for the traditions of his ancestors. Furthermore, he developed an active practice of prayer, which became one of the hallmarks of his later writings. At the same time he was outgoing, warm, enthusiastic, and had lots of friends.[4]

In 1927 he went to Berlin to study simultaneously at the Reform rabbinical school, the University of Berlin, and the Hildesheimer Orthodox rabbinical seminary, thereby receiving both an orthodox and more liberal Jewish education, as well as secular academic training at the university. He later said he felt comfortable in all three environments, but he was critical of all three at the same time. The breadth of understanding he gained in those years, plus his willingness to engage all three traditions, became an outstanding characteristic of his work throughout his life. After the Depression struck in 1929, he again experienced deep poverty but was able to complete his PhD dissertation in 1932. In Germany at that time, it was customary that one did not receive a degree until after one's dissertation was published. However, after Hitler came to power in 1933 there were no German publishers willing to publish a book authored by a Jew, so it was not until he got the book published in Poland in 1935 that he was finally granted his degree. That dissertation later was translated into English as *The Prophets*, a seminal work on the Old Testament prophets that later

---

[2] Susannah Heschel, Introduction to *Abraham Joshua Heschel: Essential Writings*, ed. Susannah Heschel (Maryknoll, NY: Orbis Books, 2011), 20–21.

[3] Ibid., 19.

[4] Susannah Heschel, personal communication, April 23, 2015.

inspired people such as Martin Luther King Jr. and Andrew Young in their civil rights endeavors.

As Hitler's rise to power continued, Jewish-authored books were burned, and Jewish academics were expelled from the University of Berlin. Heschel sought a position outside of Germany, but then was invited in 1937 by Martin Buber to succeed him as the director of the Central Organization for Jewish Adult Education in Frankfurt, Germany. However, in October 1938 he was arrested and deported to Poland. In the summer of 1939, he left Warsaw for England, just weeks before the Germans invaded Poland on September 1, 1939. Then he moved to the United States in 1940 to assume a teaching post. After leaving Poland he never saw three of his sisters and mother again (one sister had left before the war),[5] because they were killed either in the invasion of Poland or in the death camps in which six million Jews perished. Susannah Heschel reports that her father rarely spoke of leaving his family members behind, and when he did he was overcome with grief. He used to say that everyone who knew him as a child died in the war. As a result even years after the war, Heschel refused to return to Poland, Germany, or Austria. He also rarely spoke about the victims of the Holocaust but rather those who stood by while it happened choosing not to act.[6] It was out of this tragic experience that one of his famous sayings emerged: "Few are guilty, but all are responsible."[7] This phrase was to return in many ways as he became engaged in the civil rights movement.

Heschel's first appointment in the United States was at Hebrew Union College in Cincinnati, Ohio, where he worked from 1940 to 1945. The five years there were difficult because he was still learning English. He found that many of his colleagues did not share his interest in the mystical Hasidic strain of Judaism in which he was raised and that he practiced. However, while in Cincinnati he met his wife, Sylvia Straus, who was a concert pianist. In 1945 Heschel became a professor at the Jewish Theological Seminary in New York City, where he lived and worked for the rest of his life. Sylvia moved to New York to be with him, and they were married in 1946; they had one child, Susannah, who became a professor of Jewish studies at Dartmouth College.

---

[5] Personal communication, Susannah Heschel, April 23, 2015.

[6] S. Heschel, "Introduction," 24.

[7] Abraham Joshua Heschel, *The Prophets: An Introduction* (New York: Harper Colophon Books, 1962), 16.

Interfaith Relationships

Despite his scholarly Hasidic pedigree and prolific writing upon arrival in the United States, Heschel was not well received by many of his Jewish colleagues, as he taught and lived a kind of spiritual piety that was unfamiliar and somewhat disdained by most American Jews. Susannah Heschel writes that it was common among American Jews to profess a "religionless Judaism—a Judaism without God, faith or belief" and that a "rejection of Jewish mysticism, Hasidism, and even theology and spirituality were common."[8] Thus most of Heschel's work was not appreciated within Jewish circles, and it was not until the Christian ethicist and theologian Reinhold Niebuhr gave a positive review of *Man Is Not Alone* (published in 1951) that he became more prominent.[9] This review also began a long-term friendship with Niebuhr, as well as with many other progressive Christian leaders, who shared his interest in issues of Jewish-Christian dialogue and the role of religion in public life. For Heschel, "Religion . . . must rise above expediency to represent absolute values."[10] This involvement in interfaith issues eventually led him to encounter the prominent civil rights leader, Dr. Martin Luther King Jr.

Upon arrival in the United States in 1940, Heschel knew nothing about the struggles and sufferings of Black people through US history. However, while in Cincinnati he became friends with African Americans through whom he learned about some of the racial barriers they had faced all through US history. As a victim of German anti-Semitism and one who had lost so many loved ones in the Holocaust, he quickly developed a deep disgust for the racial policies and practices in the United States. However, his first public statement on the issue did not occur until 1958 at a rabbinical assembly where he chastised his fellow Jews for their "timidity and hesitance to take a stand on behalf of the Negroes."[11] After that time, Heschel's prominence grew as a respected Jewish speaker on a wide range of social issues including racism and civil rights. In that role he "sought to promote a sacred humanism, a global reverence for all individuals."[12]

---

[8] S. Heschel, "Introduction," 27.

[9] Reinhold Niebuhr, "The Masterly Analysis of Faith," *New York Herald Tribune Book Review*, April 1, 1951, 12

[10] Kaplan, *Spiritual Radical*, 183.

[11] Ibid., 215.

[12] Ibid., 206.

In March 1963 he was invited to be a keynote speaker at the first National Conference on Religion and Race, a meeting of Protestants, Roman Catholics, and Jews in Chicago to have a candid discussion as religious leaders about how to address the racial issues of the time. Another person invited to address the assembly was Dr. Martin Luther King Jr. It was at this meeting that Heschel met Dr. King, and a unique friendship developed until the latter's death five years later.

At the conference Heschel delivered the opening plenary, which he entitled "The Religious Basis of Equality and Opportunity" (it is reprinted as "Religion and Race" in Heschel's essay collection, *The Insecurity of Freedom*). In that address he referred to racism as "blasphemy," "satanism," and "unmitigated evil." He further said that the people gathered there should not only seek to help the African Americans but also attend "to the situation of the white people, to the cure of a disease affecting the spiritual substance and condition of every one of us."[13] He further described the Black civil rights struggle as the "fruit of our sins." Drawing on his work *The Prophets*, he called on religious leaders to take on the role of the prophet and to advocate on behalf of those being denied their basic rights and safety. He further chastised a noncommittal "indifference to evil" and recited his famous phrase that "some are guilty, but all are responsible." He concluded by emphasizing: "The plight of the Negro must become our most important concern. Seen in light of religious tradition, the Negro problem is God's gift to America, the test of our integrity, a magnificent spiritual opportunity."[14]

Heschel's speech incited a vigorous dialogue among the participants as to the way in which religious leaders should press for racial equality. The gathering's final speaker was Martin Luther King Jr., whose speech was titled "Challenge to the Churches and the Synagogues." Drawing on the story of the liberation of Hebrew slaves from Egypt (an image Heschel had likewise used in his address), King challenged those gathered to act on the root values of their faith and to recognize the sanctity of all people in the eyes of God. He further repeated his commitment to nonviolence. Afterward Heschel and King were introduced, and they quickly developed a partnership around their common commitments and values. They both had come from religious families and suffered racial

---

[13] Abraham Joshua Heschel, *The Insecurity of Freedom* (New York: Schocken Books, 1972), 87.

[14] Ibid., 89, 92, 93, 97.

discrimination. Like Heschel, King had risen above his own suffering to become a national leader and spokesperson for justice based in religious values and commitments.

Immersion in the Civil Rights Movement

Following that first meeting, Heschel and King formed what Heschel's daughter, Susannah, called an "extraordinary friendship" with a bond characterized by what she called "depth theology," the deep connections felt by religiously pious people because of their faith traditions. Heschel had no interest in becoming Christian, and yet through a common appreciation for the biblical prophets, Heschel and King developed a deep "religious bond."[15] In fact after meeting him, King reportedly bought copies of Heschel's *The Prophets* for the entire staff of his organization, the SCLC. In 1982 when interviewed for a retrospective look at the life of Heschel, former SCLC member James Lawson said he still had a copy of *The Prophets* in his home office.[16]

After the conference, Heschel and four hundred other religious leaders were invited to meet with Attorney General Robert Kennedy in June 1963. A day before the meeting Heschel proposed "A Marshall Plan to Aid the Negroes," calling on all religious leaders to donate one month's pay toward a fund to aid in the housing and education of Black people. Heschel was also invited in February 1964 to an ecumenical gathering on race issues in New York City, at which more than 2,000 clergy gathered. In the presence of the mayor and the New York Roman Catholic archbishop, Heschel spoke of "The White Man on Trial." Drawing on the biblical story of the Exodus, Heschel lamented that "it was easier for the children of Israel to cross the Red Sea than for civil rights legislation to pass the floor of the United States Senate." He further linked the US civil rights struggle to the plight of Jews in Russia, the Chinese oppression of Tibet, and the struggles of poor and oppressed peoples around the world. He called not just for legalized integration but a deeper integration of "fellowship, mutual respect and concern." He concluded by calling for a "spiritual revolution."[17]

---

[15] S. Heschel, "Introduction," 35.

[16] Carl Stern, "Abraham Joshua Heschel Remembered," *NBC News*, 1982, http://www.youtube.com.

[17] A. Heschel, *Insecurity of Freedom*, 103, 106–7.

Heschel's public statements were matched by his participation in local efforts in joining street protests and demonstrations. He joined others in signing a letter calling for high-quality integrated education for all children. Then on March 7, 1965, he watched a television news report from Selma, Alabama, describing the brutal events of Bloody Sunday. Ironically, that same day, ABC broadcast a documentary about the Nuremberg trial of Nazis. Heschel, like many others, could not help but see the parallels between the Nazi genocide against the Jews and the events in Selma. In response to those tragic events he helped organize a demonstration two days later in New York City with members of SNCC and the Congress of Racial Equality (CORE). They marched to the local FBI headquarters demanding protection for the civil rights workers and arrest of those who attacked them. Heschel was among a small delegation of the nearly eight hundred protesters that met with the local FBI chief. As a result, Heschel was placed on the FBI's list of potential subversives. The FBI quickly began investigating him because he had added his name to a list of three hundred signers of an advertisement in the March 10, 1965, issue of the *Washington Post* calling for the repeal of the McCarran Act. The McCarran Act required suspected Communist sympathizers to register with the government, and the ad criticized it for "[diminishing] the honor of our democracy." From that point on he was on an FBI watch list of supposed Communist sympathizers.[18]

Two weeks later Martin Luther King Jr. issued a call for religious leaders to come to Selma. King specifically asked Andrew Young to contact Heschel and urge him to join the first day of the march.[19] Several civil rights organizations joined in the effort, and the federal government promised armed protection. Even so, the atmosphere was tense, with the expectation that violence could erupt at any moment. Despite fears for his safety—since Jews were known to be discriminated against in the South as well as Blacks—Heschel traveled with an associate, Wolf Kelman, to Atlanta, and the next day they drove to Selma to join the march on Sunday, March 21. He was one of religious leaders of all denominations and faiths who had responded to King's call. King and his associates were always cognizant of the power of media images, and so it was decided that having a bearded rabbi with his yarmulke in full view of the camera would gain national attention.

---

[18] Kaplan, *Spiritual Radical*, 221.

[19] Taylor Branch, *At Canaan's Edge: America in the King Years, 1965–68* (New York: Simon and Schuster, 2006), 134–35.

Thus Heschel marched in the front line just to King's left, arm in arm with other civil rights leaders, and the image went around the globe. As the marchers processed, they passed hostile onlookers cursing, jeering, and displaying banners with racial epithets such as "Koons, Kikes and Niggers, Go Home!" After about five hours, the procession stopped to rest, and Heschel along with other prominent leaders, left to return to their homes. Others continued on the five-day march that culminated in Montgomery on the capitol steps. Reflecting on the spiritual meaning of the events, Heschel later wrote: "I felt the sense of the Holy in what I was doing. . . . Even without words our march was worship. I felt my legs were praying."[20]

In the years following Selma, Heschel continued to speak out on racial issues and deepened his relationship with King. Although he continued to teach, write, and speak out on a variety of topics, he also believed that the soul of Judaism was at stake in the fight against racism in the United States. Indeed, it is clear that a significant number of the Whites who joined the Southern civil rights struggle and joined the Freedom Rides were Jewish. So Heschel's message was being heard, and he was not alone in seeing the parallels between anti-Semitism and racism.

Linking Civil Rights and War

As the Vietnam War continued to escalate, Dr. King became convinced that he needed to speak out against the war because he increasingly saw the links between militarism overseas and poverty and injustice at home. For his part Heschel had long been a vocal opponent to the war and was a co-founder of Clergy and Laymen Concerned About Vietnam (CALCAV), which had its first meeting in October 1965. CALCAV was an organization of mainline religious leaders calling for an immediate halt to the bombing in North Vietnam and working toward a negotiated end to the war. Heschel was considered the most influential Jewish voice on the committee. King also became a supporter of CALCAV and eventually agreed to deliver a major address on the war.

So on April 4, 1967, exactly one year before his death, King mounted the pulpit of the historic Riverside Church in New York to deliver his speech "Beyond Vietnam: A Time to Break Silence," in which he clearly

---

[20] From an unpublished manuscript quoted in Susannah Heschel, Introduction to *Moral Grandeur and Spiritual Audacity: Essays by Abraham Joshua Heschel* (New York: Farrar, Straus and Giroux, 1996), xxii.

and powerfully spoke out against the war. Many of his closest SCLC advisers had advised him against making such a public statement for fear that it would weaken the alliance they had forged with the Johnson administration over civil rights, and might undercut wider public support for the civil rights movement and the gains they had achieved. However, one close friend who encouraged King's decision to speak out was Abraham Joshua Heschel. In fact, it was Heschel who introduced him to the crowd gathered that day in the church. In his introduction he decried the senseless killing done in the name of the United States and repeated his oft-quoted phrase that in a free society some are guilty and all are responsible. Following that introduction, King delivered one of the most powerfully prophetic speeches of his career, clearly showing the link between increased government spending for military efforts and decreases in spending for social programs. Likewise, he pointed out that the very same poor folks suffering at home were disproportionately represented among those who were drafted to fight and die in the war. Following King's speech there were other speeches that were then collected in a booklet called *Vietnam: A Crisis of Conscience*. Heschel himself contributed an essay titled "The Moral Outrage of Vietnam."

A Prophetic and Symbolic Friendship

The last time Dr. King and Rabbi Heschel were together occurred just ten days before King was gunned down by an assassin's bullet in Memphis, Tennessee. On March 25, 1968, King spoke to the rabbinical assembly at New York's Concord Hotel. The assembly honored Heschel on his sixtieth birthday for his activism and scholarship. As part of the tribute to Heschel, they invited Dr. King to speak, hoping to reaffirm the fraying alliance between American Jews and African Americans. In introducing his friend, Heschel said, "Martin Luther King is a sign that God has not forsaken the United States. . . . His presence is the hope of America."[21] In return King thanked Heschel for his support and presence at the march at Selma and referred to him as a "truly great prophet."[22] King further voiced his support for Israel, an issue of deep concern to all gathered at the assembly, and in return asked for their continued support in his efforts to bring about economic justice. Ten days later on April 4, 1968, Martin Luther King Jr. was dead.

---

[21] S. Heschel, "Introduction," 84.

[22] Kaplan, *Spiritual Radical*, 326.

Had he lived, King was planning to celebrate Passover with the Heschel family that year. Instead, the event was characterized by mourning the loss of a great leader and a friend. In reflecting on the relationship between the two men, Susannah Heschel writes: "Their relationship carried profound meaning for both [of them]. They seemed to have been aware of the symbolic significance of their friendship and used it as a tool to foster alliances between Jews and blacks."[23] Even after King's death, Heschel continued to support projects by King's former advisers such as Jesse Jackson and Wyatt T. Walker. Despite opposition within the Jewish community, he also continued to be a strong supporter of affirmative action programs until his death in 1972.

Much has been made of the personal, political, and theological affinities between Rabbi Heschel and Dr. King, and indeed those affinities certainly contributed to their relationship. However, it was the friendship itself that stands out as the greatest example: an older Jewish rabbi with a Polish accent and a young African American Christian preacher from the South. The picture of King and Heschel marching together in Selma, in Susannah Heschel's words, "has become an icon of American Jewish life and of Black-Jewish relations."[24] One could add that the picture has become a symbol and an example of Whites and Blacks marching side by side for the cause of justice in all places and all times.

---

[23] S. Heschel, "Introduction," 39.

[24] Susannah Heschel, "Theological Affinities in the Writings of Abraham Joshua Heschel and Martin Luther King Jr." in *Black Zion: African American Religious Encounters with Judaism*, ed. Yvonne Chireau and Nathaniel Deutsch (New York: Oxford University Press, 2000), 168.

Discussion Questions

1. What are ways that our own experiences of suffering and loss can create empathy for others?
2. What are ways that significant personal relationships between individuals of different races and/or religious faiths can be models for reconciliation?
3. Dr. King made the Exodus from Egypt the central symbol of the civil rights movement; he did not invoke Jesus in his major speeches. In so doing he welcomed Jewish participation in the movement. How do you think the Passover Seder of 1968 would have been conducted at the Heschel home with the presence of Dr. King? What questions might you have asked him about the meaning of the book of Exodus for civil rights?

Bibliography

Branch, Taylor. *At Canaan's Edge: America in the King Years, 1965–68*. New York: Simon and Schuster, 2006

Feiler, Bruce. *America's Prophet: Moses and the American Story*. New York: William Morrow, 2009.

Heschel, Abraham Joshua. *The Insecurity of Freedom*. New York: Schocken Books, 1972.

———. *The Prophets: An Introduction*. New York: Harper Colophon Books, 1962.

Heschel, Susannah. Introduction to *Abraham Joshua Heschel: Essential Writings*, edited by Susannah Heschel, 17–44. Maryknoll, NY: Orbis Books, 2011.

———. Introduction to *Moral Grandeur and Spiritual Audacity: Essays by Abraham Joshua Heschel*. New York: Farrar, Straus and Giroux, 1996.

———. "Theological Affinities in the Writings of Abraham Joshua Heschel and Martin Luther King Jr." In *Black Zion: African American Religious Encounters with Judaism*, edited by Yvonne Chireau and Nathaniel Deutsch, 168–86. New York: Oxford University Press, 2000.

Kaplan, Edward K. *Spiritual Radical: Abraham Joshua Heschel in America, 1940–1972*. New Haven, CT: Yale University Press, 2007.

Kaplan, Edward K., and Stuart Dresner. *Abraham Joshua Heschel: Prophetic Witness*. New Haven, CT: Yale University Press, 1998.

Lewis, John. *Walking with the Wind: A Memoir of the Movement*. New York: Simon and Schuster, 1998.

Stern, Carl. "Abraham Joshua Heschel Remembered." *NBC News*. 1982. http://www.youtube.com.

11

CLARENCE JORDAN (1912–1969)

*A Cotton Patch Radical**

A One-Hundred-Year Legacy

In late September 2012, more than four hundred people gathered on a farm in southern Georgia to celebrate the life and legacy of a man who had been dead for over forty years. Clarence Jordan would have been one hundred years old in that year, but he had died four decades earlier of an apparent heart attack at the age of fifty-seven. Forty-three years after his death people gathered not only to remember this humble Georgia farmer and biblical scholar but also to look forward to the work his vision still inspired.

Dallas Lee, who knew Jordan near the end of his life, described him this way:

> Tall, high-hipped, hands jammed into blue-jean pockets, floppy straw hat shading a grin—dusty from the peanut rows, greasy from the tractor shop, bespectacled from persistent study—the man was

* One-time permission to reprint image of Clarence Jordan granted by Koinonia Farm. For further information about Koinonia and/or Clarence Jordan, please see our website at www.koinoniafarm.org or write us at 1324 GA Hwy 49 S, Americus, GA, 31719, or call 229-924-0391. Visitors welcomed year round. The main sources for this chapter, unless otherwise noted, are Ann Louise Coble, *Cotton Patch for the Kingdom: Clarence Jordan's Demonstration Plot at Koinonia* (Scottsdale, PA: Herald Press, 2002); Tracy Elaine K'Meyer, *Interracialism and Christian Community in the Postwar South: The Story of Koinonia Farm* (Charlottesville: University Press of Virginia, 1997); and Dallas Lee, *The Cotton Patch Evidence* (New York: Harper and Row, 1971).

> full of the unexpected, so you listened expectantly. . . . He was a gentle man who thundered, a nonviolent man who was known to have stared down a Ku Kluxer or two, a man with much to say who listened patiently, . . . a dirt-farming aristocrat, a good ole Georgia country boy with a doctor's degree, a teacher with manure on his boots, a scholar with working clothes on his mind.[1]

He also was a man who was known throughout the South for his commitment to racial reconciliation, even though he himself saw interracial relationships and economic development not as ends in themselves but as a logical extension of his commitment to living an authentic Christian life.

Early Years

Clarence Jordan was born on July 29, 1912, the seventh of ten children born to J. W. and Maude Jordan in Talbotton, a rural town in the southern part of Georgia. J. W. Jordan was the founder of the local bank and a businessman who ran the general store with the help of his sons. As such, they were economically better off than most of the other residents of the area. The Jordans were a close-knit family, and Clarence's childhood was characterized by the safety and security of a loving home.

The Jordans were also faithful, church-going Southern Baptists who regularly practiced Bible reading and prayer in their home. Like most Southern Baptists, the Jordans taught their children that salvation was available to all who would accept the death of Jesus as the means to grace and redemption. They further believed that it was the individual Christian's responsibility to share the message and love of Christ with all they encountered. Moreover, they believed that individual Christians should live in community with other like-minded believers through their participation in a local congregation. As Tracy Elaine K'Meyer writes: "In brief the Southern Baptists have 'no mission on earth save carrying out of His [Christ's] will.'"[2] Thus, it is not surprising that at age ten, Clarence went forward at a church revival meeting where he made his own personal commitment to Christ and joined the church.

In contrast to his more outgoing siblings, Clarence was a quiet, reflective child. Although Jordan's childhood world was very secure, as

---

[1] Lee, *Cotton Patch Evidence*, 1.

[2] K'Meyer, *Interracialism*, 5.

he grew he began to notice huge discrepancies between the teachings he received at church and the way people related to one another in daily life, particularly the way White people regarded and related to Black people. Like many other White Southern families, the Jordans had a Black nursemaid and Black servants, and while they considered themselves to be "close" to these "Black friends," they treated them as subordinates whose role was to be subservient to their needs and desires. In Sunday School, he sang of how "Jesus loves the little children . . . red, yellow, black, and white, they are precious in his sight," and yet he saw that in their daily lives Black children suffered privations that caused him to wonder if in fact God did treat all children the same.

Jordan's bedroom window overlooked the county jail, which was only a hundred yards behind his home. He often stopped by the jail on his way home from school, befriended the cook, and talked with men on the chain gang, almost all of whom were Black. They told him about an instrument called "the stretcher," a bed-like frame where a man could be tortured with a series of ropes and weights. The warden of that same jail sang in the church choir, and listening to his bass voice sing "Love Lifted Me," Clarence was deeply torn by the realization that the man singing of God's love was also the one pulling the ropes and weights on the prisoners groaning in agony on the "stretcher."

Jordan noticed inconsistencies in his own family as well. One time when he was about nine or ten years old, he witnessed his father rebuking an African American man for delivering their dry cleaning to the front door, rather than the back door as was customary for Blacks to do. He was angry and embarrassed by his father's racist impetuousness, and it is said that he lectured his father for treating the man so badly. Although Jordan did not speak of these events until he was in his early twenties, it seems clear that even at an early age, he was beginning to develop an awareness that there was a gross inconsistency between the Christian message he was being taught and the ways in which Whites and Blacks actually interacted with each other.

College and Seminary

Despite his father's desire that he become a lawyer, in 1929 Clarence entered the University of Georgia at Athens to study agriculture. Already forming in his mind was the idea that he could use his education to help educate the poor tenant farmers struggling on the edge of poverty in the South. While in school he joined the Baptist Student Union and was part of Reserve Officers Training Corps (ROTC), something typical of all boys aspiring to become Southern gentlemen. In the summer of 1932 he attended a special ROTC military course at a time when he also happened to be studying Jesus' Sermon on the Mount with its emphasis on nonviolence and loving one's enemy. After one particular military exercise where he was instructed to shoot at human-shaped dummies, Jordan came out of the woods and perfunctorily resigned his ROTC commission, saying he could not be a faithful Christian and participate in war. He subsequently went to the Baptist church in Athens and asked that he be licensed to preach because he felt a call to the ministry. He had come to realize that the role he felt called to fill was to combine the work of pastoral ministry with his agricultural skills to help the rural poor.

Thus, upon graduation from college in 1933, he entered Southern Seminary in Louisville, Kentucky, where he intended to become a scholar of the Bible. While there he met Florence Krueger, who worked in the seminary library. They married in 1936, and two of their four children were born there before they left Louisville in 1939. When Clarence proposed marriage, he told Florence that he would never make much money and that he did not intend to pastor a church, that his was an unorthodox radical calling to help the rural poor; she accepted those terms, and they were married. While her part in Clarence's story is often overlooked, Florence's consistent partnership with her husband was something that sustained him in the thirty-three years they were together.

While at Southern Seminary, Clarence came under the tutelage of professors who pushed him to think more deeply about the inconsistencies between Christian faith and the racist actions and attitudes he had witnessed in his youth. His ethics professor helped him begin to think theologically about social issues, and his New Testament professor challenged him to see the connections between the Bible and current events. He also had numerous opportunities to preach in local churches where he became known as a powerful and effective speaker. However, his life began to change course when he was invited by another professor to attend a meeting of the Southern Interracial Commission, which Jordan later called "a turning point in my life."[3]

After earning his Master of Divinity degree, Jordan continued at Southern to earn his PhD in New Testament with a focus on the Greek language, the language of the New Testament. At the same time he began

[3] Coble, *Cotton Patch for the Kingdom*, 41.

teaching part time at Simmons University, a small college that trained African American pastors. On one occasion he invited his Simmons students to Southern where they held class over dinner in the seminary cafeteria; this was the first of many controversies Jordan's actions would precipitate. When word reached the administration that Jordan had invited Black students into the previously all-White cafeteria, he was informed that seminary policy forbade anyone from holding interracial functions in such a public space. However, some Southern students heard of the administration's pronouncement and protested the policy, and soon after the dinners were allowed to proceed.

Shortly after these incidents, Jordan was hired by the local Southern Baptist association to oversee its inner-city ministries, which in fact meant he was overseeing the Black churches affiliated with the Southern Baptists in Louisville (since the Whites did not want to interact directly with their Black church counterparts). In that role Jordan was able to witness firsthand the effects of segregation and deprivation experienced by many of Louisville's Black residents. He became friendly with many of the local Black ministers and sometimes worshipped in their churches. Where possible he promoted the idea that Black ministers should lead predominantly Black churches and sought to encourage Black and White ministers to meet together for prayer and study, but this effort met with limited success. Already forming in his mind was the notion that true Christian community involved Blacks and Whites living and working together despite the prevailing segregationist culture.

In Search of *Koinonia*

While in his doctoral studies Jordan became fascinated with the Greek word *koinonia*, which is often translated as "fellowship" or "community." However, Jordan developed a more radical vision of *koinonia* when he read the New Testament book of Acts, in which *koinonia* is depicted as the practice of people holding things in common, a "radical sharing of goods, worship and witness."[4] Near the end of his time at Southern, Jordan pulled a group of fellow students together who attempted to put into practice this radical ideal of community, living together and sharing many of their basic necessities in common. In the end the Southern experiment with *koinonia* failed, but Jordan remained captivated by what true Christian community could and should be.

---

[4] Helene Barnette, *Clarence Jordan: Turning Dreams into Deeds* (Macon, GA: Smith and Helwys, 1972), 17.

In 1941 Jordan read a published letter by Martin England, an American Baptist[5] missionary who was on furlough from Burma. In the letter England contended that realities such as war, racism, and economic disparity could be overcome only by small groups of people committed to living out their Christian commitments in intentional community. England's challenge dovetailed perfectly with Jordan's vision of *koinonia*. Shortly thereafter he met Martin England at a conference, and they began working together on the idea of starting a Christian community in a rural section of the South with the goal of living out a radical Christian life in community that would seek to model positive and constructive relationships between Blacks and Whites.

Though between them they had almost no money, they began looking for a farm to begin making their dream a reality. Through a tip from one of Jordan's brothers and a gracious donation from a wealthy supporter, in 1942 Jordan and England and their wives purchased a rundown farm with broken-down buildings in Sumter County, Georgia, near the town of Americus and not far from Jordan's childhood home. They called their new home Koinonia Farm.

Koinonia Farm Is Born

From his work in the Black community in Louisville, Jordan had come to believe that the struggles faced by African Americans often stemmed from rural poverty. Many of the people Jordan worked with in Louisville had come there after poverty had pushed them off their land. The rural poverty in turn was due to the fact that 65 percent of farmworkers were tenant farmers caught in a system of rising indebtedness. The average tenant farmer lived in a run-down two- or three-room structure often without electricity, plumbing, or phone service. Moreover, in Georgia the climate and soil conditions resulted in low crop yields, which only deepened their financial struggles. Excluding the county seat of Americus, the ratio of Blacks to Whites in Sumter County was two to one. The vast majority of Blacks in the county worked in some area of agriculture.[6] Combining their sense of mission with a knowledge of scientific agricultural techniques, Jordan and England saw as their mission to bring spiritual and material assistance

---

[5] The American Baptists, formerly called the Northern Baptists, broke with the Southern Baptists over the issue of slavery prior to the Civil War.

[6] K'Meyer, *Interracialism*, 39–40.

to the struggling farmers of Sumter County, while at the same time modeling racial reconciliation by developing personal relationships with local African Americans.

Even though Jordan had a degree in agriculture and England had worked in the rural parts of Burma, neither of them had much practical knowledge of how to run a farm. So they made a concerted effort to develop relationships with their neighbors, who gave them pointers on when to begin planting, harvesting, and the like. At times Jordan and England would stand on the roof of their barn to see what their neighbors were doing, and then do the same. Their first venture involved raising chickens and selling eggs to the local markets, and was relatively successful. At the same time they began running traditional Southern Baptist outreach programs, such as Sunday Schools and Vacation Bible Schools for children. Jordan also ran classes for local farmers sharing some of the latest information on effective techniques for farming, much in the same vein as county extension agents. They introduced the farmers, most of whom were Black, to new machinery, conservation techniques, and the use of fertilizers and hybrid seeds. They even opened a "cow library" where a family lacking sufficient milk could borrow a cow and milk until it was dry, and then return it. To the surprise of many local observers many of these efforts were participated in by both Blacks and Whites, and did not conform to the norms of segregation common throughout the South. At the same time, Jordan preached in local Southern Baptist churches and garnered financial support for their missionary efforts. Although the local folks thought Jordan and England a bit "odd" for their interracial mixing, as long as they stayed within the acceptable norms of doing "mission work" and seeking to provide "social uplift" for poor African Americans in the area, the local Whites accepted what they were doing.

However, soon that goodwill began to turn sour. Shortly after they began, Jordan and England hired a local Black farmer to work with them. At the lunch break the three men would sit down and share the midday meal together. A few days after they had begun doing this, a delegation from the local Ku Klux Klan visited the farm and told Jordan that the local White folks did not take kindly to Blacks and Whites eating together in such a friendly manner. Using his wit and sense of humor, Jordan was able to deflect the KKK leader's threat by pointing out that, like him, he was a good Baptist; nonetheless, this was just a forewarning of much greater stress and strife to come for Koinonia's commitment to racial reconciliation.

The Englands returned to their mission work in Burma in 1945. Local ambivalence about Koinonia and concern about their interracial mixing increased. Nonetheless, several other young Southerners, many of whom who had heard Jordan speak, came to the farm seeking to live in a radical Christian community working for racial reconciliation. As a result the group living and working at Koinonia grew to over sixty persons in the first ten years. As they continued their work on the farm and in the local community, they also struggled to actualize the vision of communal living that had drawn them together in the first place, eventually developing a policy and process for becoming full members of the community.

Struggles over Interracial Efforts

At this point the story of Koinonia and what happened in the intervening years becomes a story of the whole Koinonia community. Although Jordan continued to be the unofficial leader of the group, what occurred in the years that followed is a story of more than just one person.

In the first decade of their existence, the members of Koinonia were generally accepted by Whites in the area. Several members joined the local church, Rehoboth Baptist, and became acquainted with local folks by sharing the daily chores and struggles of agricultural life. While initially they were welcomed by the White folks, their efforts to develop relationships in the African American community were met with mixed success. Although many African Americans appreciated their efforts to improve their lives through the sharing of agricultural knowledge, others saw them as White do-gooders, and so distrusted them and kept them at a distance. After the initial visit by the KKK over their interaction with one Black field hand, many Blacks feared what would happen to them if they were caught eating with the Whites at Koinonia. Even those Blacks who did get involved with the farm were unwilling to become full members because they could not accept the requirement that they share their goods and live in voluntary poverty, having struggled to rise out of real poverty all their lives. Despite these barriers from centuries of racist oppression, the members of Koinonia developed more social relations with local African Americans and interacted in a more equitable way than was common and acceptable by the Whites in Sumter County.

The tenuous goodwill of the White community began to unravel in 1948 when one of the Koinonia members invited a Black man to attend

Rehoboth Baptist Church. Then in 1950, another member brought a dark-skinned man visiting from India, and the White church members mistook him to be an African American. This incident prompted the church members to vote to remove the Koinonia members from the membership roll of the church. The letter informing them of this action accused them of visiting African American churches, holding interracial services at the farm, and publicly disagreeing with the teachings and policies of the church. All of this was true. Ironically, on the day the congregational vote to excommunicate them was taken, Jordan was away preaching at the Dexter Avenue Baptist Church in Montgomery, Alabama, the church where, in a few years, Dr. Martin Luther King Jr. would become pastor and provide leadership for the Montgomery bus boycott, which in turn launched the modern civil rights movement.

While the external pressure on Koinonia grew, the members of the community struggled with how to work out their living arrangements together. Increased publicity and notoriety attracted long- and short-term visitors to the farm and forced the members to clearly define the requirements for full membership. This eventually led to the creation of a formal covenant and definitions of varying levels of membership and responsibility in the community. Members began corresponding with Christian communities in other parts of the country to learn from them and even to have member exchanges. These endeavors took significant time and energy and reduced the number of programs that provided for the local community. Even so, the number of people connected to Koinonia in some way (either as a member, resident, or supporter) continued to grow into the early 1950s.

Violence, Stress, and Struggle

By the mid-1950s dramatic changes in the American social and political landscape began occurring, and these changes caused Koinonia to become a target for "violence, legal harassment, intimidation and economic boycott"[7] by the local White community. During the late 1940s and early 1950s, the Supreme Court handed down several decisions that eroded segregationist policies in secondary and higher education. President Truman issued an executive order doing away with segregation in the US military. In 1950 Wisconsin Senator Joe McCarthy began holding public hearings designed to identify and root out suspected

[7] Ibid., 81.

Communist sympathizers. Many Southern politicians labeled any person, Black or White, who opposed segregation a Communist. Then in 1954 the Supreme Court issued the *Brown v. Board of Education* decision, which made any law establishing racially segregated schools unconstitutional. These events contributed to an increasingly polarized atmosphere among Southern Whites over the question of racial equality and integration. For years groups such as the Southern Regional Council and the Fellowship of Southern Churchmen had been calling for the dismantling of the Jim Crow segregation system. However, on top of all the other changes, the *Brown* decision ignited a prosegregationist reaction among many Whites who felt their "Southern way of life" was being challenged or threatened.

In 1956 Clarence Jordan "added a spark to the tinderbox of racial feeling"[8] when he attempted to help two African American students get admitted into the all-White University of Georgia business school. Even though he was unsuccessful in his efforts, a local newspaper report of the incident provoked some local Sumter County Whites to attack the farm in a variety of ways. The violence began with random gunshots and vandalism. Then Koinonia's roadside farm stand was burned, and then a sign was vandalized and torn down. At night gunshots were fired at the houses. Fifteen sticks of dynamite were exploded in front of their store. At the same time local merchants stopped selling Koinonia's eggs, and insurance companies canceled the farm's policies. To add to the level of intimidation and isolation, local police and the Georgia Bureau of Investigation refused to investigate these incidents. Moreover, the FBI also declined to get involved under the pretense that no federal laws had been broken. Even a letter that Jordan sent to President Eisenhower got no substantive response.

The few White neighbors who tried to come to Koinonia's aid were also targeted; two neighbors had their barns burned down. The KKK held a rally, burning crosses on one nearby White farmer's land, seeking to intimidate him into silence. Black residents were also threatened, especially those who worked for or had dealings with Koinonia. When they were in public, individuals from the farm were personally threatened. The KKK even offered to buy the farm out if they would leave the county; when the Koinonia residents refused the offer, the violence heightened.

Different Koinonia residents took turns patrolling the edges of the farm, hung lines of lights on the road, and sought to record license plate

---

[8] Ibid., 84.

numbers of drive-by harassers. The local officials canceled the interracial summer camp on the pretense that the farm had a lack of fire extinguishers and unsanitary health conditions. At the same time a group of local White farmers filed a suit alleging that Koinonia was operating an illegal business and contributing to the decline of children's morals. Finally, local officials initiated a grand jury investigation alleging that members of Koinonia were engaging in politically subversive activities. While no formal charges were ever brought by the grand jury, they went on record as saying they believed that Koinonia was a Communist front, committing the alleged acts of violence against itself in order to raise funds from outside sources, and brainwashing local Blacks. Even when Koinonia sent a public letter defending themselves against these spurious charges, the local White sentiment against them did not change.

However, the action that crippled Koinonia the most was a boycott of the farm; eventually they were unable to purchase supplies or sell their produce to local merchants. Insurance companies dropped individuals' policies, and banks closed their accounts. Merchants who were sympathetic to Koinonia's plight informed them that if they did do business with members of Koinonia, they themselves would become a target of the boycott. These fears were well founded. In 1957 the owner of the local feed store sought to break the boycott by selling to the farm. A few nights later dynamite was ignited on the front steps of the store, destroying it and damaging several adjoining buildings. Following this incident, a delegation including the mayor and head of the local Chamber of Commerce visited the farm imploring them to leave the area because as they saw it, Koinonia's presence was causing increasing unrest. Even the head of the local NAACP publicly distanced himself indicating he "wouldn't lower his dignity" by dealing with the farm.[9]

This intimidation and hostility was reserved not only for the adults of the community. All the Koinonia children were teased and bullied at school while school administrators looked the other way. Jim Jordan, who began high school in 1957, was physically and verbally abused every day, so much so that Clarence and Florence decided to send him to a school near a companion Christian community in North Dakota. At another point, a drive-by shooter fired a machine gun at a volleyball court on which children were playing. At still another point Clarence had to get a court order so his children could be allowed to attend the public school in Americus that had expelled them for being part of the community.

[9] Ibid., 96.

This external hostility took its toll on the members of Koinonia. They had to travel long distances to get their supplies and began selling their products through a mail-order business. As the community struggled financially, many members also suffered severe emotional stress. Relationships between members became strained, and several families and individuals elected to leave rather than continue to deal with the intimidation techniques. From a population of over sixty (a quarter of them African Americans) in 1956, the group declined to just three families by 1959.

Koinonia and the Civil Rights Movement

Despite their local struggles, Koinonia had many outside supporters. White racial progressives from around the South offered assistance where and when they could. Financial contributors responded generously to appeals for support. Others brought supplies from Florida and as far away as New England. Some local Blacks helped by purchasing supplies and then picking them up under cover of night. One local gas station operator cooperated by using subterfuge; he would fill up a parked truck while the driver from Koinonia would walk down the street to the local coffee shop for thirty minutes. Moreover, as the boycott became more widely known, civil rights leaders invited Jordan to come speak in their churches, and organizations such as the Congress of Racial Equality (CORE) and the Student Nonviolent Coordinating Committee (SNCC) offered their support. People from across the country eager to join the cause for civil rights came to Koinonia to get involved. Even with all these efforts, the operations at the farm were barely able to keep going.

Media reports caused Koinonia's struggles and its views on race relations to become more widely known, such that many outsiders misperceived it to be primarily a civil rights organization. Clarence Jordan and the other members of Koinonia shared many common values and beliefs with the leaders of the civil rights movement. Jordan had a long-standing relationship with Vernon Johns, Martin Luther King Jr.'s radical predecessor at Dexter Avenue Baptist Church, and Myles Horton, the founder of Highlander.[10] He also shared the core values of nonviolence, racial justice, and racial reconciliation that were at the heart of the civil rights movement.

---

[10] To learn more about Myles Horton, see chapter 9.

However, beneath this veneer of commonality there were some significant theological and philosophical differences. Unlike his civil rights contemporaries, Jordan's goal was not primarily racial justice and reconciliation, but rather the building of authentic Christian community in which the barriers of racial prejudice were eliminated. Thus, his work focused heavily on the building of authentic interracial relationships. Furthermore, whereas civil rights leaders sought to secure political and economic concessions from government officials, Jordan's focus was on developing a process of economic development through training and farm cooperatives that enabled Black farmers to emerge from their impoverished conditions. Although the strategy of civil rights leaders such as Martin Luther King Jr. and the members of SNCC was to nonviolently engage in direct action tactics designed to provoke a confrontation, Jordan believed in a more passive form of nonviolence that did not purposely seek to create conflict. Jordan even told his daughter that if she were arrested for participating in the direct actions being conducted in nearby Albany, Georgia, she was "on her own." When civil rights leaders in Albany called for a boycott to put pressure on the local economy, Jordan refused to endorse it, contending that as a victim himself of a boycott and as a Christian, he could not inflict on others what he himself had suffered. Ultimately, Jordan did not believe that the tactics being employed by the civil rights movement would lead to racial reconciliation; instead, he was convinced that only repentance and the spiritual conversion of Whites from their racist attitudes would bring true reconciliation.

Despite these differences Jordan worked with others in the civil rights movement toward their common goals, while recognizing they were pursuing different strategies toward those goals. Jordan attended several planning sessions and a few rallies in Albany. Other members of Koinonia actively participated in the actions, while others held back. When the movement came to Albany for an extended campaign, the farm served as staging area and a respite for those involved in the ongoing actions taking place there. Although he was never personally close to Dr. King and reportedly met him only once,[11] they corresponded and remained allies throughout the struggle. Jordan became increasingly distressed that King seemed to be more of a political than a spiritual leader. Although

---

[11] "Vincent Harding Brought Martin Luther King Jr. and Clarence Jordan Together to Discuss Their Different Approaches to a Common Goal," *Baptists Today*, April 30, 2012, http://www.baptiststoday.org.

King envisioned the "beloved community" depicted in his famous 1963 "I Have a Dream" speech, Jordan preached about a "God Movement" in which Blacks and Whites would be united. However, a final break from the movement came for Jordan when members of SNCC began to adhere to the philosophy of Black Power; Jordan believed that the goal should be racial reconciliation and saw Black Power as a barrier to that goal and contrary to his vision of Christian discipleship and community.

The Cotton Patch Version

Koinonia and Clarence Jordan entered the 1960s emotionally exhausted and financially crippled by the extended boycott and repressive tactics directed at them. However, through this period Jordan continued to speak widely, and in his sermons he often shared his personal translations of the New Testament. To help his listeners capture the power of the biblical story he would sometimes recast the biblical material from its first-century Near Eastern context to the context of southern Georgia of the 1950s and 1960s. So instead of talking about the disciples Peter and Andrew, he would tell stories of the two good ole boys, Rock and Andy Johnson; Mary the mother of Jesus became the local woman Mary Davidson. Rome became Washington, and Jerusalem became Atlanta. As early as 1955, listeners started asking for copies of his version of the Bible. So Jordan began writing what he called the "Cotton Patch" version, beginning with the letters of James and to Hebrews.

In the Cotton Patch version Jordan dealt directly with the issue of race relations by recasting the Jew-Gentile divisions in the New Testament into the divisions between Blacks and Whites of the South. For instance, in his translation of Paul's letter to the Romans (which he called "The Letter to the Christians in Washington") he equated the Jewish religious leaders, the Pharisees, with the White religious establishment, contending that despite their religiosity, the White Protestant leaders would not be saved. In his translation of Paul's letter to the Galatians, Jordan translated Galatians 3:28 as "No more is one a white man and another a Negro; no more is one a slave and the other a free man; no longer is one a male and the other a female. For you are as one in Christ Jesus."[12]

In his rendering of the parable of the Good Samaritan found in Luke 10:25–37 Jordan addressed the sin of racism head on. In his retelling of

---

[12] Clarence Jordan, *The Cotton Patch Version of Paul's Epistles* (Clinton, NJ: New Win, 1968), 99.

this famous parable the Good Samaritan is a Black man who stops to help a White man who has been beaten up by robbers on the road from Albany to Atlanta. First, a White preacher and then a White gospel song leader come along, but pass by on the other side of the road because they were on their way to a revival meeting. Then a Black man seeing the White man lying by the side of the road, stops his car, provides him with some water and drives him to the nearest hospital, promising to pay the man's bill in full on his way back through town. When Jesus asks his interlocutor (who is depicted as an adult Bible class teacher) which of the three acted as the man's neighbor, he replies "Why, of course, the nig--- I mean, er . . . well, er . . . the one who treated him kindly."[13]

Jordan even went as far as describing Jesus in Luke 15 as being depicted as a "nigger lover" and one "who associates with black people and eats with him."[14] Through the Cotton Patch translations and many of his sermons that were subsequently recorded and published, Jordan revealed the convictions that shaped and guided his life and work. Being a follower of Jesus meant that one did not compromise on essential issues, but in all ways possible sought to live out one's convictions in the vagaries and challenges of everyday life. Racial reconciliation for Jordan was not "an issue" but rather a core necessity if one was to live the Christian life with integrity and authenticity. As Coble writes, in his Cotton Patch translations Jordan was not primarily fighting racism but was demonstrating that he "was primarily a student of Scripture who wanted to live out his understanding of the biblical lifestyle."[15]

A New Chapter

During the early 1960s Koinonia continued to struggle. Membership had shrunk to its lowest level in twenty years, finances were shaky, and morale was low. Jordan himself was discontented and even talked about leaving Koinonia. However, in 1965, a man named Millard Fuller visited the farm. He was a millionaire businessman and lawyer whose firm had defended the men who beat the Freedom Riders in Montgomery.[16] At the time he arrived at Koinonia, Fuller was facing a spiritual and marital

---

[13] Clarence Jordan, *Luke and Acts: Jesus Doings and the Happenings* (Clinton, NJ: New Win, 1969), 47.

[14] Ibid., 61.

[15] Coble, *Cotton Patch for the Kingdom*, 208.

[16] Fuller was a former college classmate, business partner, and friend of Morris Dees, whose story is told in chapter 15.

crisis. A devoted Southern Baptist, Fuller had sought the counsel of his pastor, who recommended he check out a place called Koinonia. Fuller and his wife arrived thinking they would visit for a few days and ended up staying a month. Fuller spent long hours talking with Jordan about his spiritual struggles and questions. Over the next few years the Jordans and the Fullers continued to communicate. In 1968 the Fullers returned to Koinonia, and Millard and Clarence began to imagine a new venture in which they would help low-income people start businesses and build houses. Koinonia changed its name to Koinonia Partners, and eventually the organization that came to be known as Habitat for Humanity was born. After a long dry spell of struggle this transformation renewed the sense of purpose and direction for the community.

However, Clarence Jordan was not able to see this new vision come to full fruition. On October 29, 1969, he had been ill with what seemed like the flu. Over the previous few days he had started to feel better, and so returned to his study where he was working on the Cotton Patch version of the Gospel of John. A young woman named Lena Hofer, who was visiting the farm, came to talk with him about a personal matter. As he hugged her at the end of the conversion, his body began to convulse. Lena ran to get help, but when she returned with others Jordan was dead, apparently of a heart attack; he was fifty-seven years old.

Millard Fuller called the police to confirm his death, but they refused to come out to the farm, suggesting they instead call the funeral home to come pick up his body. Knowing Clarence would object to the expense of a hearse, they loaded his body in the station wagon and drove him to the funeral home themselves. His death was confirmed by the coroner, and a funeral was quickly arranged. The next day 150 people gathered on a section of the farm called Picnic Hill to say goodbye. Jordan's body was laid in a plain wooden box. Some words were said and biblical passages read, and then the group sang "Happy Birthday, Clarence" as his body was lowered into the hole that had been dug by hand.

Over forty years later Koinonia Partners and Jordan's vision for a Christian community in south Georgia continues. Despite the death of its founder, the people continued on, including Clarence's wife, Florence, who died in 1987. Several organizations have spun off to become stand-alone organizations, including Habitat for Humanity, Jubilee Partners (a ministry to refugees), and Hope House (a temporary residence for families visiting loved one in the local prison). The farm continues to do a vibrant mail order business focusing on pecans, peanuts, and related products. Clarence Jordan's books and recordings of his sermons continue to inspire and inform. In 1988 Harry Chapin and Tom Key created a musical based on Jordan's writings called the *Cotton Patch Gospel*, and in 2008 Dennis Hassell premiered *Glory Man*, a play that chronicles the life of Florence and Clarence Jordan.

As was evidenced by those who gathered in September 2012 at Koinonia, Clarence Jordan's life still inspires, still guides, and still challenges. In her study of Koinonia Tracy K'Meyer acknowledges the impact that Jordan and Koinonia has had on the local community and the South, both in terms of agricultural development and race relations.[17] At the same time she questions the efficacy of Jordan's philosophy of bringing change through intentional, interracial Christian community. She suggests Jordan may have underestimated the impact of institutional racism and the barriers to economic, political, and social equity it creates, as well as its impact on Koinonia itself. However, Jordan's legacy seems to be his continuing impact on the people directly and indirectly touched by his vision of "the God Movement." Joyce Hollyday shares the words of Carranza Morgan, whose wife worked in Koinonia's baking kitchens for thirty years. Morgan says, "When I get talking about Mr. Jordan, I can't help but just feel chills. He meant so much to my life—and to so many more in this community. He believed that you were a human being, and he thought civil rights was just treating people like you wanted to be treated. He treated you just like you were as white as he was. He was a God-sent man."[18]

[17] K'Meyer, *Interracialism*, 183-189.

[18] Joyce Hollyday, Introduction to *Clarence Jordan: Essential Writings*, ed. Joyce Hollyday (Maryknoll, NY: Orbis Books, 2003), 16.

Discussion Questions

1. Jordan believed that racial reconciliation would only come through the forming of interpersonal relationships between people of different races. He did not endorse the direct action techniques of the civil rights movement. To what extent can racism be eradicated without addressing it institutional forms?
2. Jordan believed that the way to achieve racial justice was by helping poor Black and White farmers increase their profits from farming.What is the relationship between racial reconciliation and economic development?

Bibliography

Barnette, Helene. *Clarence Jordan: Turning Dreams into Deeds*. Macon, GA: Smith and Helwys, 1972.

Coble, Ann Louise. *Cotton Patch for the Kingdom: Clarence Jordan's Demonstration Plot at Koinonia*. Scottsdale, PA: Herald Press, 2002.

Hollyday, Joyce. *Clarence Jordan: Essential Writings*. Maryknoll, NY: Orbis Books, 2003.

Jordan, Clarence. *The Cotton Patch Version of Paul's Epistles*. Clinton, NJ: New Win, 1968.

———. *Luke and Acts: Jesus' Doings and the Happenings*. Clinton, NJ: New Win, 1969.

K'Meyer, Tracy Elaine. *Interracialism and Christian Community in the Postwar South: The Story of Koinonia Farm*. Charlottesville: University Press of Virginia, 1997.

Lee, Dallas. *The Cotton Patch Evidence*. New York: Harper and Row, 1971.

"Vincent Harding Brought Martin Luther King Jr. and Clarence Jordan Together to Discuss Their Different Approaches to a Common Goal." *Baptists Today*, April 30, 2012. http://www.baptiststoday.org.

12

ANNE BRADEN
(1924–2006)

*A Life of Radical Choices**

Decision and Destiny

One sunny day in March 1954, Anne Braden came home from doing some errands. Carl, her husband of six years, had stayed home to take care of their two children, Jimmy and Anita. While Anne had been out, Andrew Wade, a young Black man with a pregnant wife and a child had stopped by to ask the Bradens for a favor. Wade was a World War II veteran who owned an electrical contracting business. He had been involved in local politics through the Progressive Party, where he had become acquainted with the Bradens. He sensed that the Bradens were a unique type of White people, known to be actively involved in efforts to secure equal rights for African Americans in Louisville, Kentucky, where all of them lived; however, the Bradens and Andrew Wade were not what one would call friends, more like acquaintances.

Andrew had come to ask Anne and Carl if they would purchase a house for him in an all-White suburb of Louisville. For months, Wade had been trying to buy a home with sufficient space for his growing family and a yard where his children could play, but because he was Black, the only homes available to him were in the poorer, older parts

* Photo of Anne Braden used by permission of the University of Louisville Anne Braden Institute for Social Justice Research. Major sources for this chapter are Anne Braden, *The Wall Between* (New York: Monthly Review Press, 1958); Cynthia Stokes Brown, *Refusing Racism: White Allies and the Struggle for Civil Rights* (New York: Teachers College Press, 2002); Catherine Fosl, *Subversive Southerner: Anne Braden and the Struggle for Racial Justice in the Cold War South* (New York: Palgrave Macmillan, 2002).

of town where the majority of the Black population lived; there was no real estate agent who would show him a house and no bank that would give him a loan when he sought to buy a house in the predominantly White suburbs. In frustration he had spoken to some of his more liberally minded White friends, but none of them had been willing to act on his behalf, until he spoke to the Bradens.

By Southern standards of the 1950s Louisville was considered a progressive town when it came to matters of racial integration. Unlike Montgomery, Alabama, Blacks and Whites rode together on the buses and shopped together in stores without incident. However, this progressive spirit did not extend to residential integration; real estate agents, bankers, and contractors had informal agreements to build and sell homes only to Whites in certain areas, effectively barring African Americans from taking part in the suburban housing expansion that followed World War II. Whereas 20,000 new homes were built in the Louisville area between 1949 and 1954, only 200 of those homes were available to Black families. Thus the only way Andrew Wade and his family would be able to secure the house of their dreams in the Louisville suburb of Shively was if a White person bought it for them.

Although Anne worried briefly over the implications of their decision and its legality, both she and Carl characterized their response to Andrew Wade's request as "automatic . . . any other answer would have been unthinkable."[1] Anne later realized how overly optimistic and naïve their decision had been, but given her commitments to racial justice, it simply seemed like the right thing to do. However, when one explores how Anne McCarty Braden had been raised and the values she had inherited from her family, such a decision not only would have been surprising, it would have been unthinkable just a few years earlier.

A Child in the Southern Way of Life

Anne Gambrell McCarty was born in Louisville, Kentucky, on July 28, 1924, the second child and only daughter of Anita and Gambrell McCarty. The McCarty family had deep Southern roots, having descended from the earliest White settlers in Tennessee. Her ancestor, Anne Poage, had been a fiercely independent pioneer woman who in 1776 had crossed the Cumberland Gap from Tennessee into Kentucky with four children in tow, had outlived four husbands in the process, and helped establish

---

[1] Fosl, *Subversive Southerner*, 139.

the community of Fort Harrod. Anne's grandmother, known as Mattie "Mama" Crabbe, often regaled her with stories of the legendary Anne Poage, who, along with her mother, provided clear examples of strong, independent Southern women. Ancestors on both sides of her family owned slaves and during the Civil War had fought for the Confederacy. Following the Civil War, her family had proudly hung on to their Southern heritage in terms of attitudes and worldview, something that Anne's mother particularly impressed upon her and her older brother. Often referred to as the "Lost Cause" mythology, Southerners sought to cast the Confederacy's loss in the Civil War as a valiant battle of sacrifice to defend and preserve basic institutions such as slavery, segregation, and the "Southern way of life."[2] Included in that heritage was a belief in the strict and complete segregation of Whites from Blacks in all areas of life.

Anne's father, Gambrell McCarty, worked as a salesman for a feed company, and in the first years of Anne's life, the family moved around quite a bit. In 1931 (when Anne was seven) the McCartys finally settled in Anniston, Alabama, where Anne grew up and lived until she graduated from high school. However, the McCarty family never completely let go of their Kentucky roots, returning for several weeks each summer to the family homestead in Eminence, Kentucky, about an hour west of Louisville.

By the time the McCarty family arrived in Anniston, the Great Depression was adversely affecting many people in the community. Almost every night, sometimes as many as twenty people came to their door asking for a meal, which they would usually provide. Rev. Jim Stoney, the rector at Grace Episcopal Church where the McCartys attended church, stressed that the well-to-do, elite members of his congregation needed to care for the poor of the community. Rev. Stoney even initiated an outreach to the people on the poor side of town involving children in the church Sunday School. However, in Anniston's segregated culture, "helping the poor" meant helping only the poor Whites who lived on the "other side" of town; it never meant helping the Black families who also were in need.

Like many elite White Southern families, the McCartys occasionally hired Black people to tend to many of the household chores both inside and outside the home. When these Black people worked for them, Anne's

---

[2] Gary Gallagher, Introduction to *The Myth of the Lost Cause and Civil War History*, ed. Gary W. Gallagher and Alan T. Nolan (Bloomington: Indiana University Press, 2000), 1–10.

parents made sure that the families of their workers were provided for, sometimes paying their rent, and often giving them the hand-me-down clothes no longer used by Anne and her brother. One of Anne's earliest memories involved seeing the daughter of a Black housemaid come to the house one time wearing one of Anne's discarded dresses. The dress was too tight on the little girl and Anne wrote, "She would sit in a straight chair in our kitchen . . . looking uncomfortable, my old faded dress binding her at the waist and throat. And some way I knew that this was not what Jesus meant when he said clothe the naked. . . . I knew that if I were in her place, if I had no clothes, I would not want the old abandoned dresses of a person who would not even invite me to come into her living room to sit down."[3]

At the time Anne did not suspect anything to be wrong about these arrangements; they were simply part of the way of life in which she was raised. However, as she grew, the incongruity of segregation caused her to question what others took for granted. One time when she was thirteen or fourteen, the church youth group was having a discussion of what they termed "the colored problem," and Anne suggested that people ought to be treated equally and fairly regardless of the color of their skin, and that there was something about segregation that did not seem right. She later wrote that people in the group were surprised by her comment, and that the assistant minister took her aside and cautioned her against making such statements lest people think she was a Communist. Anne didn't even know what a Communist was, but she assumed it must be something bad.

Although Anne's family often felt she was a bit precocious and outspoken, she later commented that her upbringing was fairly normal for children in White Southern families. Like most of the teenage girls of her class, she was concerned about doing well in school, developing friendships, and being cute for boys. The most rebellious thing she did was to begin her lifelong addiction to smoking at age fourteen. Like most adolescents she was too focused on her world to recognize the disparities and tensions in the larger world of the South. People in Anne's circle assumed they were superior to those who struggled with poverty or challenged the status quo by calling for union strikes. The discrepancies between her religious upbringing and the reality of racial segregation inevitably raised questions for her. However, by strictly limiting exposure to the negative consequences of segregation, children like Anne

---

[3] Braden, *Wall*, 23–24.

grew up believing that this was the way the world was supposed to be arranged; this was the "Southern way of life." Later in life, Anne often commented that she had grown up in a prison of White privilege that kept her from seeing and interacting with the world as it really was. However, when she left Anniston to attend college, the wall between[4] her White world and the world of Blacks began to crack.

The Awakening Years

Anne's mother had been the first woman in her family to attend college. Anne was the first woman in her family to actually graduate. After briefly considering the University of Alabama, she complied with her mother's wishes and in 1941 enrolled at Stratford College in Danville, Virginia. Stratford was a school where elite Southern families sent their daughters to become educated, cultured, and prepared for their role in society as women supportive of their husbands and indoctrinated in the Southern way of life. Within the small school Anne excelled both academically and socially, joining a sorority, becoming president of her class, and playing the lead role in the school play. Always an accomplished student, Anne relished the opportunity to learn and grow intellectually. She also greatly benefited being in the company of so many older educated women who served as role models.

During her two years at Stratford she met Harriet Fitzgerald, the sister of a Stratford professor, who became the most formative influence in her young life, and longtime friend and confidant. Anne said that Harriet "radicalized" her, though over time she became far more socially and politically radical than Harriet ever was.[5] Harriet operated an art school in Greenwich Village, but often came to Danville where she maintained a studio. She introduced Anne to the works of Karl Marx, Sigmund Freud, and other "modern thinkers," but perhaps more important, she also was the first person Anne ever met who openly opposed segregation. The bond between the older and younger woman (Harriet was twenty years older than Anne) grew such that Anne confessed "she was the first person I was ever in love with." Though their friendship never evolved into an overt romantic relationship, Harriet brought a level

---

[4] *The Wall Between* (originally published in 1958) is the title of Anne Braden's memoir of the Andrew Wade house incident, and symbolizes the wall that divides Blacks and Whites, but also imprisons Whites in their own world of racial privilege. It was reissued in 1999.

[5] Fosl, *Subversive Southerner*, 40.

of "excitement" to Anne's life that she had never before experienced. Although there appears to have been an erotic attraction for Anne, what most powerfully impressed her was the possibility that she could love someone so passionately who also stimulated her intellectually and challenged her to stretch the boundaries of her limited worldview. Although she also had a couple of serious relationships with men before, during, and after her college years, her relationship with Harriet was the most intense until she met her husband, Carl, several years later.

Harriet was an alumna and board member of Randolph Macon Women's College, and so largely owing to her influence, upon graduation from Stratford in 1943, Anne enrolled at Randolph Macon, which was located 150 miles to the north in Hanover, Virginia. Randolph Macon was much larger and more intellectually challenging than Stratford. Outwardly Anne continued to excel socially and academically, but inwardly she began to entertain questions about her direction and purpose in life. After briefly flirting with the idea of pursuing a career in the theater, Anne found that her real passion was for writing and journalism. In the summer between semesters in 1943, she landed a job at the *Anniston Star* in her hometown where she was able to write editorials, headlines, and even sports news. Many of the regular staff were men away fighting in the war, so this gave Anne the opportunity to immerse herself in the world of journalism, and she loved it.

Because she attended college during the war years, a major topic of discussion on campus was the racist and anti-Semitic ideology of Nazism. These discussions sometimes turned to the ideology of segregation, which contained many of the same White supremacist views as Nazism. Anne discovered that she was not alone in her discomfort with segregation; many of her classmates and even friends in Anniston had similar quandaries. These discussions allowed her to examine beliefs and assumptions about the relationship between Blacks and Whites that up to that point in her life were never questioned. She later described these emerging thoughts and feelings as "being bottled up in the netherland of the undiscussable."[6] Decades later in an interview she shared: "We were aware that in fighting Hitler, we were fighting a racist ideology, though I don't think we used the word 'racist.' It didn't escape people I knew that those ideas about racial superiority were akin to what we had here in the South."[7] Nevertheless, during

[6] Braden, *Wall*, 26.

[7] Fosl, *Subversive Southerner*, 52.

this period of her life, these inner rumblings never actually translated into any public words or actions. Even when one of her classmates sought unsuccessfully to bring a Black gospel group to campus, Anne remained silent and uninvolved.

In 1944 on a trip to visit Harriet in New York City she had an interaction with a Black person that turned out to be transformative for her. Harriet held a dinner party to which she invited an African American actress who at the time was cast with a small role in a Broadway play. Anne was hesitant at first to speak with her, never having actually talked in any sustained and meaningful way with a Black person, but as they talked they discovered a mutual love of theater and other subjects, and Anne felt all her fears and misgivings wash away. She wrote: "Suddenly in the midst of the conversation, the realization swept over me that I had completely forgotten there was a difference in our color. We were no longer White and Negro—we were just two young women talking about things we liked to talk about. . . . It was a tremendous revelation. It may sound like a small thing when it is told, but it was a turning point in my life. All the cramping walls of a lifetime seemed to come tumbling down in that moment."[8] Although it would be several more years before Anne would be the radical activist she later became, she marked this one evening as pivotal in her development. She wrote, "Here for a moment, I glimpsed a vision of the world as it should be: where people are people and spirits have room to grow."[9]

Within weeks of her graduation from Randolph Macon in May 1945, the war in Europe came to a close. In April of that year, President Roosevelt died, followed a few weeks later by the founding of the United Nations. The Allies had declared victory in Europe, but the battle would rage in the Pacific theater for a few months longer. Following graduation, she headed home to assume her first full-time job at the *Anniston Star*. Even though she lived at home with her parents, they and she knew she was a changed person. Anne's father later regretted sending his daughter away to college, calling it the greatest mistake he ever made as a parent. However different she may have seemed to her father, the full transformation of Anne McCarty (later Braden) had barely just begun.

---

[8] Braden, *Wall*, 27.

[9] Ibid., 27–28.

Joining the "Other America"

As Anne began her job as a reporter at the *Anniston Star*, she still was largely unaware of the changes that were beginning to take place in US society at large. African Americans had fought in the war so that others could be free of tyranny, yet they found on their return that their experiences and sacrifice held little to no significance in the Jim Crow South. Accustomed to being treated with dignity and respect overseas, many of these returning soldiers began to challenge segregationist laws and demand to be granted full rights as citizens. At the same time the Soviet Union began to expand its empire through Eastern Europe following the war, and the fear of the communism spread throughout Europe and the United States. This fear grew into a full-fledged paranoia, reaching its height during the Senate hearings headed by Senator Joe McCarthy in the early 1950s. In response to this "red scare" Congress passed bills such as the Smith Act of 1945 that made it a federal crime to advocate the overthrow of the US government; soon simply advocating changes in the current system came to be considered seditious. With the bombing of Hiroshima this fear grew into a full-scale realization that the Cold War could erupt into a nuclear holocaust at any time.

Despite these world changes swirling around her, Anne dove into her work at the *Star*, often staying late and socializing with fellow workers at the newspaper. Her articles covered a range of local issues, but reflected her hopes and idealism that the world could emerge from the war with lasting peace, economic stability, and racial harmony. However, living at home with her parents reminded her that old racist attitudes and practices were not so easily broken. In particular she had one conversation with her father that shocked her. She voiced support of an anti-lynching law that had been proposed in the Alabama legislature, and her father got so upset with her remark that in a fit of anger he blurted out, "We ought to have a good lynching every once in a while to keep the nigger in his place." Anne had never known her father to hold such views. As far as she knew he was a kind, Christian man who always went out of his way to help people regardless of race; she could not imagine him actually taking part in a murder or a lynching of a Black man, but she was left wondering, "What could segregation ever do to the Negro as terrible as the thing it had done to [her father]?"[10]

After a year in Anniston, Anne sought more challenging and stimulating work and took a position as a court reporter for the *Birmingham*

[10] Ibid., 24–25.

(Alabama) *News*. Birmingham, at the time was often referred to as the most segregated city of the South, and showed Anne a level of blatant racism she had not previously known. For instance, as the court reporter she quickly learned that in Birmingham crimes involving Whites and crimes involving Blacks received different levels of attention by the police and courts. She even had a deputy sheriff confide to her that one particular case she covered would never be solved because the victim "was a nigger, and the man that killed him was white."[11]

She also discovered she was not immune to the prejudices she witnessed in others. One morning she was meeting a friend for breakfast at a local diner. As was her custom she called her office to see if there had been any incidents the previous night that required her to go down to the courthouse first thing in the morning. When she returned to the table, she said that she had learned there was nothing important that required her attention, because all that had happened that night was "just a colored murder." Anne then noticed the quivering hands of the Black waitress who was serving their table, realized what she had said, and how she had just diminished the value of Black life as compared to a White one. This experience convinced her that unless she left the Deep South she was going to become the kind of person she did not want to be. So, after only a few months in Birmingham, she applied for a position at the *Louisville* (Kentucky) *Times* and was hired.

Compared to Birmingham, Louisville had a reputation for being a "progressive" Southern city with regard to race relations. Unlike Alabama, Louisville did not require Blacks to sit in the back of the public bus, and it had a large and active Black community that often held the swing votes in local elections. Nonetheless, Anne soon learned that beneath the "progressive" veneer, Louisville was as racially segregated and divided as any city in the South.

Shortly after arriving in Louisville, Anne met Carl Braden, a seasoned reporter who covered issues related to the local labor unions. Carl was married and ten years older than Anne. In contrast to her he had grown up in a poor, working-class section of Louisville. His father had worked on the railroad, been active in the local union, and was a member of the Socialist Party. Carl's father had named his son after Karl Marx, but later changed the "K" to a "C" when the Catholic priest refused to baptize him unless the spelling was changed. Although all his life Carl had been a voracious reader, he never graduated from high school

---

[11] Brown, *Refusing Racism*, 85.

and had gone to work for the newspaper when he was only seventeen. Like his father, Carl was an admirer of Eugene Debs, the Socialist labor leader of the early twentieth century. He took a liking to Anne, saw that she had great potential as a writer, and so began to mentor her, introducing her to local labor movement people and concerns. He also gave her books to read on labor history and the principles of the Socialist Party, and encouraged her to expand her reporting to include stories on labor-related issues.

On the surface Carl and Anne were polar opposites. He had grown up on the "wrong side of the tracks," whereas she came from an elite Southern family. He was a lapsed Catholic who had little place for religion, whereas she was devoted to her Episcopalian faith. He had not even finished high school, and she was a college graduate. However, despite these differences, they found themselves drawn to each other, and when Braden's failing marriage came to an end, he and Anne were married in a quiet ceremony at a Unitarian church in June 1948. From that day until Carl's premature death in 1975, Anne and Carl had a marriage that was bound by love and characterized by a deep mutual respect and commitment to work together for justice regardless of the consequences. As one biographer wrote, "Theirs was a partnership fired in common purpose, affirmed by personal compatibility, and sustained by something much larger than itself."[12]

In order to become more actively involved in the labor issues she was reporting on, Anne quit her job at the paper and began working a variety of manual labor jobs. Eventually she got involved with union organizing. She also joined the Progressive Party, which was mounting a national campaign for Socialist principles of government. Soon after that she started getting involved in local civil rights issues.

Her first civil rights involvement came about when a Black man who had been hurt in an auto accident was denied help at a local hospital and subsequently died before he could be taken to the hospital designated to serve Black patients. She joined with another Progressive Party member who was Black and together they launched a door-to-door petition campaign that eventually resulted in the Kentucky legislature mandating that all hospitals receiving public funds admit patients regardless of race.

A second experience that sharpened her focus on civil rights occurred in 1951. As part of a small delegation of White Southern women she

[12] Fosl, *Subversive Southerner*, 103.

traveled to Mississippi to protest the pending execution of an African American man named Willie Magee, who had been falsely accused and convicted of raping a White woman. The purpose of their trip was to show White Southern support for Magee and to encourage others like them to speak up in his defense. Anne became the spokesperson for the group and while in Mississippi was put in jail under "protective custody" by local law enforcement who feared she might be the victim of violent retaliation for her outspoken comments and actions. Three days later the women were ordered to leave the state, and as they were being escorted out, the state police officer offhandedly told her that he thought she "ought to be shot" for her betraying her Southern heritage. This experience was an "awakening" for her, as she "realized that her racial convictions placed her now—for the first time—at odds with the power structure from which she had previously benefited."[13]

Their subsequent inability to get a stay of execution for Willie Magee pushed Anne to an even more radical stance. A local African American leader and fellow Progressive Party member crystallized her understanding of what had changed for her when he told her: "You don't have to be a part of the world of the lynchers or a part of those who deny justice. You do have a choice. You can join the 'other America.'"[14] This was a choice that Anne continued to make for the rest of her life and that in many ways became the touchstone of her commitments from that point on.

The Radical Act of Buying a House

In 1951 Anne gave birth to a son, James, and then in 1953 a daughter, Anita. Anne and Carl shared family and work responsibilities equally, but Anne generally operated from home whenever she could. They were beginning their life as a family when Andrew Wade in March of 1954 came to Carl with his request to help him buy a house. Because the Bradens had been involved with the Progressive Party, one of the few political groups where Whites and Blacks worked together, and because of their involvement in the hospital and Willie Magee issues, Wade felt he could approach the Bradens with his dangerous request.

The purchase of the Wade home in the nearby suburb of Shively went relatively smoothly. Anne and Carl handled all the paperwork

---

[13] Ibid., 124.

[14] Ibid., 125.

with the builder and the bank, never revealing (nor being asked) that they did not intend to live in the house themselves but were buying on behalf of someone else. After the purchase had been made and the deed signed over to the Wades, the Wade family moved their belongings into their new home. However, on their first night in the house, a cross was burned in a field across from their house and ten shots were fired into the kitchen. A few days later a rock tied to a threatening note ordering the Wades to leave was thrown through the picture window. Six weeks after that, an explosion destroyed half the house including their daughter's bedroom; fortunately, she was not at home that night and so no one was injured. In response to these threats, the Wades organized a volunteer watch twenty-four hours a day. Local Black civil rights leaders took up defense of the Wades' decision. Even so, they continued to receive an endless string of threatening calls and letters promising all sorts of devastation and destruction if they did not move out.

Soon after the Wades had moved in, the contractor who had sold the house to the Bradens and the bank that had managed their loan went public about being deceived by the Bradens in the transactions. Soon the incident became front-page news, and like the Wades, the Bradens started receiving threatening phone calls and letters. When the Bradens were interviewed by the *Louisville Courier Journal* (where Carl still worked) they were quoted as saying: "We feel every man has a right to live where he wants to live, regardless of the color of his skin. This is a test of democracy. Either you practice what you preach, or you shut up about believing in democracy."[15] These words became a catalyst for controversy that divided the Bradens from most of White Louisville and even part of Black Louisville for years to come.

Racism was so embedded in the culture and way of life that quickly public attention shifted from the Wade family's attempt to move into a White neighborhood to the Bradens, who were being accused of manipulating the Wades so as to cause disruption in the community as part of a supposed Communist conspiracy. In the minds of most White Louisville residents it was inconceivable that a Black family would choose to disrupt the racial pecking order without the devious and seditious influence of "Communists." Eventually public rumors propagated by the local paper in Shively suggested that even the bombing of the house was part of a Communist plot, supposedly set by the Wades, the Bradens, or someone doing their bidding.

---

[15] Brown, *Refusing Racism*, 91.

At this point the state attorney general convened a grand jury ostensibly to determine the cause of the bombing. However, when the Bradens went to testify, they quickly learned that the attorney general's intent was not to investigate the harassment of the Wade family but rather to indict the Bradens for sedition, which in fact he did on October 1, 1954. In short the Bradens were accused of fomenting a Communist plot that involved the deceptive purchase of the house, the subsequent bombing, and related actions designed to create racial conflict whose purpose was the eventual overthrow of the state government of Kentucky. Fighting these outrageous charges became the focus of the Bradens' lives for the next two years. Anne issued a press statement, which in part said their indictment was the first major case where an attempt had been made to place the blame for anti-Negro violence on the people fighting segregation. She further added that the label "Communist" was a tool in the hands of White political leaders to brand anyone opposing the White supremacist sociopolitical structure of the South as an inherent threat to the stability of the community. In the years of struggle that followed, Anne often noted that the Communist label was exploited by Southern political leaders to justify their opposition to any group—Black or White—seeking to dismantle segregation.

Following their appearance before the grand jury, both Anne and Carl were arrested and put in jail. While in jail Anne realized that all the privileges that came as an aristocratic Southern woman had been stripped from her, and that the choices she had made had placed her in the center of an anti-Communist, anti-Black maelstrom. As it turned out she was bailed out by her parents, who despite their disagreement with her views and actions, could not let their daughter remain in jail. Carl was not so fortunate, and his bail was set at $40,000 (Anne's had been $10,000), and so remained in jail until his trial in November 1954. Carl was the first of seven defendants to go on trial (others included those who had helped the Wades in defending their home) and eventually the only one convicted. There ensued a thirteen-day trial in which anti-Communist witnesses from across the country were brought in to substantiate the danger Communists presented to local communities. When asked directly, Carl stated that he had never been a member of the Communist Party but had read extensively materials associated with the work of the party. Carl later regretted denying he was a member of the Communist Party, and from that time both Anne and Carl refused to answer any question about their party affiliation on the principle that answering the question was lending legitimacy to a practice in which a person's guilt or innocence hinged on whether their political views aligned with the White majority. Eventually Carl was convicted of sedition and sentenced to fifteen years in jail and a $5,000 fine.

Anne was devastated by the verdict, and anticipated that her own trial, which was scheduled to begin in February 1955, would end with the same result. However, because Carl's case was appealed, her trial was delayed, and so she spent the next eighteen months raising funds for Carl's bail, and working to have the verdict overturned. Carl ended up spending only seven months in jail because his case was thrown out when in 1956 the Supreme Court ruled that state level anti-Communist hearings were unconstitutional. Through the entire ordeal she fought for Carl's release and vindication, while maintaining contact with the Wades, who continued their own battle to remain in their house. After battling for several years, the Wades eventually decided to sell the house and move to an all-Black community. Even so, through the Wades' ordeal and Carl's trial the battle for civil rights in Louisville and throughout the South had been engaged in a new and dramatic manner. At the same time the Bradens had been going through their struggle, the Montgomery (Alabama) Improvement Association had successfully desegregated the public buses in that city after a 380-day boycott. African American communities throughout the South had begun to push for voting rights, access to public facilities, and equal treatment in all aspects of civic life. The civil rights movement had come of age and was on the move.

As might be expected, the trial and Anne's efforts at seeking clemency significantly affected her personal and family life. During much of the two years they were fighting the Wade case, the Bradens' two young children stayed with Anne's parents in Anniston. During the first summer after the Wades' house had been purchased and then bombed, Anne suffered an early miscarriage, most likely because of the stress. Anne struggled with depression, stress, and fear; she even briefly considering giving up and taking her and Carl's sentence without a fight. Because of the "Communist" label, both Anne and Carl were spurned by their former employer the *Louisville Courier Journal*. The paper stood by Carl in the early part of his ordeal, but when he was indicted, they fired him, and subsequently the paper broke all ties with the Bradens. Likewise, the local branch of the NAACP refused to let them take part in their work for fear that association with them would hurt the organization's credibility. However, many friends, as well as their pastor at the Episcopal church, turned out to be sources of great encouragement and support. In the end Anne came out of the experience more convinced than ever that she needed to work for racial justice, not just for the Black citizens of the South, but for herself as well. As she later reflected, "It wasn't that we were helping those 'poor Blacks.' . . . It was our struggle too."[16]

The Work Continues

I have chosen to focus on the early years of Anne Braden's life and the transformation that led her from being a member of the Southern elite to what Catherine Fosl called a "subversive Southerner." Yet the purchase of the Wade house and the trial were only the beginning of a lifetime of efforts to challenge, dismantle, and transform the racist culture and system of the segregated South. Despite having been legally exonerated, for years to come in their hometown of Louisville they were considered persons to be avoided. Because of the stigma created by the trial, the other five defendants chose to leave Louisville and start over in a new place, but the Bradens decided to stay.

Thus, when they went looking for work, they met many closed doors. Anne worked for a while as a receptionist at a local business, but in September 1957 Anne and Carl were hired as field secretaries for the Southern Conference Educational Fund (SCEF), an interracial reform organization working for peaceful social change within the United States. The sole goal of SCEF was to end segregation in the South through Black and White people working together. As in their other endeavors, Carl and Anne shared leadership responsibilities equally and worked together as one. Because of childcare responsibilities Anne tended to work mostly from home, whereas Carl did most of the traveling to various parts of the South to plead the SCEF cause.

The Bradens' primary task was to organize liberal-minded Southern Whites to work with African American civil rights leaders. As the Bradens had discovered in their own struggle, there was tremendous pressure on Whites to remain silent even if they did not agree with the segregationist practices and tactics of intimidation employed against Blacks marching and advocating for their rights. Both economic pressure (in the form of boycotts) and violent threats were made on Whites who

---

[16] Fosl, *Subversive Southerner*, 198.

decided to publicly support the civil rights efforts led by various African American leaders. White people who participated in civil rights actions were considered pariahs and traitors to their race, and like the Bradens were socially ostracized and regarded as seditious Communists. Thus, it was hard and often frustrating to organize Whites to stand for racial justice in such a time, but the Bradens were relentless in their efforts, and over time they were able to build a strong base of Southern Whites along with African Americans working within SCEF.

Through their work the Bradens developed many deep friendships with Whites and Blacks involved in the civil rights movement; their list of friends included Martin Luther King Jr., Septima Clark, Ella Baker, Myles Horton, Virginia Durr, and Fred Shuttlesworth. Among civil rights organizations, SCEF was considered the most radical, and therefore sometimes for political and public relations reasons groups like King's Southern Christian Leadership Conference (SCLC) had to publicly deny involvement with SCEF. However, Dr. King never broke his personal ties with the Bradens and even spoke positively of Anne in his famous "Letter from a Birmingham Jail."[17] Carl was again arrested and imprisoned in 1958 for contempt when he refused to answer questions about his political beliefs before the House Un-American Activities Committee (HUAC). Though he appealed the verdict, his conviction was upheld by the Supreme Court; he was sentenced to a year in prison and was paroled after ten months. SCEF as an organization was constantly under government scrutiny and even had its New Orleans offices raided by the FBI in 1963 for supposedly violating Louisiana's antisubversion laws. In 1965 Carl and Anne became the directors of SCEF and moved the headquarters from New Orleans to Louisville.

In the early 1960s when students formed the Student Nonviolent Coordinating Committee (SNCC), Anne served as an adviser and informal mentor to many of the White students who got involved. Through her involvement with SNCC, Anne became close friends with Ella Baker, who had left the staff of SCLC to serve as an adviser to the members of SNCC. In the mid-1960s when SNCC moved from being an integrated organization to an all-Black organization focused on Black empowerment, Anne supported this change and helped the White activists deal with the transition and form a partner organization called the Southern Student Organizing Committee (SSOC). Activists young and old, Black

---

[17] Martin Luther King Jr., "Letter from a Birmingham Jail," in *Why We Can't Wait* (Boston: Beacon Press, 1965), 85–110.

and White, were often guests at the Braden house for short and long stays. What impressed people so much about Anne was her mixture of Southern hospitality coupled with a radical commitment to overcome the evils of racism.

In 1973 SCEF folded under the tension between various factions in the organizations. Many of the African American members had been drawn away to various liberation groups such as the Black Panthers, causing SCEF to become predominantly a White organization (even though Rev. Fred Shuttlesworth was the SCEF board chair), and factions developed around various political and tactical ideologies. Carl stepped away from the group, but Anne continued to serve as the editor of the organization's newsletter, *The Patriot*. Although they could never prove it, the Bradens believed that SCEF had been infiltrated by FBI operatives whose purpose was to create dissension and eventually destroy the organization, which eventually happened when it folded in 1974. Anne believed that the vulnerability of the organization lay in its being an all-White organization and out of that experience wrote, "I made up my mind then that I would never spend another minute of my life building something all-White or predominantly White. That is just not what's going to change things in this country."[18]

In the midst of all her work Anne continued to be a devoted mother and wife. Her family continued to grow, but she also faced deep personal sadness. In 1960 the Bradens gave birth to Beth, their third child. However, in 1963, their other daughter, Anita, was diagnosed with a rare lung disease, and died in June 1964 at the age of eleven. Then in 1975 after returning from a business trip, Carl lay down to rest on the couch and never woke up, having experienced a series of quiet heart attacks that eventually took his life at age sixty. Of all the challenges Anne had faced to that point in her life, Carl's death was the most difficult. For the twenty-seven years they had been together they were "totally intertwined, like the trunks of two trees grown together."[19] She faced the challenge of reconstructing her life without her life partner while remaining actively committed to the causes and concerns that had brought them together.

For thirty years following his death she worked on building or participating in multiracial organizations. In 1975 she helped organize the Southern Organizing Committee for Economic and Social Justice (SOC).

---

[18] Fosl, *Subversive Southerner*, 321.

[19] Ibid., 322.

SOC was consciously built on multiracial leadership that focused largely on issues of environmental racism. In 1979 the Ku Klux Klan (KKK) killed an SCLC activist in Decatur, Alabama, and then killed five civil rights marchers in Greensboro, North Carolina. Anne helped organize marches against those actions and build the National Anti-Klan Network to call attention to KKK actions in the South. In 1984 and 1988 she worked on Jesse Jackson's presidential campaigns and served on the board of Jackson's "Rainbow Coalition." Back in Louisville she worked on efforts to desegregate the public schools and neighborhoods. She served on a national task force of the Episcopal Church focused on social justice and racial issues. She continued to speak out on issues of peace and racial justice and write for various Southern and social justice journals.

Despite being an activist woman for decades, Anne always had a tenuous relationship with the women's movement that emerged in the 1970s. She did not share the feminist anger toward men expressed early in the movement. Furthermore, she viewed feminism as largely a White women's movement and challenged her feminist colleagues to broaden their focus and include the concerns of Women of Color and Black men. She expressed her views in a 1972 pamphlet titled *Letter to White Southern Women*. In the letter she emphasized the shared destinies of Black and White women with these words: "We who are white will overcome our oppression as women only when we reject once and for all the privileges conferred on us by our white skin."[20]

In later years Anne's efforts were recognized and celebrated. The American Civil Liberties Union bestowed its prestigious Baldwin Medal of Liberty on her in 1990. Her alma mater, Randolph-Macon Women's College, having earlier removed her from its alumnae roll, in 1994 gave her the Alumnae Achievement Award. Various other colleges awarded her honorary doctorates. After decades of being considered a pariah, Anne was not always comfortable with such recognition and wryly insisted that these awards would not keep her from the work she was committed to doing. However on March 6, 2006, her work did come to an end when she died at the age of eighty-one. A year later in April 2007, the Anne Braden Institute for Social Justice Research was opened at the University of Louisville and continues to focus on social justice issues in the Southern United States and in Louisville, carrying on her legacy.

---

[20] Anne Braden, *Free Thomas Walmsley: A Letter to White Southern Woman from Anne Braden*, (Louisville, KY: SCEF Press, 1972), http://www.newsreel.org.

Anne Braden's Enduring Challenge

In 1958 Anne Braden published *The Wall Between*, which recounted the events and struggles of the effort to buy Andrew Wade's house and the sedition trial that followed. As one reads the book one cannot but be impressed with Anne's understanding and empathy for White Southerners and their inability to break the grip of White racism. As she often wrote, the racist, segregationist worldview in which she was raised imprisoned Whites even as it oppressed Blacks. Although she broke free from the grip of that racist Southern culture by joining the "other America," she never lost touch with it. Throughout her life she continually made choices to side and struggle with those blocked by the barriers of racism and segregation, often suffering personally for those choices. In ways big and small, personal and public, Anne Braden embodied a commitment to racial justice and in so doing provides a clear example of what it means to be a White ally for racial justice.

Discussion Questions

1. Anne Braden often referred to the segregation and White racism that characterized her early life as a "prison." In what ways do you feel like the legacy of White supremacy and racism limits the ability of White people to relate meaningfully and respectfully to people of other races and cultures?
2. Anne Braden's journey to be a strong advocate for racial justice was aided by relationships she had with such people as Harriet Fitzgerald and Carl Braden, as well as experiences with African Americans with whom worked for civil rights. Who are the people who have influenced you in your thinking and values on issue of race and difference? What are the experiences that have shaped your worldview on these issues?
3. How do you respond to Anne Braden's statement that "I made up my mind then that I would never spend another minute of my life building something all-White or predominantly White. That is just not what's going to change things in this country."

Bibliography

Braden, Anne. *Free Thomas Walmsley: A Letter to White Southern Woman from Anne Braden*. Louisville, KY: SCEF Press, 1972. http://www.newsreel.org.

———. *The Wall Between*. 1958. New York: Monthly Review Press, 1999.

Brown, Cynthia Stokes. *Refusing Racism: White Allies and the Struggle for Civil Right*. New York: Teachers College Press, 2002

Fosl, Catherine. *Subversive Southerner: Anne Braden and the Struggle for Racial Justice in the Cold War South*. New York: Palgrave Macmillan, 2002.

Gallagher, Gary W., and Alan T. Nolan, eds. *The Myth of the Lost Cause and Civil War History*. Bloomington: Indiana University Press, 2000.

King, Martin Luther Jr. "Letter from a Birmingham Jail." In *Why We Can't Wait*, 85–110. Boston: Beacon Press, 1965.

13

Viola Liuzzo
(1925–1965)

*A Malignant Martyr**

Death on the Highway

On the night of March 25, 1965, Viola Liuzzo, a thirty-nine-year-old White mother and wife from Detroit, Michigan, was driving on Route 80, which runs between Selma and Montgomery, Alabama. In the passenger seat with her was Leroy Moton, a nineteen-year-old Black community organizer from Selma. Earlier that day, they had participated along with thousands of others in the completion of the five-day, fifty-mile Voting Rights March from Selma to Montgomery. They had listened to popular singers such as Peter, Paul, and Mary, Harry Belafonte, and Joan Baez sing on the steps of the Alabama capitol. They had heard Rosa Parks, whose courageous stance against segregated busing in Montgomery had sparked the civil rights movement ten years earlier, proclaim to the mixed-race crowd, "We are not in a struggle of black against white, but rather wrong against right." The event came to a climax when the Rev. Martin Luther King Jr. proclaimed that "the arc of the moral universe is long, but it bends toward justice." Of that day Jimmy Breslin, a *New York Herald* journalist, wrote: "You have not lived in this time when

* Photo of Viola Liuzzo provided courtesy of the Levi Watkins Learning Center Digital Library, Alabama State University, Montgomery, AL. Unless otherwise noted, sources for the information in this chapter are King Encyclopedia, "Selma to Montgomery March (1965)." Martin Luther King Jr. Research and Education Institute, Stanford University, http://mlk-kpp01.stanford.edu; Mary Stanton, *From Selma to Sorrow: The Life and Death of Viola Liuzzo* (Athens: University of Georgia Press, 1998).

everything is changing until you see an old black woman with mud on her shoes stand in the street of a southern city and sing *We Are Not Afraid* and then turn and look at the face of a cop near her and see the puzzlement and terrible fear in his eyes. Because he knows and everybody who has ever seen it knows that it is all over."[1]

Truly it had been a day that had shaken the Old South culture of Alabama to its very core, and a day that history would record as a turning point in the struggle for civil rights for Black people in the United States. For Viola and Leroy, that day was almost over. They had volunteered to shuttle marchers back to Selma to collect their belongings. Viola herself planned to head back to Michigan the next morning. Although the details of what happened on the road have been disputed and debated, what is known is that about 7:30 pm as they traveled back to Montgomery to pick up one last load of marchers, a car filled with four members of the local Ku Klux Klan (KKK) pulled up alongside of them, shots were fired, the car swerved off the road, and later that night Viola Liuzzo's blood-spattered body was found in the driver's seat. Moton had either been knocked out or "played dead" and had survived. When word reached the White House, President Johnson ordered a full investigation, and to everyone's surprise, the next morning the four assailants had been arrested and detained.

Who was Viola Liuzzo? What was the path that led her to Alabama to meet her premature death? What were the confusing and painful aftereffects of her murder, some of which are still being felt decades later?

Early Life

Viola Gregg Liuzzo was born in California, Pennsylvania, on April 11, 1925. Her father, Heber Ernest Gregg, had been a coal miner who lost his hand in a mining accident and was disabled for the rest of his life. Her mother, Eva Wilson Gregg, was a schoolteacher. When young Vi, as she was called, was six years old, her parents moved to Georgia, and over the next ten years traveled and lived throughout Georgia and Tennessee looking for work, which was scarce because of the Great Depression of the 1930s. Vi had one younger sister, Rose Mary, who was born in 1936.

At an early age Vi was a strong-willed child who often challenged the norms of her parents and the mores of Southern culture. Her father considered her to be too wild and sassy, though by today's standards her

---

[1] Stanton, *From Selma to Sorrow*, 168–69.

actions might be considered common adolescent rebellion. Nonetheless, at age sixteen she ran away from home and married a thirty-four-year-old man after a night of frivolity; the next day they annulled the marriage, and a chastened Viola came home.

After the United States entered World War II, the Gregg family moved to Ypsilanti, Michigan, in search of work in the factories making implements for the war, and at the age of eighteen Viola moved to Detroit where she got a job as a cashier in a plant cafeteria. While there she met and married thirty-six-year-old George Argyris, whom she divorced six years later, after giving birth to two daughters. Shortly after her divorce, she met and married Anthony "Jim" Liuzzo, an organizer for the Teamsters Union, with whom she had three more children before her untimely death.

In 1961 at the age of thirty-six, when her youngest child, Sarah, was three years old, Viola went back to work and attended school to become a medical assistant. Though she had quit school at the age of fourteen, when she returned this time, she found learning to be exciting as it opened her up to ideas, people, and experiences she had never before considered. She got a job in a local hospital but soon found herself involved in a battle with management over unfair treatment of the female staff at the hospital. Viola knew the hardships of poverty from her childhood, and in her adulthood she became an outspoken advocate for justice and fairness for all. Her activism caused her to lose her job at the hospital, but it also started her down a path that would change her life and the life of her family forever.

A Nigerian medical researcher with whom she worked encouraged her to apply to Wayne State University. Even though she had never finished high school, she passed the entrance exams and began as a provisional student in pursuit of a nursing degree. While Detroit in the 1960s was a highly segregated city, Wayne State was a seedbed of the burgeoning Detroit civil rights movement. While at college, Viola became more sensitized to the gross disparities of treatment of Blacks and Whites. Through a Black friend, Sarah Evans, Viola joined the NAACP and attended a national convention in New York City. She also became friends with a White activist priest, Malcolm Boyd, the chaplain at Wayne State, who was her confidant and spiritual mentor.

Viola's husband, Jim, earned enough so that she did not have to work, but he came to realize that his wife was not content with the role of mother and housewife, the traditional expectations of a married woman in that era. Although he did not always understand his wife's passions, he supported her pursuit of education. He knew she was her own person, and respected and loved her for that.

Sojourn to Selma

Selma, Alabama, is a small city of just over 20,000 people located on the banks of the Alabama River, approximately fifty miles west of Montgomery. In 1965 it became the site of a vigorous campaign to secure the right to vote for local African Americans.[2] Following the post–Civil War period of Reconstruction beginning in about 1890, White Southern legislators passed various laws that made it virtually impossible for a Black person to even register to vote; if that did not work, threats and violence were used to reinforce the point that Blacks were not allowed to vote. The NAACP, CORE, and other civil rights organizations for decades had been fighting battles in the courts to reenfranchise Blacks. As the civil rights movement gained momentum in the 1950s and 1960s, the right to vote became a major issue in the movement.

In 1963 as part of its efforts to push the voting rights issue, the Student Nonviolent Coordinating Committee (SNCC) sent two staff members, Bernard and Colia Lafayette, to Selma to begin teaching classes on voting rights and procedures. Selma was chosen because it had a long history of racial intimidation. Following the bombing on September 18, 1963, of the Sixteenth Street Baptist Church in Birmingham, Alabama, people began holding mass meetings throughout Selma demanding fair treatment in all areas of life, but especially voting. Over the next eighteen months occasional actions were held in which people would march to City Hall demanding to be allowed to register to vote, always being turned away and sometimes getting arrested in the process.

Sensing that the time was right for a major push to get President Johnson and the Congress to pass a Voting Rights Act, on January 2, 1965 the Southern Christian Leadership Conference (SCLC) under the

---

[2] I am indebted to the following sources about the Selma voting rights campaign: John Lewis and Michael D'Orso, *Walking with the Wind: A Memoir of the Movement* (San Diego, CA: Harcourt and Brace, 1998); Chandler Davidson, "The Voting Rights Act: A Brief History," in *Controversies in Minority Voting: The Voting Rights Act in Perspective*, ed. Bernard Grofman and Chandler Davidson (Washington, DC: Brookings Institution, 1992), 7–51; Taylor Branch, *Pillar of Fire: America in the King Years, 1963–65* (New York: Simon and Schuster, 1999).

leadership of Dr. Martin Luther King Jr. announced that Selma would be the site of a major campaign to return voting rights to its Black citizens. At the time there were nearly 30,000 Black people of voting age in and around Selma, yet only 335 were registered to vote. King hoped the Selma campaign would dramatize the voting injustices throughout the South and thereby move Congress to action. As efforts to register intensified, law enforcement officers under the leadership of Selma Sheriff Jim Clark got increasingly violent. People were being arrested en masse, including 500 children demonstrating for their parents' right to vote.

On February 18, 1965, twenty-six-year-old Jimmie Jackson participated in a voting rights demonstration in neighboring Marion, Alabama, and was killed as he tried to protect his mother from getting beaten by a state trooper wielding a night stick. In response to this travesty, on March 7 local organizers John Lewis of SNCC and Hosea Williams of SCLC led a group of several hundred marchers across the Edmund Pettus Bridge leading out of Selma; their intent was to march fifty miles to the capital, Montgomery, in protest of Jackson's death while advocating for reformation of Alabama's segregationist voting laws. However, the marchers were met on the other side of the bridge by a blockade of state troopers on foot and horseback who attacked them with clubs and tear gas to drive them back over the bridge. "Bloody Sunday," as it came to be called, was broadcast all over the country on national news stations.

Viola was with some of her fellow Wayne State students when, following "Bloody Sunday," Martin Luther King Jr. issued a call for "religious leaders from all over the nation to join [them]" in Selma. After several days of negotiation with state and federal officials and the death of a White Unitarian minister, James Reeb, who had come from Massachusetts in response to Dr. King's call, a federal judge ordered federal troops to protect the marchers en route to the capital, and a march was scheduled for March 21, 1965. Some of Viola's classmates responded to Dr. King's call, so she decided to join them. Without discussing the matter with her husband, she got in her car, and left him a note as to where she had gone and that she would be back in a week.

Because of her medical training, Viola hoped that she could support the march with her nursing skills. However, when she arrived in Selma the day before the march was to begin, she was sent to the hospitality table where marchers could be registered and sleeping arrangements could be made. Although many religious leaders, activists, college-age students, and sympathetic Blacks from the North had responded to Dr. King's call, Viola was unique as a White mother from a working-class background. Nonetheless, she jumped right in and was well liked for her positive attitude and high energy. When the five-day march commenced, Viola continued to run the hospitality table, joined the march during the day, and then was driven back to Selma, as only a limited number of marchers were allowed to camp out overnight. On the last night of the march, she joined the nursing station at the encampment near St. Jude's Roman Catholic Church on the outskirts of Montgomery. It was during this time that she met nineteen-year-old Leroy Moton, with whom she would spend her last hours.

Although spirits were high in the encampment as singers and speakers entertained the crowd, Viola had a premonition that something violent was going to occur and that someone was going to be killed. She was not alone in her uneasiness, as rumors (that were later substantiated) circulated that the KKK was planning to disrupt the final day with violence and attempt to assassinate Dr. King. However, at the end of the rally on the capitol steps when the anticipated violence did not occur, Viola breathed a sigh of relief and offered to make several trips back and forth between Montgomery and Selma to help the marchers gather up their belongings and make their trek back to their respective homes. As it turned out, she made only one trip to Selma and on her way to pick up more marchers, she was assassinated.

Controversy around Her Death

The news of her death and the immediate arrest of Viola's KKK assassins fed into an environment that had been characterized by controversy and suspicion from the beginning. Even before the march began local media and politicians had characterized the event as an opportunity for young White women and Black men to engage in profligate and promiscuous sexual relations. On March 22, a day after the march had begun, the Alabama legislature passed a resolution (ACT 159) that asserted "there is evidence . . . of much fornication and young women returning to their respective states as unwed expectant mothers." The free interactions between Whites and Blacks evidenced in the march violated the deepest mores held by those aspiring to the Southern way of life.[3]

For this reason when Viola was discovered to have been killed while driving in a car with a Black man, local media outlets concluded she had been engaging in extramarital sex and drug use with Leroy Moton. Local authorities even circulated a story (that the local coroner flatly denied)

[3] Stanton, *From Selma to Sorrow*, 153.

that Viola's vagina had been filled with semen. Even White Southerners who openly opposed segregation, such as Virginia Durr, later stated, "Five minutes in Montgomery in those days and you knew a white woman did not ride around with a black man in her car at night."[4] As Mary Stanton writes: "Vi Liuzzo with her Michigan plates and a Black man in the front seat of her car, symbolized everything segregationists most feared and despised. Here was a White woman who had clearly stepped across the line. Her behavior removed her from the category of sacred White womanhood and motherhood (which in the chivalric code of the Southern way of life required male protection) and into the despised category of race traitor."[5]

However, an even more hideous smear campaign was orchestrated by J. Edgar Hoover, the FBI director, because one of the four KKK assailants that night had been Gary Rowe, a local man, who was acting as a paid FBI informant on the activities of the KKK. The swift arrest had been possible because Rowe had identified his three co-conspirators immediately and later became the government's chief witness to the murder. Under the Freedom of Information Act of 1966, the Liuzzo family later learned that Hoover had compiled more than a thousand pages of documents designed to discredit Viola. In these documents Viola was described as mentally ill, a drug addict, and sexually promiscuous. Her husband, Jim, was characterized as a "known Teamster strong arm with Mafia ties" and a close associate of then Teamsters president Jimmy Hoffa. Hoover insinuated such things to President Johnson, and accusations were leaked to the media, and all sorts of media stories depicted Viola Liuzzo as an immoral woman in the wrong place doing the wrong thing. As Howard Simon of the Michigan ACLU later said: "Hoover's remarks were 'designed to minimize the importance of the crime and then cover up the fact that a paid FBI informant was in the car with three other men when they opened fire on Mrs. Liuzzo.'"[6]

Back in Detroit as Jim Liuzzo and his five children tried to cope with the traumatic news of Viola's death, they also became the targets of scorn. They received duffel bags of hate mail. Garbage was dumped on their front lawn, as was a burning cross. The KKK sent a glossy magazine with graphic pictures of her dead body to their home, and the youngest child, Sarah, who was six, was harassed by classmates at school. The harassment got so great that Jim hired guards to protect the house and

---

[4] Ibid., 28. For more on Virginia Durr, see chapter 8.

[5] Ibid., 153.

[6] Ibid., 190.

changed the children's schools. Viola's friend Sarah Evans moved in to care for the children, while she screened the mail to remove the worst of it. However, the impact of Viola's death stayed with the family for decades. According to those close to Jim, he never recovered from the trauma, retired in 1975 and died in 1978. Moreover, nearly thirty years later the 1994 documentary on the Liuzzo murder, *Home of the Brave*, showed how Viola's now-grown children were still seeking to deal with the death of their mother and the controversy around it.

The trials of the defendants further enflamed the controversy. Twenty-one-year-old Collie Wilkins was the first to be tried for murder, but the trial ended in a hung jury. Gary Rowe, the FBI informant, was the government's chief witness, while Wilkins's attorney was Matthew Hobson Murphy Jr., chief legal counsel for the KKK, a man who proudly proclaimed his belief in White supremacy.[7] According to Stanton, Murphy's defense strategy hammered on two themes: "that Rowe had broken his Klan oath of loyalty in testifying against his fellow Klansman and therefore could not be trusted and that because Mrs. Liuzzo was a White woman alone in a car with a Black man at night whatever happened to her was her own fault."[8] When it became clear that there was going to be no conviction for murder at the state level, the federal government tried the men on charges of conspiracy; the men were convicted and ended up spending ten years in prison. However, in 1978 after J. Edgar Hoover had died and the three men were out of prison, the case was reopened, and Gary Rowe was indicted for Viola Liuzzo's murder. FBI investigators had learned that Rowe had been involved in several violent acts such as the 1963 Birmingham church bombing that had killed three children and attacking Freedom Riders in Alabama in 1961. However, because Rowe had been granted immunity from prosecution in the first trials, his case was never fully adjudicated. Likewise in 1982 when the family sought to bring a civil suit against Rowe, the case was thrown out and the family charged with paying Rowe's legal fees as well as their own.

A Lasting but Painful Memorial

Viola Liuzzo's name appears on a memorial to all the martyrs of the civil rights movement outside the visitor's center of the Southern Poverty Law Center in Montgomery. She is the only White woman whose name

---

[7] For more information on the trial see Jared Taylor, "The Many Deaths of Viola Liuzzo," *National Review* 47 (July 10, 1995): 38–39.

[8] Stanton, *From Selma to Sorrow*, 117.

is listed there. Her image is also part of the Civil Rights Memorial mural located at the bottom of the Edmund Pettus Bridge leading out of Selma. Likewise, in her honor a memorial was erected in 1991 by the women of the SCLC at the spot on Route 80 where she was killed. The marker was defaced several times, and so an iron rod fence was eventually put around it for protection, and the last defacing, a Confederate flag, was allowed to stay on for a while to remind people that racism still exists.[9] When I visited the memorial in the summer of 2013, the Confederate flag was gone and a beautiful pink wreath stood next to the memorial.

However, the lasting memorial is the scar and burden that Viola Liuzzo's family has had to bear.[10] Because of all the lies and distortions that followed her death, her children did not begin to pursue the real story until they had become adults, and by then many of the primary actors in her tragic trauma were gone. Viola Liuzzo's story is a reminder that an action against racism can be not only life-threatening for the person involved, but that it ripples through the relationships with the others in one's life. Viola Liuzzo was killed because of her convictions, but her family was victimized because of their connections to her.

Moreover, the reaction to her death illustrates that people are often not sympathetic to persons who challenge the established mores of their day. Shortly after her death, *The Ladies Home Journal* conducted a poll that indicated that 55 percent of those polled (mostly women) thought she should have stayed at home, while only 28 percent thought she should have gone to Selma as she had. However, Martin Luther King Jr. speaking the Sunday after her death said: "If physical death is the price some must pay to save us and our White brothers from the eternal death of the spirit, then no sacrifice can be more redemptive."[11]

History has been gentler with Viola Liuzzo than the critics of her day. Mary Stanton concludes her biography on Viola Liuzzo this way: "Viola Liuzzo possessed deep sensibilities, a short temper, an abiding warmth, painful restlessness and a strong moral compass. Once upon a time she did something extraordinary for civil rights." In that way she is like all persons of all races and ethnicities who seek to make a difference in their world.

---

[9] "Reminder of Racism," *Jet* 91, no. 14 (February 24, 1997): 22.

[10] The film *Home of the Brave* (directed by Paola di Florio [Homevision, 2004]), tells the story of Viola Liuzzo's death from the perspective of her children many years later and illustrates the devastating effect her death had on all of them.

[11] Stanton, *From Selma to Sorrow*, 176.

Discussion Questions

1. Viola Liuzzo's decision to go to Selma put her in conflict with her role and responsibility as a mother and a wife. Do you think she made the right decision? Why or why not?
2. Though Viola acted according to her values, her decision deeply affected her family. What are conflicts you may feel between your commitment to racial justice and loyalties and responsibility to your family?

Bibliography

Branch, Taylor. *Pillar of Fire: America in the King Years, 1963–65*. New York: Simon and Schuster, 1999.

Davidson, Chandler. "The Voting Rights Act: A Brief History." In *Controversies in Minority Voting: The Voting Rights Act in Perspective*, edited by Bernard Grofman and Chandler Davidson, 7–51.Washington, DC: Brookings Institution, 1992.

di Florio, Paola, dir. *Home of the Brave*. Homevison, DVD, 74 minutes, 2004.

King Encyclopedia. "Selma to Montgomery March (1965)." Martin Luther King Jr. Research and Education Institute, Stanford University. http://mlk-kpp01.stanford.edu.

Lewis, John, and Michael D'Orso. *Walking with the Wind: A Memoir of the Movemen*t, San Diego, CA: Harcourt and Brace, 1998.

"Reminder of Racism." *Jet* 91, no.14 (February 24, 1997): 22.

Stanton, Mary. *From Selma to Sorrow: The Life and Death of Viola Liuzzo*. Athens: University of Georgia Press, 1998.

Taylor, Jared. "The Many Deaths of Viola Liuzzo." *National Review* 47 (July 10, 1995): 38–39.

"The Trial." *Time* 85, no. 2 (May 14, 1965): 35–38. EBSCOhost Database.

14

Robert Graetz (1928–)

*Bridge Builder**

"A Decision That Changed Our Lives"

On December 1, 1955, Ms. Rosa Parks was arrested in Montgomery, Alabama, for refusing to give up her seat on the bus to a White passenger. Rosa Parks by vocation was a seamstress, but for over ten years she had been active in the local chapter of the NAACP. She was not the first African American to take a stand against the bus company's policies of requiring Black passengers to give up their seats to Whites, but her arrest and the protest that followed led to the Montgomery bus boycott, which in turn sparked the modern civil rights movement. On the day of her arrest, news spread rapidly through the Black community. Alabama State College professors Mary Fair Burks and Jo Ann Robinson along with other members of the Women's Political Council sprang into action, distributing flyers calling for a one-day boycott of the buses. Minsters of African American churches began calling one another in support of the boycott and to plan a mass meeting in response to the arrest.

The recently arrived pastor of Trinity Lutheran Church in Montgomery heard that someone had been arrested on the bus that day, but because he had not been part of the circle of communications, he did not know the details. Trinity was an all-Black Lutheran congregation,

* Photo of Robert Graetz used by permission of New South Publishing. Unless otherwise noted, the major sources for this chapter are Robert Graetz, *Montgomery: A White Preacher's Memoir* (Minneapolis: Fortress Press, 1991); and Robert Graetz, *A White Preacher's Message on Race and Reconciliation* (Montgomery, AL: New South Press, 2006).

but their pastor, Robert Graetz, was White. Graetz called his neighbor, Rosa Parks, to ask if she knew anything about this bus incident and of rumors that a boycott of the buses was being called for. She did. He asked: Do you know who was arrested?

"Yes, Pastor Graetz."

"Well, who was it?"

Quietly, she said, "It was me, Pastor Graetz."

Graetz later referred to Rosa Parks's decision to not give up her seat as "the decision that changed our lives" because it led him to become actively involved in the Montgomery Improvement Association (MIA), the bus boycott, and to be the only White minister in the city to take a public stand against the racist and segregationist policies of the city. Although Graetz was only in Montgomery for a relatively brief time (1955–58), his actions during that period as an ally for racial justice were characteristic of his life before and after his time in Montgomery.

Background

Robert Graetz was born May 18, 1928, in Clarksburg, West Virginia, the older of Bob and Mackie Graetz's two children. He spent most of his youth in Charleston, West Virginia, where he lived in a segregated community and attended an all-White school. The only Black people he had any contact with during his youth were school janitors and a woman named Helen who cleaned their home. Otherwise, he had no meaningful contact with African Americans in the city. Black people were often the butt of jokes among his friends, and he even participated in a minstrel show where he put on blackface and entertained youth groups and women's groups. In his segregated White environment such behavior was deemed acceptable and was not considered discriminatory or improper.

Although his father was a chemical engineer who worked in a glass company, Robert Jr. came from a long line of Lutheran ministers. Both his paternal great-grandfather and grandfather had been Lutheran ministers, and though his father had resisted the pressure to follow suit, early on Robert Jr. came under the influence of his grandfather, who taught him to read and speak German, tutored him in the Bible, and encouraged active involvement in church. By the time he was in elementary school, Robert was talking about becoming a minster. Though he toyed with the idea of becoming a doctor, in 1946 he was accepted at Capital University and enrolled as a pre-theological student.

Graetz eventually majored in social sciences with a concentration in sociology. During his junior year he was required to write a term paper, which changed his life's direction. The paper began as a research project on discrimination against Jews in higher education. However, in the course of his research, he learned that not only were there "Jewish quotas" at many colleges and universities, but also that African Americans had been totally excluded from many of the same schools; there were no quotas for Blacks because the schools intended to remain completely White. So he changed his topic and wrote a paper on the exclusion of Blacks in higher education and in his own words "crossed his Rubicon."

Within weeks of submitting the paper, he started a Race Relations Club at the school and joined the Columbus chapter of the NAACP. Through his involvement with the NAACP, he had the opportunity to meet Walter White, the national director of the NAACP. Graetz was deeply impressed with White and his commitment to racial justice. While at Capital, Robert met Jeannie Ellis, who became his wife in 1951. Jeannie came from a small town in western Pennsylvania and like Robert had grown up in an all-White environment. Contrary to her father's wishes and the customs of the time for young women, she insisted on going to college. That tenacity served her well as she became, and continues to be, Robert's constant partner in their ministry and racial justice work.

According to plan in 1951 he entered the Evangelical Lutheran Seminary located just across the street from Capital. While there he did some volunteer work with St. Philip Lutheran, an all-Black church in Columbus; little did he know that later in his career he would serve as the church's pastor. In 1952, as part of his seminary training, Graetz and his pregnant wife were sent to Los Angeles to do a one-year internship at Community Lutheran, a "small, mostly Negro congregation,"[1] in a demographically changing community. The one-year internship turned into two, as Graetz became immersed in the life of the community and the church. Under his leadership the congregation increased from 75 to 150 members and developed a children's program that outgrew their small space. Although he began his time in Los Angeles feeling conspicuously different as a White person, over time he became more at home with his African American parishioners and neighbors. However, he also witnessed racial violence firsthand when two Black families bought houses in the nearby White community and had to withstand tremendous harassment and pressure to leave. Graetz got involved in

[1] Graetz, *Memoir*, 27.

helping resolve the situation peacefully. Thus began Graetz's education in the dynamics of racism that he would battle for the rest of his life. While there his wife gave birth to the first two of their seven children.

In 1954 he returned to Columbus to complete his studies and graduated in the spring of 1955. Because he had expressed interest in doing race relations work and because the Lutheran church had few Black pastors on its rolls, when Trinity Lutheran in Montgomery, Alabama, announced a pastoral vacancy, he expressed interest in the position. Denominational officials summoned him for a special meeting, warning him that churches in the South were not always accepting of "intruders from the North" and that he should go there to be a pastor not a "[crusader] for racial justice" (i.e., don't get involved in civil rights and racial justice efforts).[2] Graetz promised to follow their advice, and he fully intended to keep that promise, but circumstances in Montgomery presented him with challenges that would change the course of his life and ministry. Later Graetz insisted that everything that transpired in Montgomery came about in the course of his pastoral duties; however, one can easily surmise that Graetz's subsequent involvement in the bus boycott was not what the church officials had in mind in their talk with him years before.

Montgomery and Trinity Lutheran Church

Trinity Lutheran was an oddity in the largely Baptist and Methodist Black church community of Montgomery. Like a typical Lutheran church of its time, Trinity's worship was characterized by a highly formal liturgy unfamiliar to most Black Christians. According to Taylor Branch,[3] the church's main attraction was its church-affiliated school supported by the World Lutheran Council; the school was "the only decent school available to Negroes" in Montgomery, and so many erstwhile Baptists and Methodists became involved with Trinity in order to send their children to the school.

Although Rev. Graetz was not the first White pastor to serve the all-Black Trinity Church, his immediate predecessor had been a Black pastor named Nelson Trout, who left Trinity to become the pastor of Community Lutheran in Los Angeles where Graetz had served his internship and eventually became the first African American bishop in the

---

[2] Ibid., 30.

[3] Taylor Branch, *Parting the Waters: America in the King Years, 1954–63* (New York: Simon and Schuster, 1988), 125–26.

Lutheran Church. Trout's White predecessors had not lived in the Black community immediately around the church, but Rev. Trout had built a parsonage in the neighborhood during his tenure there. Thus when the Graetz family moved into the parsonage in the June 1955, they were initially met with some distrust by the Black community and ostracism by the Whites. Local White store owners shunned them because of his unabashed identification with the suffering of his Black parishioners and neighbors. The Graetzes also created minor legal problems such as when they would go to the local movie theater and sit in the "Negro section" in the balcony, even though White and Black "mixing" was strictly prohibited.

Montgomery, Alabama, was known as "The Cradle of the Confederacy," as it had served as the Confederacy's first capital when the Southern states seceded prior to the Civil War. When Graetz and his family arrived, they quickly realized that "Lee may have surrendered. . . . But the South had not yet given up!"[4] Jim Crow segregation was rigidly and comprehensively enforced in stores, at lunch counters, in movie theaters, bathrooms, labor unions, and buses. Moreover, local customs dictated that Blacks were required to step off the sidewalk when being approached by a White person and to respond to Whites with deference while being humiliated in return. In addition to serving as pastor at Trinity, Graetz also had two small country churches (also all Black) that he visited and preached at once a month; as a result he saw the effects of racism in both the city and the countryside. Most of the Blacks and many of the Whites who lived in the rural areas eked out a subsistence existence as sharecroppers living in constant indebtedness to wealthy plantation owners. Yet despite these similarities, many of the poor Whites joined the Ku Klux Klan and thus participated in the harassment of their equally poor Black neighbors.

For the first few months in Montgomery Graetz immersed himself in the pastoral duties of preaching, baptizing, and visiting parishioners. Because of his unique position as a White pastor in a Black community, Graetz felt under suspicion by some in the community. Yet he set about to be a bridge builder and joined both the all-White Ministerial Association and the all-Black Ministerial Alliance. At one of the early alliance meetings he had the opportunity to meet another new pastor who, like him, was in his first pastoral charge, and who also had recently arrived in Montgomery: Rev. Martin Luther King Jr.

---

[4] Graetz, *Message*, 47.

The Bus Boycott

Everything changed for Graetz the day he learned that Rosa Parks had been arrested for refusing to give up her seat to a White passenger. Parks's arrest occurred on a Thursday, and on the following Monday, December 5, nearly all the Black citizens of Montgomery refrained from riding the buses. People with cars were urged to provide rides for those for whom walking to work would be a hardship. After consulting and praying with his wife, Graetz decided to join the drivers and cruised the streets that day offering rides to persons who needed assistance. He was impressed with the hopefulness and the determination of the walkers. That evening at the invitation of one of his members, Robert Dandridge, Graetz attended that evening's mass rally; except for reporters covering the event, Graetz was the only White person that evening in a crowd of an estimated five thousand people inside and outside the church.[5] Despite the church's being filled when he arrived, Dandridge ushered Graetz into the sanctuary since he understood the significance of a White minister's presence in that assembly. In his 2006 memoir Graetz describes the meeting in detail and concludes by saying that by the end of the rally he had moved from being an observer of the boycott to a participant.

That evening, the assembly voted unanimously to continue the boycott. After only the first day, Graetz had been identified by a local reporter as "a White man" participating in the boycott. This did not deter him, and he served as an early morning driver throughout the campaign. At the same time on December 7, two days after the decision to continue the boycott had been made, Graetz sent the first of several letters to the all-White Ministerial Association urging them to speak up on behalf of the boycott; despite his numerous appeals, the association never gave its public support. Graetz later learned that those ministers who expressed support for the boycott from their pulpits were quickly voted out or transferred out of their positions. Thus, the number of White clergy who took any sort of stand in support was small, and he was the only White pastor to take a visible leadership role.[6]

Two weeks into the boycott on December 19, as he was picking up five women who had been shopping, he was arrested by the local

[5] Virginia Durr tried to attend the mass meeting, but could not get in and so left. See chapter 8 on Virginia Foster Durr's involvement in the Montgomery bus boycott and subsequent events.

[6] Several years later, the unwillingness of White pastors to actively support the civil rights movement became the impetus for Martin Luther King's famous 1963 "Letter from a Birmingham Jail."

sheriff. His passengers were dismissed, and he was taken to the county courthouse. Alert to the fact that if held in jail, Graetz would be put in a cell with other White prisoners who would not look favorably on his pro-boycott actions, his five passengers quickly notified boycott leaders, who rushed to the courthouse to pay his bail before he was put in the jail. Graetz did not realize until later how close he had come to being put in a situation he might not have survived.

Although he had been arrested, as of yet he was not well known in the White community, so in January he surreptitiously attended a meeting of the White Citizens' Council, which he regarded as an "uptown version of the Ku Klux Klan."[7] At that meeting he saw firsthand the hatred and venom directed at the leaders of the boycott and how many of Montgomery's most powerful and prominent citizens were involved. In early January he was approached by a reporter from one of the local newspapers trying to determine who was behind the MIA. Most White city leaders assumed that the NAACP was directing the effort. However, the reporter was not satisfied and not believing that "local Negroes" could organize such an effort, he approached Graetz, who, he believed, was "uniquely qualified for the role of the hidden mastermind." However, after interviewing Graetz, the reporter concluded that "Graetz was incapable of the deviousness required to run the boycott covertly."[8] A few days later in mid-January Graetz discovered that his car had been vandalized: sugar had been poured into the gas tank, and all four tires slashed. When he filed a claim with his insurance company, he was informed that his auto insurance policy had been canceled and that no insurance company in Alabama would write him a policy. Graetz now realized he was no longer an unknown and was considered by many in Montgomery's White community as a traitor and a pariah.

In the midst of everything Jeannie gave birth to their third child, a daughter, on January 24. Six days later a bomb was thrown at Dr. King's home while his family was in the house, and he was out preaching at a local church. After that attack, it became apparent to all the leaders of the boycott that death for any and all of them had become a distinct possibility. Graetz's church members cautioned him to take circuitous routes when he visited his country churches and often sent someone to accompany him. The church had also hired watchmen to guard his house at night.

On February 21 Dr. King was put on trial in the first of a series of arrests where Black citizens were accused of breaking Montgomery's

---

[7] Graetz, *Message*, 76.

[8] Branch, *Parting the Waters*, 152–53.

antiboycott ordinance; King had been arrested for going 30 mph in a 25 mph zone. Graetz was called to testify as a witness by King's attorney. In his journals of this time he confessed to feeling a deep sense of fear, feeling isolated, and alienated from his White friends. Since the bombing of King's house, he had been receiving numerous threatening phone calls and letters every day. Every time he left his house he feared it would be the last time he would see his family. In his memoir Graetz writes: "Those times of isolation were the most depressing times of our entire Montgomery experience—not the bombs, nor the threats, nor the nasty phone calls and letters—nothing was as frightening as that feeling of total helplessness."[9]

Graetz's fears were well founded. While away with his family at a conference at Highlander[10] in August 1956, Graetz received a phone call indicating that his home had been bombed. With his family he quickly returned home only to be accused by the mayor of being involved in the bombing: the mayor suggested that the MIA had planted the bomb as a publicity stunt. Graetz openly expressed gratitude for God's protection, and as a result of the bombing, his stature in the community continued to grow. While he tried to protect his children as he continued his work, he realized years later after leaving Montgomery that all of them had been emotionally traumatized.

Because of his connections within the Lutheran church, Graetz left Montgomery several times for fund-raising trips on behalf of the MIA and the boycott. His travels took him to groups and churches in Columbus (including a student group from Ohio State University), Toledo, Anderson (Indiana), and Chicago. When possible, he took others with him, including Rosa Parks. In July 1956 he became the secretary of MIA in the midst of controversy. The previous secretary, a Baptist pastor named Uriah Fields, had quit the post, charging that some MIA leaders had mishandled funds. Fields was vilified in the Black community and later retracted his charges. Graetz was elected to replace Fields, and so became a publicly recognized leader of the bus boycott effort.

In early November 1956 the Supreme Court upheld a lower court decision making the segregation practices on the buses illegal. Yet on November 13 the local circuit court issued an injunction against the car pools providing transportation. In light of the higher court's decision the injunction was meaningless, and on November 14 mass meetings were held to celebrate the victory in two separate churches with a combined attendance of eight thousand people. Graetz was invited

---

9 Graetz, *Memoir*, 76.

10 See chapter 9 on Myles Horton for information about Highlander.

to read Scripture at Holt Street Baptist, which was pastored by Rev. Ralph Abernathy, Dr. King's close ally and friend. On December 21, 1956, the boycott officially ended as Black passengers returned to the buses. Although there were isolated incidents of violence, bus riders had undergone training to respond nonviolently to such attacks, and so the transition initially seemed to be going smoothly.

However, less than a month later their commitment to nonviolence was tested when three churches and the homes of Rev. Abernathy and Rev. Graetz were bombed at two in the morning. The Graetz family, including their ten-day-old baby, was at home asleep at the time. Investigators later found an unexploded bomb in their front yard, which if it had gone off would not only have destroyed the Graetz house but also many other homes on the block. In the ensuing weeks several other bombings occurred at other sites, including the home of Dr. King. Eventually seven men were arrested for the coordinated bombings, and four were indicted, but none were convicted. Members of the church and the Black community-at-large responded by showering the Graetzes with food and offers of help. One neighbor took up a collection, and when she handed the money over to Jeannie, she said, "When they bombed the Graetz's [*sic*] they bombed us." Graetz writes, "With those simple words we knew we had been officially accepted as bona fide members of the African American community."[11]

As the sole White person in the leadership of the MIA, Graetz became a person of great interest to friend and foe alike. Reporters from the *Minneapolis Tribune* and magazines such as *Time* and *Life* sought him out for interviews. Agents from the FBI sought to enlist him to report on any subversive activities going on in the MIA; only much later did he realize that the FBI's real mission was to discredit the movement and Dr. King. He was also visited by Paul Simon, a reporter for a Lutheran newspaper, who later would become a US Senator from Illinois, and who remained a lifelong friend. However, local Whites were not so enamored. In addition to threatening phone calls and the bombings, he was often informed by friends that there were various groups plotting to chase him and his family out of town. Once an older White man actually came to their house and said that he and his neighbors had voted that he should leave town.

Despite the threats Graetz continued to serve as pastor and as secretary of the MIA. The MIA leaders debated among themselves whether to choose another target for desegregation, such as the local airport or whether to seek to integrate the local public parks and playgrounds.

[11] Graetz, *Message*, 99.

Violence was still a major issue, and the leaders lived under the constant threat of bombings and other attempts on their lives. But there were struggles within MIA as well. In fact in August 1956 Rev. Abernathy was attacked by one of his church members for allegedly having an affair with the man's wife. Abernathy survived the attack, and the charges were later dropped. These and other sorts of internal scandals only added to the stresses they faced from the surrounding community.

Graetz continued to be actively involved in MIA, and in March 1957 he was appointed to a committee charged with developing a plan for the improvement of the Black community. A year later they presented a ten-point plan that included initiatives for voter registration, desegregating the public schools, and allowing free access to public spaces such as parks and libraries. He also chaired the planning committee for MIA's annual Institute of Nonviolence and Social Change,[12] where the nonviolent Gandhian techniques used in the boycott could be shared with others. Because of these involvements, as well as all that they had been through and all the work yet to be done, Graetz and his wife anticipated that they would be in Montgomery for a long time.

However, in January 1958, Graetz was contacted by St. Philip Lutheran Church back in Columbus to consider a call to be their pastor. Because of his involvement during his seminary years, Graetz knew something of the church, but after going to Columbus to meet with church leaders, he felt convinced that God wanted him to stay in Montgomery. However, five months later, the bishop hand-delivered a letter from the church and urged him to prayerfully reconsider going to the Columbus church. Despite protests from his wife, Jeannie, who did not want to leave, in June 1958 Graetz decided to leave Montgomery and go to St. Philip; two months later, after the birth of their fifth child, they made the move.

Much had changed in the three years since he had come to Montgomery. Black people now sat wherever they wanted when they rode public transportation. Rosa Parks and her husband had moved to Detroit because both had been fired from their jobs as well as having their lives threatened. Some Black businesses had suffered as formerly all-White establishments opened their doors to Black folks. Graetz himself continued to be under threat from the local KKK and very likely would have had further attacks against him had he stayed. Even so, Graetz left knowing that he had been part of a historic series of events that would change the nation for years to come.

---

[12] The Martin Luther King Research and Education Institute, Institute of Nonviolence and Change, http://mlk-kpp01.stanford.edu.

Ministry in Columbus

In September 1958 Graetz began his ministry at St. Philip in Columbus. As they had done in Montgomery, the Graetz family chose to live in the African American community and send their children to predominantly Black schools. Graetz joined the local NAACP and participated in a variety of community groups designed to advocate for better relations between races and improved services in the Black community. Although there were no laws in Columbus mandating segregation, by custom and practice the separation of the races and disparity of services were similar to those in Montgomery. He became involved with efforts to challenge the practice of redlining, whereby bankers, real estate agents, and political leaders conspired to limit access of Blacks seeking to buy homes in predominantly White communities. This practice adversely affected the home values of Whites living in communities, while Blacks were often forced to pay inflated prices for homes whose value had dropped. However, instead of turning their anger at those who had manipulated the process, often White and Black homeowners blamed each other for their predicaments.[13]

Graetz focused much of his community efforts on desegregating the public schools in accordance with the 1954 *Brown v. Board of Education* Supreme Court decision. As a recognized civil rights leader, he was able to serve as an unofficial adviser to the members of the Columbus Board of Education, while also meeting with African American leaders staging protests. Graetz was often able to inform board members what the protesters' demands would be, and prepare them to make an appropriate response. Eventually the board created a racially inclusive Council on Intercultural Education, which was charged with designing the steps the city should take to desegregate its schools; Graetz was asked to serve in this group. The group took their charge seriously and interviewed local residents, educational experts, and school officials. They also held hearings in both White and Black schools, where they often became the target of parental fear and frustration. The council came back with an extensive list of recommendations with a plan to help the board take small but deliberate steps toward desegregation. Their report was received, the council dissolved, and their recommendations were shelved and ignored.

---

[13] When I moved to Boston in 1975 and then Jersey City, New Jersey, in 1981, the practice of redlining was still very much alive, although it had been outlawed. In Jersey City, my neighbor, a local banker, was actually indicted for his participation in a redlining scheme.

Only when a local group brought a lawsuit a few years later, was the board forced to enact the plan that had been given to them.

During his nine years at St. Philip, Graetz was often invited to speak at conferences and with groups within the Lutheran Church talking about his role in the Montgomery bus boycott and his insights on how the church might be more responsive to the issues being raised by the civil rights movement sweeping the nation. In 1963 he represented the Lutheran Church at the National Conference on Religion and Race where both Martin Luther King Jr. and Rabbi Abraham Joshua Heschel were speakers.[14] William Stringfellow, who had organized the event, shocked everyone with his analysis that their gathering was "too little, too late and too lily-White." Graetz returned to Columbus dedicated to making a positive difference by organizing a Columbus Conference on Religion and Race.

In 1963 Dr. King saw Graetz at a church conference in Chicago and urged him to attend the March on Washington that was being held two days later on August 28. Graetz quickly borrowed money for an airline ticket. What so impressed him about the march was not the great speeches (including King's "I Have a Dream" speech), but the thousands of people who poured into Washington from all over the country. Graetz later described the event in an article he wrote for the *Lutheran Standard*. Speaking of the 200,000 peaceful marchers he wrote:

> The spirit of victory filled their hearts—not that this demonstration marked the end of the struggle—on the contrary, there was a realization that this was the beginning of a massive campaign to eradicate the evil of racism in American life once and for all. Those gathered before the Lincoln Memorial on that day gave expression to their determination to keep pressing forward until the final victory was won.[15]

For Graetz, like so many others gathered that day, it was a day when hopes for racial justice seemed possible, even if they were still out of reach.

---

[14] See chapter 10 on Abraham Heschel; this is the same conference where Heschel and King first met and developed a close working relationship until the latter's death in 1968. In fact, Graetz tells the story of interacting one morning with an unnamed Jewish rabbi, who very well could have been Heschel. See Graetz, *Message*, 143.

[15] Graetz, *Message*, 145–46.

Sadly, eighteen days later, as he was preparing to lead a Sunday School class, he learned that four girls had been killed in a bombing at the Sixteenth Street Baptist Church in Birmingham. While a national travesty, the bombing was also a personal tragedy, because one of the girls killed was the daughter of one of Graetz's former parishioners at Trinity Lutheran. Columbus, like cities around the country, sponsored marches of protest that Graetz helped organize.

In March 1965 Graetz responded to a call issued by Dr. King for clergy of all denominations and religions to come to Selma, Alabama, to protest the killing of a voting rights worker and the actions of local and state police to prevent a march from Selma to Montgomery, calling for a change in the voting rights laws. Like people around the nation, he had been horrified at the images of marchers being bludgeoned and tear-gassed as they sought to cross the Edmund Pettus Bridge leading out of Selma. Graetz flew into Montgomery on a small charter plan through a thunderstorm to join the march on the last day, as it concluded on the steps of the state capitol. As he and the others de-planed, they were threatened with arrest but were able to get out of the airport without incident. This was the first time Graetz had returned to Montgomery since leaving, and the fears he had lived with during those three years came back to him. On the night of his arrival he walked through his old neighborhood with some friends and showed them the church he had pastored years before. The next day the march concluded with a rousing challenge to Governor George Wallace by Dr. King and others. However, the need for the ongoing struggle was impressed upon him when he learned that later that night a volunteer named Viola Liuzzo had been murdered on the road back to Selma.[16]

While Graetz continued to be involved in civil rights activities on both the local and national levels, his main responsibilities centered on his pastoral duties at St. Philip. During his nine years as pastor, the church grew from 170 to 700 members. Additions were made to the building, and the ministry in the community flourished. Meanwhile, the Graetz family continued to grow, as they gave birth to two more children, their sixth and seventh.

Washington and Beyond

In 1967 Graetz was called to take part in an experimental ministry being initiated in the African American community of northeastern Washington, DC. The purpose of "Lutheran Mission 373," as it came to

[16] See chapter 13 on Viola Liuzzo.

be called, was to combine the efforts of a pastor, a social worker, and a community organizer to identify and address the needs of that community. Because of his extensive work in African American congregations, Graetz was selected to fill the pastoral role. As the work progressed, the team realized that northeast DC was well organized and that their efforts might better be focused on the northwest section of the city. So he found himself working in both communities in a variety of capacities.

While working in Washington, on April 4, 1968, Graetz learned that Dr. King had been shot in Memphis. As in cities across the country, riots erupted in DC. Soldiers patrolled the streets of his neighborhood and surveilled from rooftops; people were not allowed out of their homes to do even the most mundane tasks like shopping for food. Graetz and others went about handing out bags of food at the local Lutheran church. While he was deeply saddened by Dr. King's death, he was not surprised. Ever since the bombings in Montgomery, Graetz knew that King lived under a constant threat of death that eventually would be fulfilled. He also understood the rage in the Black community, which despite Supreme Court decisions and congressional legislation had yet to see the promise of justice and equality realized.

Just weeks before King's death, Graetz had offered to help in the efforts to plan a Poor People's Campaign, with the hope of bringing a large number of people to demand action by the federal government to address the causes of poverty. The idea was to first seek to work with legislators and then, if necessary, to engage in massive actions of civil disobedience and nonviolent direct action. Although plans were initially set aside to mourn Dr. King's death, by the end of April Ralph Abernathy and other SCLC leaders had begun to organize "wagon trains" of people from all over the country making their way to Washington. Graetz joined with other local clergy to prepare to meet the physical needs of the thousands set to arrive that summer. In July he helped organize a contingent of clergy wearing their clerical garb who packed the gallery of the House of Representatives demanding that Congress take action on legislation concerning jobs, housing, and health care.

On June 19 50,000 people congregated on the Washington Mall to construct "Resurrection City." However, soon some of the demonstrators turned violent as rain poured down on the encampment, dampening the already despairing spirits. Some of the movement's leaders abandoned the project, and, though well-intentioned, the campaign became an object of ridicule and derision. As a final insult Congress resisted passing any of the legislation that had been proposed and demanded.

By 1970 the Lutheran Church had decided that Lutheran Mission 373 was not worth continuing and informed Graetz that he needed to seek other employment. For a brief time he served as the interim pastor of a local Lutheran church. However, in October of that year, he accepted a position with the Ohio Council of Churches as the director of their Ecumenical Commission on Church and Government, which necessitated the Graetz family returning to Columbus.

Upon their return, the Graetz family faced a unique challenge. All through his time in Columbus and Washington, DC, the Graetz children had attended the local public schools, in which they had been a racial minority in predominantly Black schools. At times this had presented challenges, especially as the Black Power movement grew, and efforts were made to separate Blacks and Whites as a way of strengthening Black solidarity. Even so, living in the African American community had been the norm for the Graetz children all through their childhood. Upon returning to Columbus, Graetz did not think it wise for them to live in proximity to St. Philip since he did not want to distract from the work of the pastor who had replaced him.[17] So, for the first time since moving to Montgomery, the Graetz family moved into a predominantly White community, which in a way was a bit of "reverse culture shock" for them. Despite fears that they would encounter the kind of vicious White racism they had experience in the South, they were pleasantly surprised to learn that "not all White people are bad."

Graetz worked for the Council of Churches from 1970 to 1983 in a full-time and later a part-time position. His job involved lobbying state legislators on issues of importance to the religious community. In particular he worked diligently for the state to establish a Martin Luther King Day holiday and for passage of the Equal Rights Amendment; the former effort succeeded, but the latter did not. In 1973 he entertained an opportunity to return to pastoral ministry but was convinced to stay with the Council of Churches. For a brief time in 1976 he toyed with the idea of running for public office, but then realized he did not have the stomach for political haggling and deal making. However, while still working in Columbus, he and Jeannie bought a house in a rural area sixty miles away, and settled into a very different kind of life in a home they called "Promised Land." In 1983 he resigned from his job with the

[17] The decision to not return to one's former church is standard among most pastors in mainline White denominations. The thinking is that the presence of the former pastor might cause division in the church and undermine the current pastor's ability to lead.

Council and became the part-time pastor of a church in Logan, Ohio, near his home where he served until his retirement in 1995.

Expanding Civil Rights Activism

During his time at the Council of Churches, Graetz and his wife began to expand their concerns about discrimination to the plight of gays and lesbians. They had known since his childhood that their second child and oldest son, Robert, was gay. For years Graetz had struggled with the tension between the teachings of his Lutheran theology and his love for his son. On a trip in the late 1980s to visit "Ray" (as he came to call himself) they joined him at a worship service at the Metropolitan Community Church, a denomination that had been started by and for members of the gay and lesbian community. Their experience of love and acceptance by the members of the congregation, coupled with their love for their son, caused them to reconsider their previously held beliefs. Graetz writes: "We had come full circle. No longer suspicious. No longer judging, no longer doubting, we could love our son unconditionally."[18]

Sadly, in 1991 Ray succumbed to the HIV/AIDS virus that was decimating the gay community. His death moved them to actively participate in the AIDS Quilt Movement that was gathering momentum across the country and create a panel in memory of their son. They later became acquainted with Mel White, a gay Christian minister and founder of Soulforce, an organization dedicated to raising awareness about gay issues in the Christian community. In May 2000, Graetz and his wife joined hundreds of others in Cleveland for a Soulforce action at a Methodist Church convention that led nearly two hundred people, including the two of them, to be arrested for civil disobedience actions.

An Ongoing Advocate

To this day Robert Graetz continues to speak about his experiences in the civil rights movement and the unfinished task of securing racial justice in the United States. In 1996 beginning with a group of students from the school where one of his sons had become a teacher, Graetz began leading trips to visit the historic sites of the civil rights movement. After many years being involved in the life of their community in southern Ohio, in 2008 Graetz and his wife moved back to Montgomery

[18] Graetz, *Message*, 204.

where they are actively involved in civic activities, including a group called One Montgomery, which seeks to promote understanding and trust between people of different racial and cultural groups by offering a monthly discussion group open to the public.[19]

On Martin Luther King Day 1998 Robert Graetz was invited to speak in Birmingham on the thirty-fifth anniversary of the Birmingham campaign. Graetz began his speech by telling his story and his own awakening to the reality of racial injustice and how that eventually led him to Montgomery and involvement in the bus boycott. He went on to say that despite the fact that he himself had worked for racial justice all of his adult life, as a White person he recognized that he had been granted privileges and advantages transferred to him because of the centuries of slavery and discrimination against African Americans. As he described the litany of injustices, he confessed his participation in the sins of racism. He then said: "I am sorry. I am sorry what my people did to your people. I need to ask for your forgiveness." Soon members of the audience were shouting out, "I forgive you."

In the speech he went on to describe what it means to be an ally. "If we who are white confess our guilt that is associated with that whiteness, then it is incumbent upon you who are black to forgive us and to accept us as part of your family. We need you to recognize that not all white people are alike. Some of us are truly your allies. But we cannot work with you in a productive way until you have accepted us as your sisters and brothers, as we must also reach out to you as our sisters and brothers."[20] Graetz does not believe that racial reconciliation can be secured through words alone, no matter how sincere. He recognizes how the history of racism has created a huge gap of access and opportunity between Whites and Blacks in this country. For that reason, he believes there needs to be some kind of reparations, although he is not sure what form those reparations should take. Throughout his life, Robert Graetz Jr. has sought to be a bridge builder: from his efforts in college to start a Race Relations Club to his involvement in the Montgomery bus boycott to his efforts in the Lutheran Church and the wider religious community. Well past his "retirement," Robert Graetz Jr. continues to speak and act in an effort to build the bridge between races that has yet to be fully constructed.

---

[19] Wikipedia, "One Montgomery," http://en.wikipedia.org.

[20] Graetz, *Message*, 235.

Discussion Questions

1. At critical junctures in his life, Robert Graetz Jr. made choices that allied himself with the suffering of the Black community. What opportunities exist today to ally ourselves with people suffering oppression and racism?
2. How do you respond to Graetz's confession and request for forgiveness? What must White people do to contribute toward the process of racial reconciliation and justice in the United States?

Bibliography

Branch, Taylor. *Parting the Waters: America in the King Years, 1954–1958*. New York: Simon and Schuster, 1988.

Graetz, Robert, Jr. *Montgomery: A White Preacher's Memoir*. Minneapolis: Fortress Press, 1991.

———. *A White Preacher's Message on Race and Reconciliation*. Montgomery, AL: New South Books, 2006.

Hare, Kenneth M. *They Walked to Freedom 1955–56: The Story of the Montgomery Bus Boycott*. Champaign, IL: Spotlight Press, 2005.

The Martin Luther King Research and Education Institute. Institute of Nonviolence and Change. http://mlk-kpp01.stanford.edu.

Wikipedia. "One Montgomery." http://en.wikipedia.org.

Contemporary White Allies

15

Morris Dees (1936–)

*Lawyer on the Offense**

A Foiled Assassination

In May 1984 a small group of White supremacists called The Order gathered in Boise, Idaho, to plan an assassination. According to the White supremacist "bible" called *The Turner Diaries*, assassinations are necessary to incite revolution. Leading the meeting was thirty-one-year-old Robert Matthews, who had formed The Order in September 1983. He pulled out a slip of paper with names of three possible targets: television producer Norman Lear, Denver radio talk show host Alan Berg, and Morris Dees, lawyer and founder of the Southern Poverty Law Center.

One month later on June 18, 1984, as Alan Berg was pulling a grocery bag out of his car parked in his driveway, Matthews and another man jumped out of a vehicle across the street and fired several shots into Berg, who fell to the ground and died instantly. A can of dog food rolled down the driveway as the two assailants and their driver drove off.

In August Robert Matthews met with two leaders of the Carolina Knights of the Ku Klux Klan (CKKKK) in the small town of Angier, North Carolina. At the time the two CKKKK leaders, Glenn Miller and Stephen Miller (no relation to each other), were involved in a trial in which Dees was representing the family of a young boy who had been brutally tortured and murdered by some Klansman connected to the CKKKK. The agenda of the meeting was simple: to put in motion a plan to kidnap, torture,

---

* Photo of Morris Dees used by permission of Southern Poverty Law Project and Morris Dees. All information in this chapter, unless otherwise noted, comes from Morris Dees and Steve Fiffer, *A Lawyer's Journey: The Morris Dees Story* (Chicago: American Bar Association, 2001).

and kill Morris Dees. On Christmas Eve 1984 guards hired to protect Dees and his family flushed out gunmen in the grass around his spacious farmhouse outside of Montgomery, Alabama. Gunshots were fired, but no one was hurt. Dees himself ran out searching for the assailants, but they got away. The assassination attempt failed, but over the years at least thirty different people have been arrested in conjunction with plots to kill Dees or bomb the Southern Poverty Law Center buildings.

Who is Morris Dees that people would go to such great lengths to assassinate him? Why is he so despised by White supremacist and hate groups, as well as many conservative talk show hosts? What has he done to provoke such hostility and ire?

Early Years on the Farm

From his background, one would not predict that Morris Dees, who was called "Bubba" by his friends, would become a prominent civil rights lawyer and target of right-wing hate groups. He was born on December 16, 1936, in the rural Alabama town of Mt. Meigs, to Morris and Annie Ruth Dees. He grew up on the farm where his father raised cotton on rented land that was part of a larger estate. His father eventually partnered with a couple of other businessmen to purchase a cotton gin, which enabled them to move to a larger rented house on another estate. Eventually, his father saved enough money to buy his own land, so the family moved again. Despite the relative success, farming was still a difficult way to make a living, so the family always lived on the edge of debt and poverty.

Like all farming operations in this time, the Dees farm was a family affair, and so the younger Morris spent many summers in the fields picking cotton alongside the White and Black hands hired to harvest the crop. Like his father, Dees interacted freely with the Black farmers and workers in the area. While working in the cotton fields, he learned the Negro spirituals being sung by the workers.

As was customary with many families in the Deep South, the Dees family belonged to the local Baptist church. Since it was located in a remote rural location, the congregation only had a preacher from the city come out to speak to them once a month. The rest of the time the congregation ran its own affairs. Consequently, Morris's introduction to religion came largely through his third grade Sunday School teacher, who also happened to be his teacher at the local public school. He counted her as his primary influence outside of his family. Because of her he became quite knowledgeable about the Bible, and by the time he was in high school began to think he wanted to become a preacher.

However, his father always wanted him to be a lawyer. When Dees was sixteen, his father sent him on an errand to impress upon him why effective lawyers were so necessary. He sent his son into town to advocate for a Black man who had been wrongly arrested by a state trooper for driving while intoxicated. Because the man worked on the Dees farm, and they knew him to be a hardworking, teetotaling father of nine children, they assumed the charges were a form of the harassment regularly endured by Black residents at the hands of the local White police officers. So Morris went before the judge fully expecting to set the matter right. Despite making a strong argument for the man's innocence, he lost the case, and when he shared his frustration, his father told him that the judge earned his fees only when a guilty verdict was rendered. His father's lesson was simple: justice was secondary to profit. Dees's father used this experience to show how being a lawyer might enable him to challenge and change the unjust practices of the Jim Crow South.

However, this experience also illustrates the kind of "White moderate" environment in which Dees was raised. On a personal level his father treated everyone fairly and respectfully regardless of race, so much so that his father's brother, Uncle Lucien, called him a "nigger lover." Moreover, he demanded that his workers be treated with respect. Morris learned the hard way how deep his father's commitment to respect of all persons was when he called one of the African Americans on the farm a "black nigger." Following that comment he received "the first whipping of [his] life." As indicated in the case of the unjustly treated worker, the elder Dees also recognized the basic unfairness of the Jim Crow system. In a similar way, his mother felt her Christian faith required her to be kind to all persons regardless of race. She had grown up in a home with an outwardly racist father who belonged to the Ku Klux Klan and sought to consciously treat Blacks differently from the way she had been raised to do. Among the Black folks in the area she was known as "Miss Annie Ruth" because she never hesitated to help someone in need, Black or White. Yet their kindness and concern on an individual level was never translated into actions against or speaking out against the unjust system they knew was there.

From his work in the fields Dees earned about three dollars a day, which he carefully saved. To earn more money he picked up and recycled old Coke bottles from the side of the road, delivered newspapers, sold fruits, and did odd jobs. When he became a teenager, his father gave him a small plot of land on which to grow vegetables. The entrepreneurial Dees used the produce from that plot to start a business selling his vegetables until he had earned enough to buy a calf. He then mated the calf with one of his father's bulls, and soon he had developed small herd of cattle. Later he purchased pigs and chickens, which along with the cows raised for slaughter, earned him even more money. Fearing that his son would be looked down upon for his enterprising ways, his father chastised him for "always selling something." In that small town society where a man's image was critical to his standing in the community, his actions had tarnished his father's public image. Having a son who was always seemed to be hustling to make a dollar, the elder Dees feared people would think his son was forced to work in order to supplement the family income. However, his father's warnings did not slow the younger Dees down, and in fact his early sales experiences turned out to be only the first of many money-making schemes he would develop in college and beyond.

Marriage, College, and Fleeting Awareness

In the spring of 1955 while he was still in high school, he married his high school sweetheart, Beverly Crum. That summer the new couple entered the University of Alabama with its Whites-only student body. That same week in neighboring Mississippi a fourteen-year-old boy named Emmett Till was brutally lynched by two White men on August 28, 1955, for allegedly speaking to a White woman. Although Dees did not speak of Till's death until years later, the racist brutality of that murder affected him deeply.

The year before he entered college the Supreme Court had handed down the *Brown v. Board of Education* decision, which effectively outlawed racial segregation in all public institutions. Based on that landmark decision, a 1956 federal court ordered the University of Alabama to admit an African American student named Autherine Lucy. On the day Lucy attempted to register for classes school authorities warned students to remain in their dorm rooms. Dees watched from his dorm window as an angry mob of nearly a thousand Whites yelled, "Nigger, go home," when Lucy, accompanied by a local Roman Catholic priest, drove up to enroll at the school. This was the first time Dees had seen the KKK and its ilk in action. Although the experience did not shake his belief in segregation, the crowd's vitriol made him nauseous. On the Sunday following the incident, good Southern moderates Dees and his wife spoke to their Married Couples Sunday School class about the discrepancy between the Christian teaching to love all people and the kind of hateful action they had witnessed on campus. Having heard of his speech to the class, the church's pastor, apparently not convinced the Christian gospel called for moderation in matters of race, relieved the Dees of their roles as class leaders, saying the church wanted to take the class "in a new direction." Needless to say, Autherine Lucy was not enrolled at the University of Alabama either.

While he sometimes was moved to speak up after events like Autherine Lucy's victimization, he was far from being the civil rights activist he would later become. He was generally oblivious to the events and changes taking place all around him, even though his hometown of Montgomery became the epicenter of the burgeoning civil rights movement in 1955. Dees admitted: "Although the birth of the modern civil rights movement took place in my backyard, I didn't pay much attention to it. The 381-day Bus boycott . . . passed me by completely."[1] Overly focused on his career advancement and family concerns, the awareness and activism that would come to characterize his life occurred much later.

A Successful Business and Personal Changes

In fact Dees spent much of his free time in college coming up with ways to make money. He teamed up with a fellow student named Millard Fuller, and together they developed the "'Bama Birthday Cake Service," whereby parents could order cakes on special occasions to deliver to their children who were students. While still students, Dees and Fuller spawned several other businesses and even bought some buildings, all of which they eventually sold to other students. Like Dees, Fuller had grown up on an Alabama farm with a father who wanted a better life for his son. The two shared an interest in politics as well as business, and became inseparable, attended law school together, and upon graduation jointly developed a successful mail-order cookbook business.

While the business was his main preoccupation, occasionally Dees practiced law on the side. One of his early cases occurred in 1961 and involved defending Claude Henley, a White man who had assaulted a news reporter covering the Freedom Riders. The Freedom Riders were thirteen Black and White students who attempted to ride a commercial bus from Washington, DC, to New Orleans for the expressed purpose of challenging the segregated bathrooms and waiting rooms in Southern

[1] Ibid., 78.

city bus stations. When the Freedom Riders arrived in Montgomery (having already been severely attacked in nearby Anniston), they were accosted by a screaming, club-wielding crowd of about a thousand Whites who beat them while the police passively looked on.[2] Henley, a pot-bellied, cigar-smoking used-car salesman was photographed by a *Life* magazine photographer as he kicked and beat a newsman covering the event. Though Henley was charged both in a federal lawsuit and a criminal charge of assault, he got off with a mild injunction to refrain from any further mob actions.

For representing Henley, Dees earned the hefty fee of $5,000. As he walked out of the courtroom, he was met by two Black men, who questioned why he was willing to defend someone who had obviously been involved in denying African Americans their basic civil rights. Dees was taken aback by their words and realized that although he counted several Black people as his friends and saw himself as basically a decent Christian person, in defending Henley he had transgressed his own moral values. That brief encounter was a turning point, and after that he vowed to never again take cases that ran contrary to his basic beliefs and values.

Despite these few forays into law, Dees focused on the business of publishing and marketing recipe books and other mail-order items. The joint venture with Fuller was extremely profitable and made both of them quite wealthy. However, Fuller had been questioning his values and direction in life, and so in 1965 he left the business, leaving Dees solely in charge, and joined Clarence Jordan and Koinonia Farm in south Georgia.[3] While at Koinonia Millard Fuller founded Habitat for Humanity, a nonprofit organization that enabled poor people with the help of volunteers to build and own their own homes. (Fuller served as executive director of Habitat until his death in 2009.) Around the same time, Dees divorced his wife, Beverly, with whom he had raised two sons. Shortly thereafter, he married a woman in his company named Maureen Buck. When Beverly moved to Louisville, their two children continued to live with him, along with Maureen's two children by a previous marriage; subsequently Dees and Maureen had a child together, so there were five children in the household. These changes in his life reflected and foreshadowed deeper personal changes that had been brewing in his consciousness in ways that would transform his life.

---

[2] For a full history of the Freedom rides, see Raymond Arsenault. *Freedom Riders: 1961 and the Struggle for Racial Justice* (New York: Oxford University Press, 2006); also see chapter 8 for Virginia Durr's experience of the same event.

[3] For more on Millard Fuller and Koinonia, see chapter 11 on Clarence Jordan.

A Rising Consciousness

Like most White Alabamans, Dees had grown up without questioning the segregationist practices of the Jim Crow South. He espoused the respect and fair treatment of Blacks that he had learned from watching his parents, and he held to his Baptist upbringing that Christians were supposed to love all people. However, until his commitment to fairness had been challenged by the onlookers at the Claude Henley trial, he had never seriously questioned the injustices and inequity built into the Jim Crow system. Like many "White moderates," he held naively to the idea that Blacks and Whites would gradually come to a place of reconciliation, and all that was needed was patience.

His belief in slow progress was shaken on September 15, 1963, when four African American girls preparing to lead the youth service were killed as a bomb went off in the Sixteenth Street Baptist Church in Birmingham, Alabama. It was later was determined that the bomb had been planted by members of the local KKK. On the following Sunday, Dees stood up in front of the small rural Baptist congregation of which he was a member and invited the people in the congregation, many of whom were people he had grown up with, to join him in taking up a collection to help rebuild the Birmingham church. Dees later wrote that the congregation "quickly fell into two camps—those who were angered by the suggestion and those who were too shocked to be angry."[4] When he realized that there were no respondents to his call for financial support, he invited folks to join him for a time of prayer between the worship service and Sunday School. Dees wrote: "My words hit their frozen hearts and fell to the floor. Head bowed, I prayed silently." When he looked up, everyone had left the sanctuary.[5] From that point on Dees knew his life had to change.

Two years later (March 1965) Dees and Fuller joined several thousand civil rights marchers as they completed the five-day, fifty-mile trek from Selma to Montgomery, and then listened to a stirring address by Dr. Martin Luther King Jr. on the steps of the Alabama state capitol building calling for full voting rights for Black citizens across the South. Earlier in the week Dees and Fuller had served as volunteers driving people from the Montgomery airport to Selma to take part in the march. As he drove past state troopers along the road on one of those trips, he recognized some of them as friends of his family. He realized

---

[4] Dees and Fiffer, *Lawyer's Journey*, 87.

[5] Ibid.

that these were the same men who only two weeks earlier had beaten the marchers on "Bloody Sunday" as they crossed the Edmund Pettus Bridge leading out of Selma; ironically a court order now required them to protect the same marchers they had beaten. As Dees walked with the crowd on the final stage of the march onto the steps of the state capitol in Montgomery, on the side of the road he spotted his Uncle James, who screamed: "You're nothing but a bunch of nigger lovers. I oughta take this gun and kill you both here on the spot."[6] Afterward, as his involvement in the march became known throughout the city, he became the target of several other disparaging remarks and found himself disinvited from many of the Whites-only social functions and clubs which had previously been open to him.

Shortly after the incident in the Baptist church, he and his wife began attending a Unitarian Fellowship that seemed to practice justice as well as preach it. Through connections in the church, Dees got involved with the local chapter of the American Civil Liberties Union (ACLU), which gave him the opportunity to occasionally do legal work on local civil rights cases. However, the demands of running a business, especially after Fuller left for Koinonia, made it difficult for him to give a lot of time to this work.

Yet that was soon to change. On a business trip to Chicago in February 1968 he bought a paperback copy of Clarence Darrow's biography, *The Story of My Life*. Dees stayed up all night reading the book, and when he was finished, he felt his life had "changed forever." Like Darrow, he realized that his deepest sympathies were with the poor, marginalized, and suffering people of society. Like Darrow, he often found himself challenging the dominant worldview of the people around him. Like Darrow, he was involved in business. However, unlike Dees, Darrow had broken away from his corporate law practice, in order to try cases that aligned with his deepest values. So on his way back from Chicago, Dees decided to set in motion a process to sell his company so he too could follow his passion and specialize in civil rights law.

As serendipity would have it, when he returned to his office in Montgomery, there was a message from Fred Gray, a Black lawyer who had defended Rosa Parks and Martin Luther King Jr. during the bus boycott and who had become one of the most prominent civil rights lawyers in the state. Gray asked Dees to assist him in a lawsuit filed by the Alabama State Teachers Association, an all-Black organization, seeking to block Auburn University from building a campus in Montgomery. The

[6] Ibid., 92.

suit alleged that if the expansion was allowed to go through, it would perpetuate racial segregation on college campuses by undercutting the previously all-Black Alabama State (located in Montgomery) that at the time was seeking to attract White students. Though the three-judge panel ruled in favor of Auburn, this case inducted Dees into the world of civil rights law that would consume him for the rest of his career.

Complex negotiations required that Dees continue to run his business, while still practicing law until 1970. However, in that year the sale of his business was complete, and a new career and chapter in his life began.

Early Cases

One of his earliest cases occurred in 1969 while he was still untangling himself from his business, and involved the Montgomery YMCA. In the wake of the 1956 federal court injunction banning segregation on all public buses, the city commissioners of Montgomery passed ordinances banning African Americans from using parks, pools, and other public spaces designated as "Whites only." Members of the Montgomery Improvement Association (the organization responsible for the bus boycott) filed a suit alleging that the segregation policy violated the US Constitution.[7] Before the case was decided (which the plaintiffs eventually won), the city of Montgomery responded by closing all its public facilities to both Blacks and Whites, going so far as to bulldoze the city's fourteen public swimming pools. In a secret deal that was to become public through Dees's efforts, the city then redirected its public recreation funds to the YMCA, which in effect became the entity responsible for the city's recreational programs. However, because the YMCA ostensibly was a privately funded organization, it was allowed to admit or exclude anyone it chose to, and thereby was not bound by federal antisegregation laws. At the time the YMCA operated eight different facilities around the city, and only one was designated as "Black."

Dees invited Fred Gray, who had called on him earlier, to assist in a case involving two seven-year-old African American cousins (Vincent and Edward Smith), who had not been allowed to enroll in the YMCA summer camp closest to their home. The plaintiffs alleged that the boys were rejected for being Black and that therefore the YMCA was violating the Civil Rights Act of 1964 that asserted that no one could be discriminated against on the basis of race. Because the YMCA was private, and

---

[7] Robert Graetz, whose story is told in chapter 14, was actively involved as a member of the MIA in the efforts to desegregate all the public spaces in Montgomery.

because he was not aware of the secret deal between the city and the YMCA, Dees hoped only to make the case more of a media event that would shine a negative light on the YMCA and the city; he did not think they could actually win the case. As the case proceeded, Dees discovered that there was a concerted effort by some of his former high school classmates to defame and discredit him in the public eye. This tactic of intimidation was one of the most common and often effective ways in which moderate Whites in the South were kept from "stepping out of line"; however, it only made Dees more determined to pursue justice.

During their research in preparation for the trial, Dees and his team accidentally discovered a document from 1958 detailing the contract that had appointed the YMCA to run the city's recreational programs and that public funds were to be diverted for that purpose. Because this was legal documentation of a formal (though secret) arrangement between the YMCA and the city, it meant that the YMCA was required to follow federal law regarding segregation. When news of the secret deal was made public, the YMCA quickly settled and agreed to integrate all of its facilities in accordance with the law.

For Dees, this case had a deeply personal dimension in that the executive director of YMCA, a man named Bill Chandler, was someone Dees had known and respected for a long time. The case compelled Dees to publicly confront his friend, whom he described as a "good Christian" and a decent human being. Although following the settlement Chandler expressed strong animosity toward Dees and had even participated in the effort to discredit him, years later he personally thanked Dees for forcing him and the YMCA board to do the right thing.

The Southern Poverty Law Center

In 1969 Dees formed a partnership with Joe Levin, a lawyer with whom he had worked on other civil rights cases. From the beginning, as a matter of policy the firm of Levin & Dees charged clients who could afford their fees while offering their services without charge to those who could not. Several of their early cases focused on issues involving freedom of speech, women's rights, and rights for racial minorities. They also decided to turn their law practice into a nonprofit corporation, trusting in Dees's ability to raise necessary funds. Consequently, in 1971 Levin & Dees became the Southern Poverty Law Center (SPLC), and the noted civil rights activist Julian Bond agreed to be the first chairman of the board. From the beginning their goal was to use innovative legal strategies to fight the effects of poverty and to promote education on various racial and justice issues. Their strategy was to choose cases that could establish important legal precedents for basic civil and human rights, which in turn could lead to broad-based legal changes. Levin and Dees served as co-directors in the first few years, but eventually Levin left to run his own private practice in the mid-1970s, and Dees became the sole director.

The SPLC docket included a wide variety of cases. In 1972 they successfully challenged a redistricting plan established by the Alabama legislature designed to divide the votes of African Americans, thereby keeping any Black politicians from getting elected to public office. In 1974 they were able to free three Black men in Tarboro, North Carolina, who had been given death sentences for raping a White woman, proving that in fact no rape had occurred. In a high-profile 1975 trial they successfully acquitted a Black female inmate named Joanne Little who had killed her White jailer when he tried to rape her in her cell.

In accord with his early commitment to act according to his values, Dees litigated these cases because of his basic commitment to fairness and justice. For instance, his initial reason for taking the Tarboro case was that he opposed the North Carolina law that made the death penalty an automatic sentence for rape cases. Likewise, in the Joanne Little trial he was motivated by his belief in the right of a woman to defend herself against sexual predators. He further believed that conditions in many prisons were inhumane, and that in many states the death penalty was used in a discriminatory way against People of Color.

Taking on the KKK

After Levin left the practice, Dees and the board of SPLC added a new dimension to their work when they decided to specifically focus on cases involving the terrorist activities of the KKK. In 1981 SPLC created a program called Klanwatch, which was specifically designed to monitor the activities of White supremacist groups in the United States, especially various regional branches of the KKK. Their first Klan case focused on a group of Vietnamese fishermen in the Galveston, Texas, area who were being threatened by members of the Texas Knights of the Ku Klux Klan (TKKKK). Members of the TKKKK had told the Vietnamese to get out of the fishing industry or suffer the consequences. These recently arrived refugees made up only a small percentage of all shrimpers fishing in Galveston Bay and did not pose an economic threat to their White counterparts.

However, when one of their boats was set on fire, they understandably felt vulnerable and made arrangements to shut down their operations. Hearing of their plight, Dees offered to plead their cause so they could stay in business. Recently escaped from the trauma of the Vietnam War and hoping to start a new life in a new country, the Vietnamese fishermen became increasingly hesitant as the threats and intimidation continued. Dees called a meeting of the elders of the community and was able to convince them to see the case through. Eventually with Dees's help the Vietnamese won a court injunction against the TKKKK and were able to continue their fishing work without further intimidation. However, this case put Dees on the KKK's list of "enemies."

In 1983 SPLC took on the case of Bobby Person, an African American, North Carolina prison guard who was threatened by the local KKK when he applied for a promotion. In this case Dees faced two infamous White supremacists, Glenn Miller and Stephen Miller (not related, and mentioned above), who headed up the Carolina Knights of the Ku Klux Klan (CKKKK). Through an arduous process of investigation, Dees and his associates discovered a whole network of illegal Klan activity that existed throughout the state, and eventually the Millers decided to settle the case rather than go to court. One of the key revelations unearthed in the investigation was that the CKKKK was training its members to overthrow the US government and establish a new country or state for Whites only. Thus, key elements of the settlement mandated that the CKKKK cease to operate as an organization and that the Millers no longer be involved in offensive paramilitary training practices. However, shortly after the case had been settled, the Millers started a new organization called the White Patriots Party, which held weekend military training sessions led by army officers from nearby Fort Bragg. Dees was able to prove that this activity was in direct violation of the previous settlement, and so the Millers were eventually convicted and sentenced to prison in 1985.

At the same time the Bobby Person case was going on, Dees and the SPLC got involved with a lawsuit against the United Klans of America (UKA). The UKA had been implicated but never convicted in numerous acts of racial violence over the years, including the beating of Freedom Riders in 1961, the bombing of the Sixteenth Street Baptist Church in Birmingham, the murders of Viola Liuzzo and Rev. James Reeb in conjunction with the march from Selma to Montgomery,[8] and the attempted murder of the director of the Birmingham NAACP. In 1983 the UKA was implicated in the murder of a fourteen-year-old African

[8] For the story of Viola Liuzzo, see chapter 13.

American boy named Michael Donald from Mobile, Alabama, who had been abducted and lynched by three Klansman "simply because he was black." Michael Donald's death was a response to a case in which a court had rendered a "no decision" in the case of a Black man accused of murdering a White man; in response the UKA wanted to display their "disgust with blacks" by "hanging a nigger,"[9] who unfortunately turned out to be Michael Donald.

In conjunction with Michael Donald's grieving mother, Dees brought a lawsuit against the UKA with the objective of putting the organization permanently out of business by getting the court to issue a financial penalty so high they would not be able to pay. After a four-year process that involved not only investigating the Mobile murder, but also the Liuzzo and Reeb murders, Beulah McDonald, Michael's mother, won a $7 million settlement against the UKA. However, because the case had bankrupted the organization as planned, in reality she only received the UKA's building, which she sold for about $50,000. Additionally, several key UKA leaders were put in jail, and the UKA, the largest KKK organization at the time, was put out of business.

In 1983 while these cases were going on, the offices of SPLC were burned when three members of the local Montgomery KKK, working under direction of national KKK leaders, entered the building through a sewer tunnel, doused the offices with gasoline, and set the building on fire. When asked later why they did it, the assailants said that they wanted to destroy key files because "Dees was aggravating the hell out of [them]."[10] While the building was destroyed and had to be rebuilt, the important files on KKK activities had been locked in a fireproof file case and were preserved. During this same period, the assassination plot mentioned at the beginning of this chapter was launched and successfully contravened. Despite these threats, through the 1990s Dees continued to take on and win significant cases against various branches of the Klan, but to this day he travels with bodyguards and keeps his house under constant security.

Ironically, throughout these ordeals Dees refrained from demonizing his adversaries and rather chose to see them as fatally flawed but not inherently evil individuals. For example, following the meeting where the settlement with the CKKKK was reached, he asked one of the defendants, Glenn Miller, for a ride to the airport. He even joked with Miller, asking how he could believe in the superiority of the Aryan race when he had brown hair

[9] Dees and Fiffer, *Lawyer's Journey*, 211–12.

[10] Ibid., 225.

and black eyes. Drawing on his Baptist background, Dees even sought to "convert" Miller, asking him to consider changing his violent racist ways. As Dees stepped out of the car, Miller told him he liked him as a person and warned him that people were out to kill him. This was not the last time Dees faced Miller in court, and eventually Miller was sent to jail, but Dees never ceased to see Miller and those like him as human beings in need of change, rather than devils beyond hope of transformation.

The SPLC Today

Since its inception, the SPLC under Dees's leadership has litigated civil rights cases of various kinds. In the beginning, most of the cases involved racially based injustices. In more recent years they have also taken on cases involving the rights of gays and lesbians, as well as litigating organizations that have taken advantage of undocumented immigrants. Klanwatch, which changed its name in 1998 to The Intelligence Project, has expanded its focus beyond White supremacist groups to various forms of "hate groups," which it defines as groups that "have beliefs or practices that attack or malign an entire class of people, typically for their immutable characteristics."[11] On their list of groups are included not only White supremacist groups but also antigay and Black separatist groups like the New Black Panthers and the Nation of Islam. Also included are paramilitary militias and nativist groups that attack immigrants (most often of Latino origin). In 2012 SPLC listed nearly two thousand such organizations throughout the United States and noted that since the election of President Barack Obama, there has been a 50 percent rise in hate groups.[12]

In 1991 SPLC initiated "Teaching Tolerance," a program that provides materials for teachers and students on developing tolerance and acceptance for people of different races, genders, cultures, orientations, and physical abilities. Materials are provided free of charge to teachers, and programs are designed to bring diverse groups of students together to learn to interact constructively across difference. In 2012 Teaching Tolerance was honored by the National Association for Multicultural Education for its work in helping children "appreciate and respect differences."[13]

[11] From SPLC website, http://www.splcenter.org.

[12] Morris Dees, Presentation at the University of Michigan Martin Luther King Symposium, January 21, 2013, http://www.youtube.com.

[13] See http://www.splcenter.org.

On the site of the former offices destroyed by fire, SPLC now operates a visitor center that seeks to highlight its work and educate the public on activities of hate groups. Across the street from the visitor center now sits a tall glass building with a state-of-the-art security system that serves as the organization's headquarters. In 1989 a Civil Rights Memorial was dedicated, which lists the names of people who were killed for their work during the civil rights movement and evokes the words often quoted by Dr. Martin Luther King Jr. from the biblical book of Amos: "Let justice roll down like waters, and righteousness like an ever flowing stream."[14]

Controversies

Morris Dees continues to be a controversial figure. A simple Google search will reveal any number of Dees's critics, from conservative commentators who accuse SPLC of being a "hate group" itself to various religious and political groups opposed to gay rights and gay marriage. For instance, in 2010, SPLC added the Family Research Council (FRC) to its list of hate groups because of public statements that were made calling for homosexual behavior to be outlawed. FRC responded by calling SPLC "reckless" for its statements, and accused SPLC of demonizing conservative political groups. The SPLC director, Mark Ogden, defended the designation by referring to SPLC's definition of "hate groups" (see above) and clarifying that the designation did not imply FRC was engaged in violent attacks against LGBT persons, but that their statements could incite such actions.[15] In a 2010 interview, Dees himself surmised that the rise in conservative political groups, along with a precipitous rise in hate groups since President Obama's election, was in many ways racist in its origins.[16] In a 2013 address he further suggested that the increasing racial and cultural diversity of the US population is causing more fear among many White Americans.[17] These sorts of comments are often the kinds of statements that lead to the reactions of his conservative critics.

---

[14] Katie Day, "Southern Poverty Law Center," *Encyclopedia of Alabama*, 2007, http://www.encyclopediaofalabama.org.

[15] David Sessions, "Is the Family Research Council Really a Hate Group?" *Daily Beast*, August 16, 2012, http://www.thedailybeast.com.

[16] Mike Light, "Diversity Conversation: Morris Dees," Grand Rapids Community College, April 1, 2010, http://www.youtube.com.

[17] Dees, Presentation at the University of Michigan, 2013.

Although political bantering is to be expected, a more serious allegation has come from Ken Silverstein, an editor with *Harper's Magazine*, which tends to have a politically liberal perspective sympathetic to issues important to Dees and SPLC. Silverstein charges that SPLC spends most of its resources on "peddling memberships in the church of tolerance" while engaging in "relentless fund-raising"; Silverstein quotes a former SPLC lawyer, Millard Farmer (not to be confused with Millard Fuller), who called Dees "the Jim and Tammy Faye Bakker of the civil rights movement." For example, Silverstein claims that SPLC has raised $27 million through fund-raising and another $17 million in investments, but has spent only $13 million on civil rights programs. Silverstein also cites the Michael Donald case in which Beulah Donald received only a little over $50,000 from the sale of the UKA warehouse, but that in the subsequent year Dees and the SPLC raised $9 million from fund-raising solicitations that featured the Donald case; none of those funds were shared with Mrs. Donald. Although Silverstein does not accuse Dees and SPLC of any legal wrongdoing, he does question the ethics of raising such huge amounts of money from other people's suffering. Silverstein's criticisms are not new; in 1988 John Eggerton wrote a similar article in *The Progressive* titled "Poverty Palace: How the Southern Poverty Law Center Got Rich Fighting the Klan," in which he made many of the same claims as Silverstein.[18]

Silverstein claims that the American Institute of Philanthropy (AIP) gave SPLC one of its lowest ratings, and that in 1998 Dees received a salary higher than the top officers of similar advocacy groups.[19] However, Charity Navigator, a website that rates charities for potential donors, gives SPLC a 3 out of 4 rating, and despite its criticism, AIP indicates that SPLC has been transparent in all its financial dealings. In part at issue is a commitment Dees made early in SPLC's life that when the organization's endowment reached $50 million, the organization would have enough money so that fund-raising would not be necessary; but the fund-raising has continued well past $50 million, and in 2011 the Morris Dees Legacy Endowment Fund reported over $223 million in

---

[18] Ken Silverstein, "The Church of Morris Dees: How the Southern Poverty Law Center Profits from Intolerance," *Harper's Magazine* 301, no. 1806 (November 2000): 54–57; John Eggerton. "Poverty Palace: How the Southern Poverty Law Center Got Rich Fighting the Klan," *Progressive* 52, no. 7 (July 1988): 14–17.

[19] Silverstein, "Church of Morris Dees."

assets.[20] Since Dees is considered the face of SPLC and is a consummate fund-raiser (having even assisted in several political campaigns), it would appear he is working to ensure that SPLC can continue long after he has passed on.

An internal rift occurred in the organization in 1983 following the arson attempt on the center. Many in the staff were leery of the efforts to prosecute members of the KKK and instead wanted to focus on the conditions that led disenchanted White people to join groups like the KKK, such as poverty and ignorance. Dees attributed some of their reactions as a response to the fire and fear of what could happen to them. Dees admitted that the fire ended SPLC's "age of innocence." However, he held firm and insisted that pursuing the Klan and groups like them through the courts needed to continue.[21] Silverstein asserts that several significant leaders within the organization resigned when Dees refused to address these concerns and remained focused on pursuing the KKK.[22] When one reads Dees's memoir there is no question that he has a clear focus on the Klan, and that like many determined leaders he has both strong supporters and strong detractors.

Today, Morris Dees continues to take on cases, though not as many as earlier in his career. In 1979 he divorced Maureen Bass,[23] with whom he had a daughter. He subsequently married Elizabeth Breen.[24] Despite the death threats and the many battles he has fought, as well as the recent resurgence he sees in racism and hate groups, Dees remains hopeful about the future and committed to the legal process as a way of achieving racial justice. Citing his civil rights forebears, Dees writes, "If Dr. King could have faith in our justice system and democracy . . . how can any of us fail to have faith today?" He advises young lawyers "to learn your client's story. Then fit it into the bigger picture of what we believe in as a people and a nation." Like his inspiration Clarence Darrow, Dees believes that "trial lawyers hold the keys to gates of justice," and he has given his life to fight against injustice, especially racial justice, for the whole of his adult life.[25]

---

[20] SPLC 2011 Annual Report, http://www.splcenter.org.

[21] See Dees and Fiffer, *Lawyer's Journey*, 199–201.

[22] Silverstein, "Church of Morris Dees," 165.

[23] Tuscaloosa News, "Dees Divorce Case Settled," *Tuscaloosa News*, September 27, 1979.

[24] Bill Shaw, "Morris Dees," *People Magazine* 36, no. 2 (July 22, 1991).

[25] Dees and Fiffer, *Lawyer's Journey*, 344, 348.

Discussion Questions

1. Dees grew up believing he should treat all persons with decency and respect, regardless of their race. Only later did he see that racism was embedded in culture and the legal system. Why do you think it is inadequate for White allies to solely focus their antiracist work on an interpersonal level without addressing the larger systemic issues?
2. Throughout his work as a civil rights lawyer Dees has had to endure rejection from friends and family and death threats from enemies. What is the cost for White people today to work for racial justice in our US society?
3. Morris Dees dedicated his legal career to identifying and prosecuting White supremacist and other hate groups. What are some overtly racist and hate groups in your state or local area? What can be done to minimize their impact on people's lives and safety?

Bibliography

Day, Katie. "Southern Poverty Law Center." *Encyclopedia of Alabama*, 2007. http://www.encyclopediaofalabama.org.

Dees, Morris. Presentation at the University of Michigan Martin Luther King Symposium, January 21, 2013. http://www.youtube.com.

Dees, Morris, and Steve Fiffer. *A Lawyer's Journey: The Morris Dees Story*. Chicago: American Bar Association, 2001.

"Dees Divorce Case Settled." *Tuscaloosa News*, September 27, 1979.

Eggerton, John. "Poverty Palace: How the Southern Poverty Law Center got Rich Fighting the Klan." *Progressive* 52, no. 7 (July 1988): 14–17.

Light, Mike. "Diversity Conversation: Morris Dees." Grand Rapids Community College, April 1, 2010. http://www.youtube.com.

Sessions, David. "Is the Family Research Council Really a Hate Group?" *Daily Beast,* August 16, 2012. http://www.thedailybeast.com.

Shaw, Bill. "Morris Dees." *People Magazine* 36, no. 2 (July 22, 1991).

Silverstein, Ken. "The Church of Morris Dees: How the Southern Poverty Law Center Profits from Intolerance." *Harper's Magazine* 301, no. 1806 (November 2000): 54–57.

Southern Poverty Law Center 2011 Annual Report. http://www.splcenter.org.

16

Curtiss Paul DeYoung (1957–)

*Reconciler on a Journey**

A Long Journey to Now

On a gray and rainy Saturday morning in March 2013, I met Curtiss Paul DeYoung in a quaint bakery-restaurant in south Minneapolis, Minnesota. He had just flown in the night before after speaking the previous week at a church conference. He looked tired. Dr. DeYoung and I had never met before. I had only contacted him a couple weeks earlier when I realized I was going to be in the Minneapolis/St. Paul area where he lived and worked.

On that dreary March morning Curtiss DeYoung had come a long way from his birthplace in northern Indiana to a career and calling that had taken him from Harlem to South Africa to the hills of Israel's West Bank and many places in between, teaching about and working for racial reconciliation. Despite his apparent fatigue that morning, as he talked I could tell that he was not an "average White guy" but rather someone who had a grasp and grit about the reality of racism in the world that could not be ignored.

* Photo used by permission of Curtiss DeYoung. The information in this chapter comes from Curtiss Paul DeYoung, *Homecoming: A White Man's Journey through Harlem to Jerusalem* (Minneapolis: Jezi Press, 2009); Frank Clancy, "The Reconciler," *Minnesota Monthly*, June 2004, 56–61; and an interview with DeYoung conducted by the author on March 9, 2013.

Early Years

Curtiss Paul DeYoung was born on November 26, 1957, to Arnold and Marylin DeYoung in LaGrange, Indiana. His father, a pastor in the Church of God denomination, is the grandson of Dutch immigrants who had come to the United States in the late 1800s, and his mother (whose maiden name is Curtiss, from which he got his first name), is of English and Irish ancestors who had been in the United States for several generations. In his adulthood DeYoung learned that one of his ancestors from the 1700s had been Thomas Bedoonah, a free Black man from Massachusetts, who had married a White woman named Lydia Craft in 1703 in defiance of laws prohibiting interracial marriage in Massachusetts. However, as is the case with many White families, that part of his history had been lost or forgotten, and was only acknowledged long after the Bedoonahs had passed on. Nonetheless, Thomas and Lydia's relationship foreshadowed his own interracial marriage centuries later.

When Curtiss was very young, his father pastored a multiracial church for a brief time, but by the time he was five, the family had moved to Portage, Michigan, an all-White suburb of Kalamazoo, where he grew up. Although his parents were not activists, they were sympathetic and quietly supportive of the civil rights movement sweeping the American South in the 1960s. Their one act of visible support was the placing of a sign in a house window in support of open housing in their community. Describing his childhood, DeYoung writes, "My family . . . provided me with building blocks for a foundation that has produced my current worldview. Yet my family of origin did not have all of the resources I needed."[1] In a sense Curtiss DeYoung has spent his adult life filling in the pieces of wisdom and understanding his family could not provide him.

The assassination of Dr. Martin Luther King Jr. in 1968 had little impact on DeYoung at the time (as was common for most people in predominantly White communities in the North at the time), but two years later, when he was twelve, he watched the 1970 documentary on King's life and work titled *King: A Filmed Record . . . Montgomery to Memphis*. The film piqued DeYoung's interest and prompted him to learn more about Dr. King. However, until he went to college his engagement with People of Color and their struggle against racism occurred solely at a distance through reading and occasional television programs.

In the late 1970s DeYoung attended Anderson College, the denominational school of the Church of God (North America) in Anderson,

[1] DeYoung, *Homecoming*, 31–32.

Indiana. According to DeYoung, the Church of God has always had a larger percentage of African Americans than the national average for predominantly White denominations in the United States. Since its founding in the late nineteenth century, nearly 20 percent of the congregations and 15 percent of the membership in the Church of God have been African American, according to Cheryl Sanders.[2] Although the interactions between the African American and White churches in the denomination have been minimal, and while Anderson College was 95 percent White when DeYoung attended, the campus pastor and a professor of biblical studies was Dr. James Earl Massey, the prominent African American pastor and former confidant of Dr. Martin Luther King Jr. DeYoung considered Massey a mentor who was crucial to his development in the years that followed.

"Minister Curt" in New York City

In 1979 during his junior year DeYoung went with a small group of Anderson students on a class trip to New York City. Visiting a number of churches and social agencies, he was exposed for the first time to the diversity and struggles of urban life among the working class and the poor. He saw the dilapidated buildings of the South Bronx and the underserved neighborhoods of New York's poorer sections. Reflecting on the many privileges of his upbringing, he recalled the words of Jesus, "to whom much is given much is required," and vowed one day to return. After graduating from college in 1980, he spent a year working as a youth pastor in Michigan, but in 1981 he fulfilled his vow by moving to New York for a one-year stint working with runaway youth in a shelter called Covenant House.

Covenant House was founded in 1972 by a Franciscan priest named Bruce Ritter and was located near Times Square.[3] At that time Times Square was the center of Manhattan's sex and drug trade. On a daily basis DeYoung interacted with youth who were on the streets because of physical and sexual abuse, drug addiction, and poverty. Most of the youth were either Latino or African American. Of that time DeYoung writes, "Every night I could peer out my window and observe a sordid world where people were stripped of their dignity and sense of humanity."[4]

---

[2] Cheryl Sanders, *Saints in Exile* (New York: Oxford University Press, 1996), 22.

[3] "Covenant House History," http://www.covenanthouse.org.

[4] DeYoung, *Homecoming*, 13.

Because Covenant House was a Roman Catholic organization, staff members were required to attend daily Mass as part of their employment, but because he was not Catholic, DeYoung was not allowed to fully participate in the Eucharist, and so he felt excluded. Very quickly he began to feel lost and alone and took steps to find some like-minded people.

This longing for familiarity prompted him to search out a Church of God congregation in the city that he could attend for Sunday worship. He reasoned, "If I could just enjoy an hour or two with people who looked like me, believed like me, and worshipped like me, I could better maintain the rest of my life."[5] His search led him to the Congregational Church of God located in the northern section of Harlem, which at the time was a center for African American life in the city. When he was greeted by the usher at the door, he explained that he was relatively new in the city and a member of the Church of God, and so was ushered into the sanctuary. Not only was he the only White person in the congregation, but he was probably the only White person to have entered the door of that church in a long time. What started as an attempt to find comfortable similarity launched him on a path toward diversity and reconciliation that has characterized his life ever since.

Less than five minutes after he had been seated, he was summoned to the office of the pastor, Rev. Levorn Aaron, who greeted him warmly. Noting that he had been a student at Anderson College, Rev. Aaron asked him, "Do you know my boy, Jim?" (referring to James Earl Massey). When Rev. Aaron learned that DeYoung had been licensed as a Church of God minister, he invited him to preach two weeks from that Sunday. Then because it was the tradition of the church to seat all ministers on the dais behind the pulpit, DeYoung spent his first Sunday sitting in full view of the congregation at the front of the church. Although he could have chalked up that Sunday morning to an interesting cultural experience, he chose instead to spend his year in New York immersing himself in the life of the church while being mentored by Rev. Aaron. On average he preached about once a month and found himself fully embraced by the members of the church.

The year he spent with the Congregational Church of God was transformational for DeYoung. Never once did he feel singled out for being the only White person in the congregation. In the congregation's eyes he was "Minister Curt," another young person being mentored for

---

[5] Ibid., 15.

ministry by their pastor. Parallel to his outward experience, DeYoung experienced an inward change. He later noted in his journal that in the early weeks of his involvement with the church, he often referred to the church as a "Black" congregation, with a "Black" pastor and a "Black" gospel music. However, as the year progressed he noticed that the adjective "Black" disappeared from his vocabulary and he was "able to relax in that context." He saw that the us-and-them mentality common in interracial settings faded from his mind-set. Furthermore, he found that his stereotypes about African American life were challenged and his view expanded. In the end he writes that during that year he "learned what it meant to accepted unconditionally as a human being."[6]

Howard Divinity School

Following his year in New York, DeYoung returned to Anderson to pursue a seminary degree, but he soon realized that he longed for the urban context, and so made plans to transfer to Union Seminary in New York. However at the urging of Rev. Massey he went to Washington, DC, to spend a summer working under Rev. Samuel Hines, pastor of the Third Street Church of God. Born and raised in Jamaica, Hines believed that "God has a one-item agenda: reconciliation."[7] To that end he dedicated his ministry to building bridges across cultures (his congregation was made up of African Americans and Jamaicans), dismantling apartheid in South Africa, and finding ways to bring rich and poor, the powerful and the powerless together. One of his efforts was an urban prayer breakfast program that regularly brought the Washington politicians and bureaucrats together with the homeless of DC for a shared meal.

Before the summer was over, DeYoung had begun dating a young woman from the church named Karen McBee, who would eventually become his wife, and he decided that he did not want to leave DC. At the advice of Rev. Hines and through the intervention of some of the church leaders, he was able to enroll at Howard Divinity School that fall. Because Howard is a historically Black university, he was often the only White person in his classes and one of only a handful of Whites attending the school. Although he was initially uncomfortable with his minority status, he soon realized that he was being afforded an inside

---

[6] Ibid., 17.

[7] Ibid., 35.

look into African American thinking and cultural life hidden from most Whites. In his classes he was able to listen in on honest conversions about the impact of racism on the average African American, and the ways his classmates and teachers responded to that reality personally and theologically. Despite being a racial minority on campus, DeYoung realized that as soon as he stepped off the campus, he reentered a society where his White skin gave him unquestioned superior status. This dual understanding has consistently served as a check and balance that has informed his racial reconciliation work. He writes, "I may have acquired an intellectual stance usually reserved for persons of color and even acculturated some patterns from other cultures . . . but I will never experience life as a person of color."[8]

While at Howard, DeYoung continued to worship and work under the leadership of Dr. Hines. In that context he acquired the skills required of an urban pastor. However, another mentor that affected his life at that time was Dr. Calvin Morris, who oversaw the field education work of seminary students. Raised in Philadelphia, Dr. Morris had served in Chicago with the Rev. Jesse Jackson and Dr. Martin Luther King Jr. as the national coordinator of Operation Breadbasket. In 1976 he came to Howard where he served for sixteen years as an associate professor of pastoral theology and the director of field education. He later left Howard to be the dean of the Interdenominational Center in Atlanta, and then the director of Chicago's Community Renewal Society.[9] However, for DeYoung he was another mentor who brought "a razor-sharp ability to cut to the real issues when dealing with individuals aspiring to leadership."[10]

Morris saw part of his role with students to be to "push their buttons" on those issues where he thought they needed to grow personally and professionally. In DeYoung's case he wanted to make sure he was not just a "daddy's boy" who had imbibed some legalistic fundamentalism in his personal and spiritual development. Moreover, he wanted to be sure DeYoung was more than just another White liberal do-gooder not really committed to the work of reconciliation over the long haul. Because of the constant pressure and challenge from Morris, DeYoung came to feel deep anger and resentment toward him, and near the end of his tenure at Howard went in to confess his negative feelings

[8] Ibid., 46.

[9] The History Makers, "Rev. Dr. Calvin Morris," http://www.thehistorymakers.com.

[10] DeYoung, *Homecoming*, 32.

to Morris. The professor responded to the confession by saying, "I've been waiting for you to come," and he proceeded to tell DeYoung that he had wanted to test his ability to deal with "an angry Black man" before he went on to work on racial reconciliation. At first DeYoung felt Morris's response was arrogant and unnecessary, but later he came to see that in fact Morris was even then pushing him to mature. DeYoung writes, "Calvin Morris performed surgery on my psyche. . . . What I experienced as a confrontation was really an act of love."[11] Throughout his career DeYoung has continued to communicate with Dr. Morris and has confessed that "he's still messin' with me."

Another significant influence on his life while at Howard was the New Testament professor Dr. Cain Hope Felder who showed DeYoung how education could be a force for social change. Felder is editor of the *Original African Heritage Bible* and has written books on African influences in the Bible in such books as *Stony the Road We Trod* and *Troubling Biblical Waters*. Through ground-breaking anthropological study, Felder has shown that mainstream biblical studies have largely been caught in a Eurocentric reading of the Bible, which has blinded scholars from seeing the Bible's deep African and Asian cultural roots. Felder profoundly shaped DeYoung's reading of the New Testament and led him to argue in his book *Coming Together* that the Old Testament Jews and Jesus were culturally Afro-Asiatic Jews in which Jesus is not the central figure in a "White man's religion," but rather a multicultural figure much more akin to the oppressed Persons of Color in Asia, Africa, and around the world. Dr. Felder wrote the foreword to *Coming Together* in which he described DeYoung as "a minister who has sought aggressively to bring together diverse racial and ethnic groups so that they may better understand one another."[12]

DeYoung's three years in Washington, DC, were instrumental in his development as an activist, advocate, and author on racial reconciliation. Although his family was instrumental in his growth, DeYoung often reflects on the continuing impact of his African American mentors, who not only served as role models for him but also "connected [him] to an expanded and very rich legacy" of African American leaders

---

[11] Ibid., 33.

[12] Cain Hope Felder, foreword to Curtiss Paul DeYoung, *Coming Together: The Bible's Message in an Age of Diversity* (Valley Forge, PA: Judson Press, 1995), xii. There is now a revised version, *Coming Together in the 21st Century* (Valley Forge, PA: Judson Press, 2009), for which DeYoung added chapters written by a racially diverse collection of biblical scholars.

through history—such as Sojourner Truth, Mary McLeod Bethune, Howard Thurman, and Martin Luther King Jr. This legacy was to lead him into the work that consumed him for the next twenty-five plus years.

While in Washington, DeYoung and Karen McBee were married, and Rev. Hines officiated. DeYoung's relationship with his wife further deepened his awareness of racism's dimensions. Although they were generally well received by close friends and family, in public they sometimes had difficult moments. One of the more painful confrontations occurred when DeYoung was invited by the White pastor of a multiracial church to consider becoming the church's youth pastor. However, prominent White members of the church rejected DeYoung because he was believed to have a "personal problem," which turned out to be his African American fiancée. Although DeYoung simply wanted to move on from the incident, passing the comment off as coming from a "racist jerk," Karen took it much more personally. She pointed out to Curtiss that her skin color would always be a "problem" in certain circles and that although he could pass off the comment as ignorant bigotry, she had to constantly live with the reality that she was the target of such bigotry. Through these and other incidents DeYoung more fully realized that while he could be justifiably angry at incidents of racism, he also was often spared the pain of that racism because of his White privilege.

Change and Conflict in First Church

Upon graduation from Howard in 1986, DeYoung went with his new wife to serve as pastor at the First Church of God in Minneapolis, Minnesota; there they faced a new set of challenges. First Church of God had been founded in the 1930s by prominent Scandinavians and Germans, including the legendary author of the *Peanuts* comic strip, Charles Schulz. By the time DeYoung arrived, the church had experienced a long numerical decline while situated in a neighborhood of south Minneapolis that was changing racially, ethnically, and economically. DeYoung entered his new role with energy and idealism, convinced that God's presence was most palpably found among the marginalized of society. In his zeal, he failed to notice that the congregation had a distinctly different perspective than he did on church life and faith. The congregation had a practice of not discussing controversial public issues and thought of their faith in largely personal rather than social or political terms. They had hired him in the hopes that as their new pastor he could revive their declining congregation by attracting a younger and more diverse crowd, which in fact he did; however, neither DeYoung nor the congregation anticipated how this influx would significantly challenge the prevailing culture of the church and that there might be conflict.

Within eighteen months of his arrival the congregation had nearly doubled in size, attracting African Americans and Asian Americans to the previously all-White congregation. People in the immediate neighborhood had begun attending, some of whom struggled with addictions, mental illness, English as a second language, and the ravages of poverty. DeYoung helped start a Sunday School modeled on the twelve-step program familiar to recovering addicts. For the move to a more multiethnic congregation, DeYoung was an ideal person to be the pastor. His training in the traditions and practices of the historic Black church made his leadership style familiar to many Persons of Color, while his White face was less threatening to the older White members. Initially, the older White members were quite supportive of these changes and were involved with the efforts to reach out to people in the community; however, soon some of the long-standing members became troubled as they saw the overall ethos of the church begin to take on a multicultural feel. The children's choir at one point was almost entirely composed of Hmong children. African Americans who attended the church brought their call-and-response worship style into services, and DeYoung himself often preached on issues of justice and reconciliation.

Soon amid these demographic and cultural changes racial tensions began to emerge in the church's life. DeYoung was accused by some Whites of spending too much time with the African American members, and complaints were heard about his continued focus on racial reconciliation. These tensions caused the older White members to question who the "real members" of the church were, and to assert their desire for ultimate control of the church's ministry. Although these actions were rarely overt, DeYoung realized that some of the church's long-term members were deliberately and subtly subverting his efforts to renew the church through his commitment to cultural diversity. As a young pastor, DeYoung was not prepared to deal with the resistance in an effective way, and so five years into the ministry he was mentally and emotionally exhausted, resigned his position in the church, and decided to leave pastoral ministry.

TURN to a Wider Ministry

DeYoung left the church questioning his call to pastoral ministry and wondering if the racial reconciliation work he wanted to do could be realized in an institutional setting. Although he had entered First Church of God with a great deal of hope for creating a space of human community and flourishing, he left with more questions than answers. Coming out of that painful experience, he wondered if institutions, especially churches, "could be places of care, concern and compassion."[13] For a year after leaving the church he worked on various projects and did some teaching, and then in 1991 he was hired as the first full-time staff person of the Twin Cities Urban Resourcing Network (TURN, which later became Twin Cities Urban Reconciliation Network), which provided him a second opportunity to work with faith-based organizations to see if he could find a way to make them places of healing and hope rather than division and disappointment.

Started by a group of urban evangelical leaders in 1981, TURN had mostly focused on sponsoring several self-contained events in the course of a year. In hiring DeYoung, the board of TURN wanted to shift the focus from events to a concerted effort to unite Christian leaders across a diversity of cultures, races, and denominations. Upon his arrival, DeYoung realized that within TURN there was little involvement of African American, Roman Catholic, and mainline Protestant churches. So for the first few years he focused his attention on building relationships with church leaders across Minneapolis and neighboring St. Paul. He had a passion to reach across previously uncrossable lines, and having a Howard Divinity degree opened doors for him with many of the African American leaders. He likewise spent a great deal of time building relationships with groups and individuals who had previously not been involved with TURN in order to broaden its constituency.

TURN was a nimble enough organization that it was able to respond to social crises in a relatively short period of time. For instance in 1992, after the uprising in Los Angeles following the Rodney King verdict, TURN sponsored a dialogue involving many key city leaders on racism and rage. That same year DeYoung spoke at an interfaith gathering following the murder of a local police officer. TURN cooperated with groups like SCUPE and Call to Renewal[14] to address issues of violence

---

[13] DeYoung, *Homecoming*, 68.

[14] SCUPE (Seminary Consortium for Urban Pastoral Education) is an ecumenical network in Chicago for training urban church leaders (http:// www.

and poverty. Soon TURN's reputation had shifted from being an event-driven organization to a movement for social justice and reconciliation. Under DeYoung's leadership the organization began to flourish, the staff expanded, and programs for job training, youth development, multi-cultural education, child care, and pastoral training were developed. However, what made TURN work was that it was the "glue for a relational network"[15] bringing diverse organizations and persons together for the common purpose of improving life in the metropolitan area.

During his time at TURN DeYoung began to write. In his first book, *Coming Together: The Bible's Message in an Age of Diversity*,[16] he grounds the concern for racial and cultural reconciliation in his understanding of the Bible. Building on the work of his former professor, Cain Hope Felder, DeYoung argues that the Bible was written in a culturally diverse context, and that Jews, and in particular Jesus, were part of and influenced by both Asian and African cultures. He then contends that these insights should inform the church's work in racial reconciliation. His second book, *Reconciliation: Our Greatest Challenge—Our Only Hope*,[17] was written as a companion to the first book to "further 'unpack' the meaning and scope of reconciliation"[18] by looking at factors that impede reconciliation and outlining the steps that individual, groups, and institutions must take to pursue reconciliation. Like the previous book, *Reconciliation* reflects his belief that reconciliation is central to the Christian message. Thus, through his work with TURN and his writing, DeYoung was becoming a recognized authority on racial reconciliation in Christian circles and beyond.

However, in 1999 his views on reconciliation began to be expanded further. In that year he was invited to attend a prestigious seminar in Salzburg, Austria, on the topic "Race and Ethnicity: Social Change through Public Awareness." The Salzburg Seminar, begun in 1947, was designed to be a gathering place for intellectuals to discuss pressing issues of the day. Up to this point in his career, DeYoung had worked in settings dominated by a Christian worldview. However, in Salzburg he found himself in an

---

scupe.org/). Call to Renewal is an ecumenical network started by *Sojourners Magazine* in Washington, DC, that seeks to bring awareness and action among Christians on issues of social justice (http://sojo.net).

[15] DeYoung, *Homecoming*, 73.

[16] DeYoung, *Coming Together: The Bible's Message in an Age of Diversity.*

[17] Curtiss Paul DeYoung, *Reconciliation: Our Greatest Challenge—Our Only Hope* (Valley forge, PA: Judson Press, 1997).

[18] Ibid., x.

intellectually and culturally diverse setting where his Christian perspective was not dominant and at times was openly challenged.

During the one-week seminar, he interacted with such leading thinkers as the multicultural historian Ronald Takaki, the civil rights leader Lani Guinier, the British-Indian Muslim journalist Yasmin Alibhai-Brown, and the South African author Njabulo Ndebele. He was challenged to think about his Christian faith from an interfaith perspective and quickly realized that his religious convictions could not be expressed in words alone but had to be evident in his attitudes and actions. Although he had been involved in interfaith settings prior to 1999, the Salzburg Seminar affected him at a deeper and more emotional level, and furthered his interest and respect for the value of other faith traditions. Though he had been working in multicultural settings for over fifteen years, he wrote that Salzburg "was the most diverse multicultural and international experience of my life."[19]

At this same time DeYoung began to feel his work with TURN coming to an end. The scope of the organization's work expanded significantly, and the board had gone from being overwhelmingly White to 90 percent Persons of Color. However, the internal dynamics of the organization were often tense and did not reflect the commitment to reconciliation that TURN outwardly promoted. By his own admission, DeYoung was not effective in dealing with these conflicts and often thought that good intentions alone would enable people to work effectively across racial and cultural differences. Just as he had ten years earlier at First Church of God, DeYoung felt himself burning out, discouraged by his inability to fully make his commitment to reconciliation an actuality in the organization he led. So in 2001, "confused and dispirited,"[20] he resigned as TURN's executive director. Following his departure, the organization continued to experience conflict and within a few years lost funding and ceased to exist.

Black Jesus in South Africa

However, as one door in his life was closing, another was opening. In 2000 two South African participants of the Salzburg Seminar invited him to present a four-day workshop with the title "The Bible and Culture in the Twenty-First Century." It had been only ten years since Nelson

[19] DeYoung, *Homecoming*, 95.

[20] Ibid., 76.

Mandela had been released from his nearly thirty-year imprisonment, and six years since he had been elected as South Africa's first Black president. In 1995 the South African government had established the Truth and Reconciliation Commission (TRC) led by Archbishop Desmond Tutu, which had begun investigating atrocities committed against Black South Africans by the former apartheid government. The purpose of the TRC as expressed by one official was "to enable South Africans to come to terms with their past on a morally acceptable basis and to advance the cause of reconciliation."[21] Thus for South Africans, reconciliation was synonymous with social justice.

During his workshop DeYoung drew largely on his earlier work in *Coming Together* in which he debunked the largely White images of Jesus that dominate mainstream Christian thinking. In its place DeYoung proposed that Jesus was an Afro-Asiatic Jew who in contemporary racial terms would be considered Black. To many of the workshop participants who had been raised on the image of a White Jesus, this was both surprising and liberating. The workshop was so well received that he was invited back in 2002 to repeat it; during that second visit he had an opportunity to meet Archbishop Tutu. Then in 2003, his hosts arranged a far more extensive speaking schedule, which they titled the "Jesus Is Black Tour." During the tour he spoke in Black and White settings and visited many of the poor Black townships in South Africa's four major cities—Johannesburg, Cape Town, Port Elizabeth, and Durban. Over the course of sixteen days he spoke nineteen times to a variety of organizations and in a variety of settings. His purpose "was to counter and dispel the belief that Christianity is an exclusive faith and to restore the biblical truth that people of all races and cultures are created fully in the image of God,"[22] and to challenge the apartheid theology that had dominated the White Dutch Reformed Church for decades.

The prospect of a White American preaching about a Black Jesus in South Africa created an interesting dynamic. As DeYoung said, it "used racism against racism." Because he was a White Christian leader, his words carried a certain authority that might have been challenged had he been Black. At the same time, the very fact that a White Christian leader could understand the deep racial and cultural dynamics at work in the Bible and in South African society provided hope for many of his Black listeners, whose experience with White Christians had been

---

[21] Truth and Reconciliation Commission at http://www.justice.gov.za/trc/.

[22] DeYoung, *Homecoming*, 103.

extremely negative. Furthermore, the fact that he was partnering with Black South African leaders provided a model of what reconciliation could and should look like.[23]

Reconciliation and Interfaith Work

Meanwhile, after leaving TURN in 2001, he briefly led an organization called Citygate Project, which helped Christian colleges and seminaries involve their students in urban ministry. However, in the fall of 2002 he was hired by Bethel University in St. Paul as a professor in Reconciliation Studies, a unique program with a "focus on diversity, conflict mediation, social justice, and reconciliation theology."[24] In 2004 he completed his doctorate at the University of St. Thomas in St. Paul, and his dissertation became the basis for another book, *Living Faith: How Faith Inspires Social Justice*.[25] In this book, DeYoung focuses on the lives and work of three individuals—Dietrich Bonhoeffer, a Christian; Malcolm X, a Muslim; and Aung San Suu Kyi, a Buddhist—whom he calls "mystic-activists." DeYoung describes the mystic-activist as one "whose activism consumes them yet is deeply rooted in their faith and in the mystery of the divine."[26] In addition to exploring the role of faith in the lives of his three main characters, he also explores similar characteristics in well-known activist figures such as Martin Luther King Jr., Dorothy Day, Rigoberta Menchú, Mohandas Gandhi, Thich Nhat Hanh, and the Dalai Lama.

This study of individuals beyond the Christian faith coincided with another life-changing trip. DeYoung visited Israel in 2006 for a program hosted by the Christian development organization World Vision. On this trip he had an opportunity to meet with Christian leaders, most of whom were Palestinian in both the West Bank and the Gaza Strip, as well as Jewish peace activists in Jerusalem. He also visited several historical Christian sites, always cognizant of the ubiquitous Israeli military surveillance and presence. He was struck by the passion for justice and peace among the Palestinian Christians and Israeli Jews he met, but also realized "that sharing the same space does not automatically translate

---

[23] These comments came during my interview with DeYoung in March 2013.

[24] From the website of the Bethel University Department of Anthropology, Sociology, and Reconciliation Studies, http://cas.bethel.edu.

[25] Curtiss Paul DeYoung, *Living Faith: How Faith Inspires Social Justice* (Minneapolis: Fortress Press, 2007).

[26] Ibid., 7.

into peace and reconciliation."[27] In 2007 he returned to continue these conversations and also took a trip to Tekoa, the ancestral home of the Old Testament prophet Amos, to meet with an Orthodox Jewish Rabbi named Menachem Froman. Rabbi Froman lived in one of the more controversial Jewish settlements that had displaced Palestinians on the West Bank and sought to work for peace among Christians, Jews, and Muslims in the area. While on the way to meet the Rabbi, DeYoung's Sufi Muslim companion was threatened by four Jewish vigilantes and then challenged by an Israeli police officer. However, when the Jewish member of their team explained that they were a Jew, a Muslim, and a Christian working together for peace, they were allowed to pass. Thus DeYoung's passion for reconciliation placed him in yet another context beyond his original intent.

The Journey Continues

Throughout his career, DeYoung has shared this journey with his wife, Karen, and their two children. They often have been able to accompany him on his trips abroad, and Karen in particular has helped him understand racism from the perspective of a Person of Color. DeYoung points out that because he is in an interracial marriage does not mean he has overcome his inherited racial prejudices and stereotypes. Moreover, when as parents they have had to help their children contend with the prejudices they face as biracial persons, DeYoung has often followed Karen's lead. In contrast to his own upbringing, Persons of Color are taught by their parents how to contend with the dynamics of racism, and the parents "give [the children] the hard lesson of how our society works around race." Thus, he recognizes that Karen has been given the tools to address such issues in ways he can never fully comprehend. Together DeYoung and his wife have sought to situate their children in neighborhoods, schools, and multiracial churches that affirm their identity rather than criticize it.

DeYoung has continued to write, having authored or coauthored ten books and numerous articles. He regularly is invited to lead workshops and speak on topics of reconciliation, justice, and diversity. His position at Bethel afforded him the opportunity to travel with students to different places around the world. He hopes to expand his work on interfaith reconciliation, as well as develop relationships and do work

---

[27] DeYoung, *Homecoming*, 117.

with Native American leaders. He has also begun to explore the dimension of diversity that is not particularly racist but nonetheless culturally different and strange; he wants to help people learn how to "relax into culture" that is not their own, so as to build meaningful relationships and do effective work. In June 2014 he left Bethel to become the executive director of the Community Renewal Society in Chicago, an organization dedicated to "[empowering] people to build just communities by working to eradicate racism and poverty."[28] At some point DeYoung says he will retire from paid employment, but he never sees himself "retiring from the journey."[29]

In the epilogue to *Reconciliation* DeYoung says that people who are committed to the work of racial justice are artisans of reconciliation who "devote [their] lives to becoming more skilled at the art of relational bridge building."[30] When asked how he viewed himself, he replied that he sees himself in the role of the "serious empathetic" one who has the ability to imagine and feel another's pain, even though he himself has not experienced it firsthand. He also aspires to be the mystic-activist described in *Living Faith*. What is clear is that from his first encounter in the Congregational Church of God in Harlem, Curtiss Paul DeYoung has been on a pilgrimage to bring hope and reconciliation to a racially, culturally, and religiously divided world, and as he says, the journey continues.

---

[28] From website of the Community Renewal Society, http://www.communityrenewalsociety.org.

[29] Interview by author with DeYoung, March 9, 2013.

[30] DeYoung, *Living Faith*, 137.

Discussion Questions

1. DeYoung's story is characterized by a pattern of putting himself in situations where he was in a racial and cultural minority. What might be the value for White people to place themselves in situations where they are a racial and/or cultural minority?
2. In Salzburg DeYoung realized that he was in a setting where the Christian worldview was not dominant. What are your experiences with interfaith settings? What can we learn from such settings?
3. What might the work of reconciliation (racial, cultural, interfaith) look like in your context (home, work, church, etc.)?

Bibliography

Boesak, Allan Aubrey, and Curtiss Paul DeYoung. *Radical Reconciliation: Beyond Political Pietism and Christian Quietism*. Marynoll, NY: Orbis Books, 2012.

Boyd, Drick. Interview with Curtiss Paul DeYoung in Minneapolis, Minnesota, March 9, 2013.

Clancy, Frank. "The Reconciler." *Minnesota Monthly*, June 2004, 56-61.

Community Renewal Society. "Rev. Curtiss DeYoung Named Executive Director of Community Renewal Society" (January 29, 2014). http://www.communityrenewalsociety.org.

"Covenant House History." http://www.covenanthouse.org.

DeYoung, Curtiss Paul. *Coming Together: The Bible's Message in an Age of Diversity*. Valley Forge, PA: Judson Press, 1995.

———. *Homecoming: A White Man's Journey through Harlem to Jerusalem*, Minneapolis: Jezi Press, 2009.

———. *Living Faith: How Faith Inspires Social Justice*. Minneapolis: Fortress Press, 2007.

———. *Reconciliation: Our Greatest Challenge—Our Only Hope*. Valley Forge, PA: Judson Press, 1997.

Felder, Cain Hope. Foreword to Curtiss Paul DeYoung, *Coming Together: The Bible's Message in an Age of Diversity,* ix–xiii. Valley Forge, PA: Judson Press, 1995.

History Makers. "Rev. Dr. Calvin Morris," http://www.thehistorymakers.com.

Massey, James Earl. Foreword to Curtiss Paul DeYoung, *Reconciliation: Our Greatest Challenge—Our Only Hope*, ix–xi. Valley Forge, PA: Judson Press, 1997.

Sanders, Cheryl J. *Saints in Exile: The Holiness-Pentecostal Experience in African American Religion and Culture*. New York: Oxford University Press, 1996.

17

Tim Wise
(1968–)

*Speaking Treason, Speaking Truth**

No Joke

Tim Wise has been called "one of the most brilliant, articulate and courageous critics of white privilege in the nation" and "a national treasure" (Michael Eric Dyson). It has been said that "he tells the truth, no matter how inconvenient that truth might be" (David Sirota). One of his strongest critics has called him "the Uncle Tom of the white race" (Dinesh D'Souza). Wise himself has referred to his work as "treason" against White privilege, and Whiteness (which he distinguishes from being against White people) in the United States.[1] The author of numerous books and articles, and a nationally known speaker, Tim Wise is probably the most outspoken White critic and speaker on issues of White privilege and power in the United States today. He can also tell a good joke.

Tim Wise was once invited to speak at a college in Montana. After the presentation he joined a group of students who went out to a local

* Photo used by permission of Tim Wise. The subtitle of this chapter plays on the title of a book by Tim Wise, *Speaking Treason Fluently: Anti-racist Reflections from an Angry White Male* (Washington, DC: Soft Skull Press, 2008). The information shared in this chapter comes from Tim Wise, *White Like Me: Reflections on Race from a Privileged Son* (Brooklyn, NY: Soft Skull Press, 2005): *White Like Me: Reflections on Race from a Privileged Son; The Remix: Revised and Updated Edition* (Berkeley, CA: Soft Skull Press, 2011); and an interview conducted by the author on November 13, 2013.

[1] These descriptions are found on the back cover of the first edition of *White Like Me* (2005).

establishment. As the evening progressed, a young man joined the gathering who knew some of the students, but not Wise, or his reason for being there. The newcomer told an overtly racist joke. After an awkward silence, there was some nervous laughter and a few gently chided the joke-teller not to say such things. Wise, however, laughed as if it was the funniest thing he had ever heard, and then said, "Did you hear the one about the white guy who told this really racist joke because he assumed that everyone he was hanging out with was also white?" The joke-teller nervously said, "No, I haven't heard that one." Tim replied, "It's no joke because my mother's black," at which point the young man apologized all over himself. Wise then revealed that in fact his mother was not Black and proceeded to question him as to why telling such jokes was acceptable in all-White settings but not when Blacks were around.[2]

Just as he shook up the embarrassed young man at the table that night, Tim Wise has been shaking up Whites about racism for most of his life.

All in the Family

Tim Wise was born on October 4, 1968, the same year that two champions of civil rights, Martin Luther King Jr. and Robert Kennedy, were assassinated. He was born in Nashville, Tennessee ("just a few hours and half a state away" from where Dr. King was murdered),[3] to a Jewish father (Michael Julius Wise) and the daughter of a conservative Southern White family (Lucinda McLean Wise). As he later wrote, it was a time of "great turmoil, none of which had been of my own making, but which I could hardly escape."[4] In fact the tension around racial issues in his family in many ways was a microcosm of the struggles facing the South then and now.

His father's side of the family arrived permanently in North America in 1910. Jacob Wise, Tim's great-grandfather, who had been living in the United States for several years, was deported in 1901 in a wave of xenophobia against East Europeans following the assassination of President William McKinley. However, Jacob's desire to escape czarist Russia and come to the United States was so strong that nine years later he completed a successful reimmigration with a wife and children.

---

[2] Wise, *White Like Me Remix*, 195–97.

[3] Ibid., 23.

[4] Ibid., 2.

Tim's grandfather, Leo, born in 1919, graduated from college and ran a successful liquor business in the heart of Nashville's Black community, where he enjoyed a close and constructive relationship with the people there.[5] Leo married Mabel McKinney, who had been born in Detroit, Michigan, where her father was an active member of the local Ku Klux Klan. Her family moved to Nashville, and, at age fifteen she met and then later married Leo, a Jew. Her relationship with Leo compelled her to stand up to her racist, anti-Semitic father, telling him "either he was going to burn his Klan robes, or she was going to do it for him."[6] This resistance and abhorrence of bigotry is something that was passed on to their grandson, Tim.

Tim's paternal grandparents had a profound influence on his life, particularly his perspectives and attitudes about race. Despite his strained and difficult relationship with his father, his grandparents provided a safe and secure space when life in his home got tense and abusive, as it sometime did. He spent many enjoyable hours in his grandfather's store where he was able to casually interact with many of the African American customers. Likewise, from his grandmother he learned a "deep abiding contempt for bigotry, for racism, of any form."[7]

Tim's maternal family line could not have been a greater contrast from the Wise side of the family. The McLean ancestors first arrived in the United States in 1750 from Scotland. Ephraim McLean became a surveyor in his newly adopted country and soon received 12,000 acres of land in Tennessee and North Carolina for his service in the Revolutionary War. The McLeans went on to be prominent wealthy Southern slave owners and passed that inheritance down through the generations. Although his mother's parents and grandparents were never involved in the KKK, they worked hard to preserve the "Southern way of life" with its degradation of and segregation from African Americans.

In reaction to her traditional Southern upbringing, Tim's mother consciously and deliberately sought to build a life for herself and her family that challenged and countered the segregationist and racist attitudes of her family. She was not close to her family and, as a result, neither was Tim. Speaking of his mother, he wrote, "She deliberately set

---

[5] Later recognizing the deleterious effect of alcoholism on the African American community, Wise tells the story of a man who grew up in that community who affectionately but seriously referred to Tim's grandfather as a drug dealer, but a legitimate kind.

[6] Wise, *White Like Me Reflections*, 129.

[7] Ibid.

out to ensure I would not be raised amidst such attitudes. Her defiance rubbed off on me in any number of ways."[8]

Tim learned to carefully avoid conversations about politics and race with the McLean side of the family. However, he noticed that the family matriarch, Aunt Isabel, departed from the family narrative, by telling stories about one prominent ancestor named Elizabeth Angel, who had been an outspoken abolitionist, and who even convinced her family to free their slaves in the pre–Civil War era. However, instead of being a family hero, Elizabeth had been reduced to a footnote in the official McLean family history, as if her abolitionist acts were of no significance, and perhaps an embarrassment. Yet it was from that hidden tradition of Isabel and Elizabeth that Tim's mother drew her values and worldview.

Tim's parents had met when they were in eighth grade, but their relationship was often strained and difficult. Because his father was Jewish, and the son of a liquor store owner, the McLeans never warmed to Michael, and in fact moved to West Virginia their senior year in part to get Lucinda away from him. For three years the separation strategy seemed to work, as she went off to college, and he went to California to begin his career as a professional comic and actor. However, in 1967 they found each other again and were married.

Early Memories

Michael Wise was a stand-up comedian who traveled a great deal. With Michael getting sporadic gigs in his career, Lucinda doing whatever paid work she could find, and Michael's parents providing financial support, the Wise family was able to eke out what would have been considered a working-class level of income. The first eighteen years of Tim's life were spent living in a small apartment with few amenities.

Tim's father was an alcoholic, and he often came home drunk and got into fights with his wife. The thin walls in their apartment allowed Tim to hear the fights and violence that became more frequent and intense as the marriage deteriorated. As his father's drinking increased, so did the abuse. However, the long periods when his father was traveling to various venues provided Tim and his mom periodic respites of relative peace. When Tim was in middle school his father's alcoholism increased, as did the verbal abuse directed toward his mother. Tim would stay awake at night until his father would stumble home so he could know

[8] Ibid., 72.

that his father had not killed himself for one more night. He grew up also fearing that the verbal abuse would escalate to physical violence and that his mother might be killed in a drunken rage. Eventually after a particularly traumatic episode when Tim was in college when his father in a drunken stupor tried to kill himself, his mother separated from him, and Tim no longer felt threatened

For these reasons it was Tim's mother who shaped his early views on the world around him, and this applied particularly on matters of race. For example, when he was two and a half years old, his mother enrolled him in a preschool where he was one of only three White kids and where all the teachers and aides were African American. From his earliest memory Tim regarded People of Color as authority figures, and some of his earliest friendships were with his Black peers. Although many of those relationships did not persist into middle school and high school, they left an indelible mark on his view of the world. Reflecting on this experience, Tim writes: "My ability to resist racism, to speak out against it, has much to do with the decision to expose me to a different community than the one in which I was born."[9]

His first awareness of skin color occurred when he was only two years old as he looked out a window and saw a forty-year-old man known to the White community as "Mr. Tommy." Noticing the man's dark skin, Tim asked his mother who the "brown man" was. His mother corrected him and said that Mr. Tommy was not brown but rather Black. Tim objected, insisting that according to the colors in his crayon box, Mr. Tommy was more brown than black. At this point Tim's mother gave him his earliest lesson on race dynamics explaining that while Mr. Tommy looked brown, people who looked like him referred to themselves as Black. Many years later Tim came to appreciate both his mother's directness and the courage of a people so long denied basic rights to claim the right to define themselves as they saw fit.

School Years

When Tim entered grade school, he continued to have friends who were African American, but began to recognize the preferential treatment he received because he was White. By his own admission he was something of "class clown" and an underachiever. One time in first grade he and a Black student named John disrupted class and were sent to the

[9] Ibid., 69.

principal's office; he was given a warning, while John was paddled for his misbehavior. As it turned out, the difference in treatment was not strictly racial, because John's parents had given the school permission to paddle him whereas Tim's did not. Even so, it began to make him aware throughout his school experience how Blacks and Whites were treated differently.

When he was eleven years old, Tim played on a mixed-race baseball team, where four of the players were White and the rest were Black. One time they played an all-White team from a rural community thirty miles outside of Nashville. After the game as his team got in the van to return home, some players of the other team and adults began pounding on the van calling the Black kids "niggers" and the White kids "nigger lovers." Describing this event, Wise wrote: "I'm sure this was terrifying for the Black kids; it was certainly terrifying for me. . . . I had made the ultimate mistake in the eyes of these White kids and their parents: I had transgressed against my group; I had transgressed against whiteness, even though I didn't know what whiteness was at age eleven."[10]

In grade school he also played on a predominantly Black basketball team where "the advantage of racist stereotypes [worked] in [their] favor."[11] Wise's team mostly played teams from private schools made up of White players who had been brainwashed with the stereotype of Black athletic prowess. Wise learned that having a predominantly Black team in black uniforms would cause a "bunch of pasty white boys to damn near piss themselves."[12] Wise also tended to prefer the so-called Black music of funk and hip-hop. These associations and behavior caused him to become a "concern" to his White teachers. One particular teacher chastised Wise's mother for sending him to public school where he would be interacting with Black peers. Wise's mother promptly petitioned to have the teacher dismissed for her racist attitude and succeeded in doing so.

By the time he was in sixth grade Wise became aware of the race-based tracking taking place in the school. All the White kids would be sent off to the "Very Exceptional" class while the Black kids were left behind in the regular classroom. The one exception was a very dark-skinned girl who had recently moved from Zimbabwe, whom his teachers seemed to adore. He noticed that the White people in his life often rationalized

[10] Cooper Thompson et al., *White Men Challenging Racism: 35 Personal Stories* (Durham, NC: Duke University Press, 2003), 154.

[11] Wise, *White Like Me Remix*, 44.

[12] Ibid.

away their racism by pointing to their acceptance of people from Africa, while denigrating their African American counterparts of equal skill and intelligence. This practice of tracking and differential racism continued into middle school and high school, making meaningful interaction between the Black and White kids increasingly strained. He began to realize that the differences between Blacks and White had less to do with personal interaction and more to do with a system that favored the White students over the Black students.

When he was in eighth grade his parents sent him to Sabbath school to be instructed in the Jewish religion of his father, even though his father was far from devoted to his own religious practice. Most of the students in the Sabbath school attended Jewish private schools and came from upper-middle-class homes. Being only one of a handful of Jewish kids in the public schools, he felt discriminated against for being of a lesser class when he went to the Temple. By the time he had reached the ninth grade, the tension got so great that he walked out never to return. While today he acknowledges his Jewish heritage, religiously Wise considers himself an agnostic.

Despite developing cross-racial friendships early on, they did not always last, and Tim found that despite his best efforts at being honest and open with folks, he still got caught up in the racial dynamics of the larger society of which he was a part. When he was in third grade, two of his Black friends referred to him as their "nigger" on the playground. Although his friends seemed to be getting a good laugh at calling him that, Tim felt increasingly uncomfortable because they were using a word that he had been forbidden to utter. Many years later Wise realized that his Black friends had innocently "flipped the script" of racial dynamics by calling him their "nigger." He wrote: "What I realized is that even at the age of nine . . . they had known what it meant to be someone's nigger."[13] At that young age Wise didn't have the language to express what he was feeling, but during these years his consciousness had begun to develop.

When Wise got to high school his academic performance was sporadic, not for lack of intelligence, but because of lack of interest and a lack of effort. Where he found his greatest joy was participating on the debate team. In contrast to his involvement in sports, which tended to be dominated by Black kids, the debate team was an activity largely pursued by White kids. Sports and theater had served as an escape from his troubled

[13] Wise, *White Like Me Reflections*, 26.

home life when in middle school, and debate became his refuge in high school. By the end of high school he had become a successful debater, a skill he would eventually develop into a career of public speaking.

Wise was also regularly involved in the party scene at his high school. Even here he noticed racism at work. Although the local police routinely raided the poor and African American neighborhoods in the "War on Drugs," those same police looked the other way when parties were held at homes in predominantly White neighborhoods.

In high school Wise began to develop the political sensibilities that came to characterize his career. One of the only Black students on the debate team, James Bernard, who was three years older and an activist, inspired Tim. He also found inspiration listening to punk music, which not only spoke to his adolescent alienation but also made him aware of burning political issues. Through his involvement with punk music, he became aware of the antiapartheid movement in South Africa, which in turn led him to read a collection of essays by martyred South African activist Stephen Biko. Biko's book *I Write What I Want* served as an example of one who spoke his truth without reservation, something Tim would later do.

Following in the fashion of Biko, Wise wrote a 350-word essay in an underground school newspaper when the high school administration suspended a cross-dressing male student who came to school wearing a skirt; the administration had threatened similar action to anyone who came to the young man's defense. So Wise was not surprised when he was summoned to the principal's office, expecting he too would be suspended. Instead, after talking briefly about the essay, the principal said to him: "I don't think you recognize your power," and described how he felt Tim could persuade the student body to just about anything he wanted them to do. He concluded by warning Wise to be careful how he used his persuasive powers. From that point Wise knew his "road was coming clear."[14]

In high school as in middle school he also saw that Black students and White students were often tracked on the basis of perceived differences in their academic potential. So although he was a less-than-stellar student, was a party-er, and took joy in annoying White teachers with his use of "Black English" and his love of rap music, he was placed on the advanced track, while more studious African American students were put on the lower track.

---

[14] Wise, *White Like Me Remix*, 80.

Getting Schooled at Tulane

Despite substandard SAT scores and a spotty academic record, Wise received a scholarship to Tulane University. He lived on a dorm floor where marijuana use was rampant among the White students. As in high school, he noticed that when it came to drug and alcohol use, the predominantly White Tulane students got a pass in contrast to the residents of the largely Black neighborhood near the university. Although White students were warned about staying out of certain areas of the city that were predominantly Black and poor, he noticed that the Black students were not warned about staying out of the racially hostile White suburbs. These sorts of discrepancies stayed with him and heightened his racial consciousness.

By the time he arrived at Tulane in 1986 he considered himself to be "hip, liberal, aware of racism and committed to fighting it,"[15] and yet found during those years that his commitments, however strong, lacked a certain depth and breadth. He got his first taste of activism when he became involved with protests against US support for right-wing regimes in Central America. In 1987 he joined a student campaign to persuade the university trustees to divest from companies conducting business in the apartheid regime of South Africa. In this campaign the White activists were joined by several Black student organizations linking the protest against South Africa to a call for restoring the university's African American studies program and increasing their commitment to recruit students and faculty of color. One of their early successes in this campaign was to persuade Archbishop Desmond Tutu, who was scheduled to speak on campus, to refuse the invitation until the university's board of trustees divested of companies doing business with the apartheid South African regime.

After working together for about a year, the alliance between the White activists and the Black organizations fell apart. As the alliance dissolved, so did the White students' commitment to addressing the other issues raised by the African American students. Even so the predominantly White Tulane Students Against Apartheid (TUAA), as they came to be called, continued to hold demonstrations, even constructing shantytowns on the college green, and participating in a hunger strike asking for the trustees to accede to student demands to divest; eventually the students successfully persuaded the trustees to reinvest the university's investment portfolio.

---

[15] Wise, *White Like Me Remix*, 95.

In the excitement of the seeming victory over the divestment issue, Tim was confronted in a public meeting by an African American student from a neighboring college. She questioned why he and the others could have a deep concern for apartheid in South Africa, while ignoring the apartheid in New Orleans all around them. The question hit him like a punch in the stomach because he "had been doing all this work against racism half a world away, but frankly had done nothing to speak of in opposition to the racism in the town where [he] was living."[16] He realized that even in his liberalism and overt antiracist efforts he could perpetuate White privilege and power. The commitment to work against racism overseas without having an equal passion for racial justice at home made him acutely aware of his inherited, but largely unconscious, racism, and moved him on the path to becoming an outspoken antiracism advocate. As he reflected on the incident for weeks following, he realized he "had been completely oblivious to the way in which [his] own privilege . . . had obscured [his] understanding of issues as accountability, the need to link up struggles . . . and the need to always have leadership of color in any antiracist struggle."[17]

Another pivotal experience occurred the summer of 1989, between his junior and senior years, when he and his mother visited Philadelphia, Mississippi, to attend the twenty-fifth anniversary of the deaths of James Chaney, Michael Schwerner, and Andrew Goodman, three civil rights volunteers with the Student Nonviolent Coordinating Committee (SNCC), who had been killed while participating in Freedom Summer 1964.[18] The event held at a Baptist church in Philadelphia was attended by numerous civil rights leaders, celebrities, and people who had been involved in the events twenty-five years earlier. What was most profound for Wise was the vast number of White people present that day who had participated in the civil rights movement. He wrote, "I had never, in my life, been in the presence of so many white allies in one place, so many whites who had put their lives on the line for justice."[19] Like so many others, he had not been taught that many Whites also joined in the struggle for civil rights under the leadership of their Black coun-

---

[16] Wise, *White Like Me Reflections*, 115.

[17] Wise, *White Like Me Remix*, 123–24.

[18] Freedom Summer was an effort organized by SNCC to register Black voters in Mississippi. Chaney, Schwerner, and Goodman were murdered within three days of their arrival. Their story is told in Kirk Mitchell, *Mississippi Burning* (New York: Signet, 1989).

[19] Wise, *White Like Me Reflections*, 83.

terparts. Coming away from that event, he noted that "when people of color, in positions of leadership, can count on and call upon the efforts of committed whites . . . real change is possible."[20] In essence Tim Wise has sought to fulfill this statement in over twenty-five years of antiracist work all over the country.

Organizing in New Orleans

In 1989 avowed White supremacist and former Grand Wizard of the KKK, David Duke, successfully ran for a seat in the Louisiana House of Representatives. A year later he ran in the Republican primary for a seat in the US Senate. While still in college Wise had worked on the campaign with the Louisiana Coalition Against Racism and Nazism to defeat Duke. This experience not only expanded his activism into the political realm but also helped him develop his ability to talk about political and racial issues with the working-class Whites that tended to support a David Duke candidacy. Owing to a challenge from a girlfriend, Wise began entering bars in Metairie, Louisiana (which was in Duke's state legislative district), and engaging the customers in conversations about the issues Duke had highlighted in his campaigns, such as immigration, affirmative action, welfare, and poverty. Although he was not successful in changing anyone's mind, he learned a valuable lesson: "that there are ways to talk to people, even truly tough cases, and make some headway, break down defenses, get people to at least begin to question the things they have always taken for granted."[21] He came away realizing that treating people with respect and love is necessary if White allies will ever be able to persuade other people to change their deeply embedded stereotypes and racist perceptions.

Upon graduation from Tulane, Wise continued to work on the campaigns to defeat David Duke's respective runs for Senate, governor, and president. Out of a job in 1992, he followed a girlfriend to Houston, Texas, where he worked various odd jobs. In May of that year because of his work on the Duke campaign, he received a call to appear on the *Jane Whitney Show*, a syndicated television talk show where he appeared with two former KKK members and two current KKK members to talk about the White supremacist movement. For Wise, though the show had a short run, it initiated him into the public realm and showed him even committed racists could be transformed. Then in 1993 Wise was invited

---

[20] Ibid., 84.

[21] Ibid., 90.

to testify as an expert in racial discrimination in the case of Jimmy Jackson, a Black football coach who was suing the National Football League for racial discrimination. These two incidents were formative for Wise in helping get a firsthand look into the complex dynamics of systemic racism.

In 1994 Wise and his girlfriend returned to New Orleans, where he worked a number of part-time jobs until April 1995 when he was hired as a researcher and community organizer for Agenda for Children, an antiracist child advocacy organization. This job put him in direct contact with individuals and families living in low-income housing units in the city. For the first time in his life, Wise got to hear firsthand the stories of the community residents, and he saw the human toll that racism takes. At the same time he was seeing the depth of poverty in the city, he also was moved by the wealth of grassroots knowledge and wisdom these same residents had to cope with the conditions and challenge the structures and policies oppressing them.

As part of his employment at Agenda, Wise was required to attend an "Undoing Racism" workshop sponsored by People's Institute for Survival and Beyond, a New Orleans based antiracism training organization. Although initially anticipating that the purpose of the training was to stir up his White guilt, the workshop helped him for the first time to see clearly that racism was harmful to White people in a way he had not considered. Like his great-grandfather Jacob Wise, who had given up his name when he came to the United States, Europeans had been forced to let go of their unique cultures and the customs, traditions, and practices of their ancestors, as part of the process of assimilating into White culture. Thus, not only was Whiteness linked to discrimination toward People of Color, but also it had robbed Whites of their unique cultural identities.

Speaking Out

While still working for Agenda, Tim was invited to add his name to Speak Out, a California-based organization that provided speakers for colleges and other organizations looking for presenters with a politically progressive viewpoint. His first speaking opportunity came in March 1995 at two colleges in the Chicago area. By the end of that year he had gone on a number of speaking engagements and found that he enjoyed sharing his views with others and meeting young activists all over the United States. By early 1996 he realized that his traveling was disrupting his work in New Orleans, and that while he loved the organizing work, he wasn't particularly good at it. So by mid-1996 he left Agenda, and returned to Nashville to begin what would be a new phase in his life.

By this time he had left his longtime girlfriend, but shortly after arriving in Nashville, he met Kristy Cason, the woman who eventually became his wife. Kristy impressed him as someone who shared his values and supported his work, but at the same time let him know that she had her life too, and as their relationship developed, he came to appreciate how she kept him grounded. They eventually married and now have two children, Ashton and Rachel.

By this time, Tim had decided to try to make a career out of speaking and writing. This track provided an unsteady income, and so occasionally he picked up jobs with local political organizations. One such job was as the director of the Tennessee Coalition to Abolish State Killing (TCASK), a statewide anti-death penalty organization. However, after only eight months he resigned in April 2000, realizing his talents did not lie in management. So he decided to focus on what he loved: speaking and writing.

White Privilege, White Power, and the Pervasiveness of Racism

Wise addresses a wide range of issues, but three consistent subjects characterize his messages: the nature of White privilege, an analysis of the White power structure, and the pervasiveness of racism in White culture. When speaking about White privilege, Wise often uses his own experience as an example. In his memoir, *White Like Me*, which has been updated and revised two times, Wise couches his personal story in the context of the White privilege in which he was born and raised. In *White Like Me* he points out that on the surface his circumstances at birth did not appear to be privileged, because he had been born into a family with an alcoholic father, and they lived in what many would consider a working-class neighborhood. However, being White gave him advantages that were not enjoyed by many of his African American peers, such as being able to trace his lineage back to Europe, being given deference in school despite his underachieving performance and wisecracking attitude, being able to attend college by using his grandmother's house as collateral for school loans, seeing underage White Tulane students use drugs and drink alcohol while the authorities looked the other way, and so much more.

Wise continually emphasizes that while their privilege is largely invisible to Whites, it is blatantly evident to People of Color, and if Whites want to challenge racism and dismantle White supremacist structures, they need to start with themselves. In one of his early speaking engagements an African American college student responded to a talk he gave on racism by stating that as an African American she hated and distrusted him and other White people. Wise responded to the woman's challenge by acknowledging the justification for her feelings, and then said: "I mean no disrespect [but] I am not fighting racism to save you. That would be paternalistic. . . . I fight racism because racism is a sickness in *my* community, and it damages me." He went on to say: "Challenging racism and white supremacy is what we *should* be doing. Resistance is what we need to do for *us*."[22]

Wise's second common theme follows very closely: an analysis of the White power structure. In his book *Between Barack and a Hard Place*,[23] Wise analyzes the presidential election of 2008 through the lens of racism: how Barack Obama was able to rise to the nation's highest political office as the first biracial or Black president. While acknowledging the truly historic nature of Obama's victory, Wise notes that from early on his candidacy was framed by the media by how White Americans would respond to a Black president, and whether or not they were ready for that. He points out that the election demonstrated the precipitous decline of overt race-based bigotry (Racism 1.0) in favor what he refers to as "black exceptionalism" (Racism 2.0). In this new form of racism Whites see Obama as the exception to their general perception of Black men as violent, dangerous, unmotivated, and not to be trusted. Obama succeeded in large part because he helped White people "feel comfortable" with him as a Black man in contrast to their general disdain of the Black population. When he did speak on racism, he did so in way that did not confront White folks with the historical legacy or present reality of racism.

Wise then goes on to point out that following the election many commentators, both conservative and liberal, celebrated that American society had "gotten beyond race," even though clearly racist tactics were used by Obama's opponents and critics from Hillary Clinton to Rush Limbaugh. Moreover, despite his election, huge disparities by race still exist in health care, education, housing, employment, income,

---

[22] Wise, *White Like Me Remix*, 182.

[23] Tim Wise, *Between Barack and a Hard Place: Racism and White Denial in the Age of Obama* (San Francisco: City Lights Books, 2009).

and criminal justice. While acknowledging that in order to get elected Obama may have had to employ the tactics and framing of this message as he did, Wise concludes:

> We must at least recognize what his need to pander to the perceived needs of the white electorate means about race and racism in this country. It means nothing more and nothing less: White folks are still calling the shots. White folks still hold the power. White folks still get to call the tune.[24]

The very fact that Obama was able to "transcend race" demonstrates how intact the White power structure still is.

A third common theme is the pervasiveness of racism in White culture. One story Wise uses to illustrate this point involves his paternal grandmother, who, in her later years, was diagnosed with Alzheimer's disease. For much of his life, his grandmother had instilled in her children and grandchildren "a deep and abiding contempt for bigotry and racism."[25] She had been a strong supporter of Wise's career choice and had made choices throughout her life to follow a different path from her racist upbringing. Yet in the latter days of her life, with her mind deteriorating, she could be heard shouting racial epithets at the Black nurses attending to her. As Wise wrote: "She could not remember how to feed herself. She could not go to the bathroom by herself. She could not recognize a glass of water for what it was. But she could recognize a *nigger*."[26] The fact that virtually all memory could be lost, and yet deep-seated racism would still remain was a sign to him of how pervasive and all-encompassing racism is in the White cultural psyche.

Controversy

Since the decision in 1996 to focus on speaking and writing, Tim Wise has become a nationally recognized spokesperson on issues related to White racism in the United States. While he has never been seriously harmed, he has received death threats and been the focus of bomb scares that occasionally required the presence of special security guards and at times even the FBI. He has been accused of being "anti-White and anti-American" and the focus of numerous protests when speaking at

[24] Wise, *White Like Me Remix*, 91.
[25] Ibid., 199.
[26] Ibid., 200.

particular venues. He has been confronted by White supremacists, neo-Nazis and KKK-ers, though more often than not the resistance he has experienced has been more passive from people who don't think of themselves as racists. His blogs and Facebook pages often receive comments critical of statements he has made or written. Wise recognizes that in his messages he is betraying the unwritten and often unconscious rules of Whiteness. As he says, "To speak against the prerogatives of Whiteness, or merely break the silence about white racism, is at some level to engage in 'race treason.'"[27] However, he is quick to add that his treason is against Whiteness—White privilege and White supremacy—and not White people, who are victimized by Whiteness as are People of Color.

While Wise understandably upsets many conservatives, he has also been criticized by antiracist activists of color. A critic of other antiracist activists is a blogger named Trudy, who identifies herself as a Black Jamaican woman and is the author of a blog called *The Gradient Lair*. In a 2013 posting, *The Gradient Lair* criticized Wise for lashing out on Facebook at a Person of Color who felt that he was taking speaking opportunities and venues that could have justifiably gone to a Person of Color. Wise was further criticized for not acknowledging that his ability to do antiracist work is due to the privilege he enjoys as a White male. The blogger than questioned why Black people look to a White person like Wise to speak on their behalf, when there are numerous Persons of Color doing the same work and saying much the same thing as Wise. Wise later apologized for his "rant" on Facebook, but it did not appear to mollify his critics.[28] Ewuare Osayande has been Wise's most outspoken critic. Osayande has noted that because of his privilege Wise has received speaking engagements that activists of color could (and in Osayande's view should) be taking. He further criticizes Wise for failing to accompany his words with public actions, demonstrations, or even civil disobedience against institutional racism.

These observations and criticisms illustrate the fine line that an antiracist activist like Tim Wise walks between those whose minds he is trying to change and those with whom he considers himself an ally. Wise himself acknowledges his own privilege in his speaking engagements and concedes that sometimes as a White antiracist activist he is perceived as less threatening to the audiences (often on college campuses)

---

[27] Tim Wise, *Speaking Treason Fluently: Anti-Racist Reflections from an Angry White Male* (Washington, DC: Soft Skull Press, 2008), 4.

[28] The Gradient Lair, "I Don't Want Tim Wise as an Ally. No Thanks," blog posting September 17, 2013, http://www.gradientlair.com.

where he is invited to speak. However he is quick to add that at times it is important that White people hear from other White people as to the nature and damage of the White supremacy that permeates the American system. Osayande contends that Wise has not said anything that has not been said before and often by others; the difference is that he is White.[29] Wise would not disagree, but feels where he is given an opportunity to speak and challenge racist policies, he should take it. As the fellow antiracist author and speaker Curtiss DeYoung notes, even when White antiracist allies are seeking to address areas of racism, racial dynamics come into play, and so it is important that Whites like Wise and DeYoung make themselves accountable to people of color.[30] What Wise critics most want him to acknowledge is the validity of their concerns; and he does.

The Ongoing Struggle

Tim Wise has made a career out of being an antiracist speaker and author. On average he has about seventy-five engagements, traveling 80,000 miles a year. His work has enabled him to share the stage with renowned civil rights leaders, such as Jeremiah Wright Jr., Michael Eric Dyson, and Angela Davis. Following the tragic events of September 11, 2001, Wise sought to raise awareness of the racist implications of profiling and blaming all Arab Americans and Muslims for the bombing of the World Trade Center. In 2008 when Rev. Jeremiah Wright Jr. came under public attack for statements he had made criticizing the United States while Barack Obama was a member of his congregation, Wise publicly supported Rev. Wright and the views he expressed. Wise now maintains a rigorous speaking schedule nine months of the year and takes the summers off, and has written nine books, including three editions of his memoir, and maintains a regular blog (timwise.org).

As a father, a new dimension to Wise's antiracism work now involves conveying antiracist values to his children. He and Kristy take an active role in providing natural opportunities for their children to interact with children of other races through school and extracurricular activities. They also try to expose them to positive authority figures who are

---

[29] Ewuare Osayande, "Word to the Wise: Unpacking the White Privilege of Tim Wise," Ewuare X. Osayande Website, August 23, 2013, http://www.osayande.org; Rosemary McClure, "Does Tim Wise's Success Marginalize Anti-racist Activists of Color?" *Scripps Voice*, April 3, 2013, http://www.scrippscollege.edu.

[30] Interview with Curtiss DeYoung, March 9, 2013.

People of Color. They also pay close attention to the media images their children take in. For instance, Wise shared that when the Disney movie *Pocahantas* came out, he gave in to his daughters' desires to watch it, but then afterward Tim and Kristy sat with them and deconstructed the racist images portrayed in the film. Even so, he knows he cannot prevent his daughters from absorbing White racist cultural images. Altogether, Tim and Kristy realize that more than anything, the most important lesson will be the example they set living day in and day out as parents.

Knowing how important his children are to him, I find it unsurprising that in the years ahead Wise hopes to do more work in schools with younger children. He also has sought to inject more humor into his presentations, recognizing that humor can often make his message easier to receive. He continues to speak and teach, and, while he has no grand plan, hopes to continue doing so for many years to come.

At the end of *White Like Me*, Wise sums up how he sees the ongoing struggle to eradicate racism in the United States. He writes:

> Let's be honest; there is no such place called "justice," if by that we envision a finish line, or a point at which the battle is won and the need to continue to struggle is over. After all, even when you succeed in obtaining a measure of justice, you're always forced to mobilize to defend what you've won. There is no looming vacation. But there is redemption in the struggle.[31]

As to whether or not racism can ever be eradicated, he writes:

> I have no idea when (or if) racism will be eradicated. I have no idea whether anything I say, do or write will make the least bit of difference in the world. But I say, do or write it anyway, because as uncertain as the outcome of our resistance may be, the outcome of our silence and inaction is anything but. We know exactly what will happen if we don't do the work: nothing. And given that choice, between certainty and promise, in which territory one finds the measure of our resolve and humanity, I will opt for hope.[32]

To that end, Tim Wise keeps speaking the truth about racism in the United States.

---

[31] Wise, *White Like Me Remix*, 270.

[32] Ibid., 271.

Discussion Questions

1. Wise attributes his early awareness to relationships he developed with People of Color in childhood. What are some the relationships you have developed with people of other races that have informed your understanding of racism in America?
2. At different times Wise was confronted with the unconscious racism and privilege in his life. If you are White, what are some experiences that made you aware of your White privilege?
3. How do you respond to the criticisms of fellow antiracist activists who believe Tim Wise is able to write and speak largely because of White privilege? Can Whites acknowledge their privilege and still be allies of People of Color in the struggle for racial justice?

Bibliography

Boyd, Drick. Personal interview with Tim Wise, November 13, 2013.

Gradient Lair. "I Don't Want Tim Wise as an Ally. No Thanks." Blog posting September 17. 2013. http://www.gradientlair.com.

McClure, Rosemary. "Does Tim Wise's Success Marginalize Anti-racist Activists of Color?" *Scripps Voice* 16, no. 10 (April 3, 2013): 6–7. http://www.scrippscollege.edu.

Osayande, Ewuare. "Word to the Wise: Unpacking the White Privilege of Tim Wise," Ewuare X. Osayande Website, August 23, 2013. http://www.osayande.org.

Thompson, Cooper, Emmett Schaefer, and Harry Brod. *White Men Challenging Racism: 35 Personal Stories*. Durham, NC: Duke University Press, 2003.

Wise, Tim. *Between Barack and a Hard Place: Racism and White Denial in the Age of Obama*. San Francisco: City Lights Books, 2009.

———. *Dear White America: Letter to a New Minority*. San Francisco: City Lights Books, 2012.

———. *Speaking Treason Fluently: Anti-racist Reflections from an Angry White Male*. Washington, DC: Soft Skull Press, 2008.

———. *White Like Me: Reflections on Race from a Privileged Son*. Brooklyn, NY: Soft Skull Press, 2005.

———. *White Like Me: Reflections on Race from a Privileged Son; the Remix: Revised and Updated Edition*. Berkeley, CA: Soft Skull Press, 2011.

Conclusion

From Sympathetic Awareness to Active Alliance

> Therefore, since we are surrounded by such a great cloud of witnesses, let us throw off everything that hinders and the sin that so easily entangles. And let us run with perseverance the race marked out for us.
>
> — *Hebrews* 12:1

A Cloud of Witnesses

The challenge of writing a book relating the stories of White allies involved in the struggle for racial justice is that many people whose stories are worthy of telling have not been included. I am acutely aware that the list of individuals I have chosen to write about in this book is incomplete. The stories related here are representative, rather than exhaustive, and consequently I have provided a brief list of other White Allies in the Appendix. Fortunately, recent scholarship has begun to explore the stories of White individuals who have worked for racial justice,[1] and some activists still living have recorded their stories.[2] Moreover, others have begun researching current White advocates for racial justice and

[1] Some recent works telling these stories include Cynthia Stokes Brown, *Refusing Racism: White Allies and the Struggle for Civil Rights* (New York: Teachers College Press, 2002); Cooper Thompson, Emmett Schaefer, and Harry Brod, *White Men Challenging Racism: 35 Personal Stories* (Durham, NC: Duke University Press, 2003); Robin K. Bertson, *Marching to a Different Drummer: Unrecognized Heroes of American History* (Westport, CT: Greenwood Press, 1994); Barbara Barnsby, *Deep in Our Hearts: Nine White Women in the Freedom Movement* (Athens: University of Georgia Press, 2000).

[2] Many of these personal accounts have served as sources for this book.

the motivations behind their choices and actions.[3] The purpose of these studies is not only to tell a history of White antiracist activism that is unknown in US history but also to provide models and a way forward for White individuals to likewise engage themselves in the pursuit of a racially just society.

As Mark Warren[4] points out, despite centuries of effort to eradicate racial injustice in US society, it continues to persist albeit in a subtler form. Significant disparities in education, economic opportunity, health care, incarceration rates, and housing quality continue to exist in the United States between most Whites and most People of Color. Despite heroic efforts to undo Jim Crow segregation, Whites and People of Color continue to reside in largely separate communities, attend separate schools, worship in separate communities of faith, and socialize in separate networks. Even so, the vast majority of White Americans repeatedly express disapproval of overtly racist statements or acts, and believe racial reconciliation is a desirable, if elusive, social goal.

One limitation in the way a majority of Whites think about racism is that they see it solely on an individual, personal level, and do not recognize its systemic and cultural dimensions. Whites tend to espouse what Eduardo Bonilla-Silva calls "colorblind racism" claiming they don't "see color," yet ignoring the way in which the structures, policies, and institutional practices continue to discriminate along the lines of race.[5] Because they do not acknowledge the institutional nature of racism or practice racism on a conscious interpersonal level, Whites tend to think of the racial disparities that exist in US society as due to a lack of individual initiative or effort, rather than societal norms or institutional practices. Moreover, Whites point to the two-time election of an African American president as evidence that we as a nation have moved past racism, but we still are ignoring or explaining away the disparities mentioned above.

Most Whites today look at the three centuries leading up to the current era as a period when racism was far more overt, violent, and

---

[3] Two recent studies include Mark Warren, *Fire in the Heart: How White Activists Embrace Racial Justice* (New York: Oxford University Press, 2010); and Becky Thompson, *A Promise and a Way of Life: White Antiracist Activism* (Minneapolis: University of Minnesota Press, 2001).

[4] Warren, *Fire in the Heart.*

[5] Eduardo Bonilla-Silva, *Racism without Racists: Colorblind Racism and the Persistence of Racial Inequality in America* (Lanham, MD: Rowan and Littlefield, 2006).

clearly unjust. What these same Whites fail to take into account is that in the times of slavery, Jim Crow, and the civil rights movement, the vast majority of Whites did not see the racist practices and structures of their time as any more unjust than most Whites do of the unjust systems and practices today. Just as Whites concerned about racial justice today must fight the complacency within the status quo, so too the people in this book had to challenge the comfortable status quo of their times. In addition, many Whites in times past who recognized that the practices of their times were fundamentally unfair to People of Color did not act to eradicate those injustices. They either rationalized the status quo on the basis of other priorities, or they chose to believe that the racial disparities of their time would eventually dissipate on their own.

However, one thing that is clear from these stories is that racial injustice is pervasive and pernicious and does not dissipate of its own accord. Rather, institutional racism must be dismantled through concerted, deliberate action. The people in this book were persons who joined with others to actively dismantle the racist practices and structures of their time. They paid dearly for their actions. All of them encountered strained family relations and friendships, as well as a loss of social status and political influence. Some struggled with financial solvency, and others endured physical injury, in some cases to the point of death.

What Motivated Them

The question I try to address in this chapter is "Why?" What motivated them to move beyond an awareness of racial injustice to actively seeking to undo it? What motivated them to act in ways that were contrary to their personal self-interest? Why were they willing to endure societal scorn, social alienation, and in some cases physical harm, while most White people of their day considered their actions to be unwise, immoral, and subversive?

In his study of contemporary White racial justice activists, Mark Warren presents three sociological models used to explain the actions of White antiracist allies.[6] The first model is the interest-convergence model put forth by Derrick Bell and other Critical Race theorists, which asserts that Whites support Black demands and projects when they converge or coincide with White self-interest. For instance, from the perspective of the interest-convergence model White Democratic leaders in the

---

[6] Warren, *Fire in the Heart*, 15–22.

1950s and 1960s supported civil rights legislation because it converged with their desire to project a positive image abroad. In contrast to the concept of interest convergence is the altruistic model, which suggests that Whites work for the benefit of People of Color because in some way they see it as the morally right thing to do. So in the case of civil rights legislation, the changes in law were the right thing to do to address the concerns of Black people, but did not seriously challenge the White power structure that created the injustices in the first place. The limitation of the altruistic view is that it assumes that racial justice is not something that Whites need or want for themselves; it is just for others. Warren puts forward a third model, which draws from both the interest-convergence and altruistic models. Based on scholarship on why individuals join social movements, this alternative model proposes that when Whites authentically work for racial justice, they do so because they see that it is beneficial both for them and for the People of Color with whom they are allied. Warren suggests that the key elements of this alternative model are a sense of moral shock at injustice, personal relationships with People of Color suffering under that injustice, and a vision of what a racially just society might look like. By and large and in varying degrees, the stories in this volume make the most sense in light of this third model. Admittedly, most of the people whose stories are told in this book first became involved in the struggle for racial justice because of self-interest or a noble sense of altruistically helping the disadvantaged People of Color in their midst. However, although that may be where they started, it is not where they ended up; in the end they saw their destinies inextricably bound with those they were seeking to help. As Anne Braden admitted about her own journey, she started with "a mission consciousness," but in the end came to believe "it wasn't that we were 'helping those poor blacks.' It was our struggle too."[7]

The distinction between acting out of self-interest or altruism and this more authentic form of active alliance can be seen in James Cone's critique of Reinhold Niebuhr.[8] Niebuhr was widely influential in shaping social and political attitudes, as well as Christian responses

[7] Catherine Fosl, *Subversive Southerner: Anne Braden and the Struggle for Racial Justice in the Cold War South* (New York: Palgrave Macmillan, 2002), 102, 198.

[8] James Cone, *The Cross and the Lynching Tree* (Maryknoll, NY: Orbis Books, 2011), 30–64.

to social and political problems, in the mid-twentieth century. Many have considered him to be the most influential Christian thinker of his time. He began as a pastor in Detroit from 1915 to 1928 ministering among workers, and then went on to be a professor of Christian social ethics and theology at Union Theological Seminary in New York from 1928 to 1960. Niebuhr wrote numerous books, edited the progressive journal *Christianity and Crisis*, and was a widely sought-after speaker and adviser to preachers, educators, and political leaders.

Niebuhr spoke out on many issues of his day, including the role of democracy in achieving justice, the Nazis' treatment of the Jews, and poverty and economic injustice. Cone points out, however, that when it came to racial issues, Niebuhr was far less articulate, forceful, and insistent on the need for change. Niebuhr acknowledged the scourge of segregation, the tragedy of lynchings, and other forms of race-based violence in some of his writings, but responded by calling for gradual change, patience, and prudence on the part of the African American community that was the target of these injustices. In Cone's words "had eyes to see black suffering but . . . lacked the heart to feel it as his own."[9]

Cone asks: "How could anyone be a great theologian and not engage America's greatest moral issue?"[10] Although Niebuhr wrote extensively about the "Jewish question" and developed significant relationships with prominent Jewish leaders, he had few if any such relationships with prominent African Americans, even though his office at the time was less than a mile from Harlem, the "capital" of Black America. According to Cone, he lacked true empathy for the suffering and injustice faced by African Americans in the mid-twentieth century, and therefore lacked the passion to speak out against the evil they were enduring. Late in his life Niebuhr himself admitted his failure to address the gross injustices of systemic racism and his fear of speaking out on issues that ran counter to the prevailing opinion of White Americans in the 1940s and 1950s. Despite his influence on African American leaders such as Martin Luther King Jr., Barack Obama, and even Cone himself, Reinhold Niebuhr did not use his considerable influence to act and speak in ways that addressed the injustices he saw, keeping him from ever truly becoming what one would call an activist ally.

---

[9] Ibid., 41.

[10] Ibid., 51–52.

From Awareness to Activism

So what moves a White person from simply being aware of racism and being sympathetically concerned to taking concerted steps to ally themselves with People of Color in combating the racist practices and structures of their time? In the lives of the people whose stories are told in this book, there are at least five factors that seem evident.

The first and most compelling factor is the *development of authentic personal relationships* with People of Color. With the exception of Elijah Lovejoy and John Woolman, every person in this book had at least one, and in many cases several, significant relationships with People of Color. Abraham Joshua Heschel developed a close friendship with Martin Luther King Jr., so much so that he was compelled to go to Selma when the call went out. John Rankin worked closely with John Parker to assist slaves escaping the South for freedom. Angelina Grimké and Theodore Weld offended the people of Philadelphia by inviting several prominent African Americans to their wedding. Anne Braden was a close, personal confidante to Ella Baker. Curtiss DeYoung was mentored by African American pastors and teachers, and married an African American woman.

As Warren points out, the development of significant personal relationships across racial lines is critical in part because such relationships give Whites "approximating experiences of racism."[11] Anne Braden was told that when she and she husband endured harassment because of their efforts to purchase a house for Andrew Wade in a White suburb, that she had become part of the "other America" where African Americans lived. When J. Waties Waring was ostracized by the White community of Charleston, South Carolina, he and his wife were sustained by relationships with Black leaders such as Septima Clark who understood the struggle they were facing. Viola Liuzzo was inspired to join the march from Selma to Montgomery through the influence of her African American classmates at Wayne State University.

In some cases their relationships with People of Color helped these Whites to more clearly understand the dynamics of racism. Curtiss DeYoung shared with me that his wife has helped him know how to effectively guide their two biracial children in dealing with the prejudice they face in their lives. Likewise, Mary White Ovington was mentored by W. E. B. Du Bois in her efforts to understand the plight of Negroes

[11] Warren, *Fire in the Heart*, 20.

in New York. Du Bois allowed her to be one of few Whites and the only White woman to attend meetings of the Niagara Movement. Robert Graetz was guided and helped by the members of his all-Black congregation, as he sought to find his place in the Montgomery bus boycott.

A second key factor moving White people from awareness to activism is a *compelling moral conviction*. Despite the acquiescence of their respective communities to the justification and common acceptance of racist practices, the people in this book acted out of a deep sense that their White community was essentially wrong in its acceptance of racist practices. For some, this sense of outrage came as a result of their religious faith. John Woolman's Quaker belief in the dignity of all persons moved him to travel tirelessly to convince Quaker slaveholders to release their slaves. Clarence Jordan and Martin England founded Koinonia Farms from the dream of establishing a radical Christian community that would model positive relationships between Blacks and Whites in rural Georgia. Abraham Joshua Heschel continually spoke about his work on behalf of the Black community as integral and consistent with his Jewish faith.

While many of those whose stories are told in this book rooted their convictions in their religious faith, the religious communities of which they were a part ostracized them for the application of the very truths those communities had taught them. Angelina Grimké, who was a deeply religious person, left the Presbyterian church when the elders refused to see the inconsistency of their Christian faith and slaveholding, and then left the Quaker community when they criticized her for acting out publicly on the abolitionist spirit that the Quakers said they had. Clarence Jordan and his family were kicked out of the Baptist church in Americus because of their commitment to racial reconciliation. Morris Dees and his wife were ostracized when they dared to stand up in their rural Alabama church and invited people to pray for the victims of the Sixteenth Street Baptist Church bombing. Levi Coffin was forced to start the Indiana Meeting of Anti-Slavery Friends when the regular Indiana Meeting ordered him to cease his Underground Railroad activities. In each case these individuals chose to suffer rejection rather than renounce their conviction to resist the racist practices of their religious communities.

Others, though not motivated primarily by religious convictions, had a deep sense of the immorality of racism. Tim Wise inherited his mother's passion for racial justice from the time she placed him in the nearly all-Black preschool at Tennessee State University, and where some of his earliest friendships were forged with children of color. Myles Horton grew up in a family where he learned to respect the inherent wisdom of common people of all races. Likewise, Mary White Ovington was the daughter of abolitionists and from her earliest days believed that people of all races were worthy of respect.

In having such convictions, these folks were not unique; what caused them to stand out is their willingness to live out those convictions despite vigorous and often violent opposition to their views. At different times Anne Braden, Myles Horton, and Virginia Durr had to respond to charges that they were Communist subversives seeking to overthrow the US government because of their commitments to racial justice. Morris Dees has been the target of an estimated thirty assassination attempts because of his ongoing efforts to prosecute White supremacist hate groups. Robert Graetz had his home bombed, Clarence Jordan's farms came under repeated attack, and Viola Liuzzo and Elijah Lovejoy paid the ultimate price of death. Yet in each case they remained steadfast.

Even if their convictions did not lead to death, often they led to family estrangement. Angelina and Sarah Grimké were never able to return to their home of Charleston, South Carolina, because of their abolitionist views. Anne Braden lived in constant tension with her parents, despite the love and care they had for each other. Viola Liuzzo's husband objected to her actions, and he and her children had to live with the ignominy of her death for decades. Virginia Durr broke away from all the traditions and expectations of an aristocratic Southern woman by choosing to work for racial justice, effectively isolating herself from friends and family.

A third factor that may seem obvious but that can be so easily overlooked is deliberately *making a choice to act and speak against racism publicly* even in the face of opposition. In his "Letter from a Birmingham Jail" Martin Luther King Jr. was pointedly critical of so-called White moderates who said they were sympathetic to the cause of racial justice but failed to act on their convictions. Such persons were "more devoted to 'order' than justice," and he found their "lukewarm acceptance . . . much more bewildering than outright rejection."[12] The persons whose stories are told here move beyond words of support to explicit actions to dismantle the structures of racial injustice.

Although the process of enlightenment leading to action may have been gradual, at some point in their lives each of the persons whose

[12] Martin Luther King Jr., "Letter from a Birmingham Jail," in *Why We Can't Wait*, by Martin Luther King Jr. (New York: Signet Classic, 1963), 73.

story is told here made a deliberate decision to act on his or her convictions. As was said earlier, these were not the only ones in their time who *thought* about such things, but they were distinguished by their *decision to act on the convictions they had*. After the uncomfortable experience of writing a bill of sale for a slave woman, John Woolman made the decision to visit Quaker meetings and individuals to try to persuade them to free their slaves. J. Waties Waring wrestled with the conflict between his elite White upbringing and his understanding of true justice, and then ruled on cases in a way that changed the political landscape in South Carolina. Though she was shy and reserved, Angelina Grimké spoke out on abolition in the face of opposition to her views on slavery, as well as her status as a woman speaking to "promiscuous audiences," that is, those made up of both men and women. Despite her responsibilities as a wife and mother, Viola Liuzzo chose to join the march on Selma to act out her convictions. Morris Dees left a lucrative life as a successful businessman to practice law against some of the most violent, virulent racists in the South.

Closely related to the deep sense of moral conviction is a fourth factor: *a commitment to perseverance over the long haul in the struggle for racial justice*. Much like what was expressed by Rev. Martin Luther King Jr. on the eve of his assassination, all of these folks may have "seen the promised land" but they did not live to see their dreams fulfilled.[13] Many, like John Woolman, Elijah Lovejoy, Viola Liuzzo, and Clarence Jordan, died at a relatively young age in the midst of their work. Others, like Anne Braden, Myles Horton, John Rankin, and Virginia Durr, were active well into old age but expressed a sense of disappointment at how little change their efforts had brought about. Often it has been left to others to point out what was accomplished through their efforts, things they themselves could not see in their own time. As Warren points out, many racial justice activists have a vision of a more just society,[14] but at least in the lives of those told here, the convictions that motivated people often issued from a vision that outlived them. What they had struggled so long and hard for was left to others to continue.

The fifth factor evident in these stories is the *willingness of these White folks to use their privilege and power* where possible and to

---

[13] Martin Luther King Jr., "I See the Promised Land," April 3, 1968, in *A Testament of Hope: The Essential Writings of Martin Luther King*, ed. James W. Washington (San Francisco: Harper and Row, 1986), 279–86.

[14] Warren, *Fire in the Heart*.

revoke that privilege where necessary. Because of scholarship over the last twenty-five years, the prevalence of White power and White privilege is well documented.[15] Once they are made aware, many Whites desire to divest themselves of their privilege and power because with it comes tremendous responsibility. However, the people in this book did not shirk from their power and privilege but used it where appropriate to achieve their goals. John Woolman used his role as a visiting minister to enter homes and meetings where he could express his antislavery views. Mary White Ovington used her extensive network of friends and associates to call together the founders of the NAACP. Because of her time in Washington, DC, Virginia Durr had contacts with many politically powerful people, whom she was not shy about calling on when their assistance and resources were needed. J. Waties Waring used his powerful position as a federal district judge to abolish the Whites-only Democratic primary in South Carolina and voted on school desegregation, setting the stage for the *Brown v. Board of Education* decision in 1954. Robert Graetz drew on his role in the Lutheran Church to raise funds for the Montgomery bus boycott. Whether it was their social status, their personal networks, or simply the access granted to them by their White skin, all of these allies used their place in the sociopolitical and economic system to work against White supremacy and fight for racial justice.

However, there were just as many times when these Whites needed to relinquish the power and privilege that society had granted them. Paul Kivel points out that in a culture that routinely diminishes and devalues the contributions of Persons of Color, it is important for White allies to support People of Color in leadership.[16] He also emphasizes that allies should not do so uncritically, but should respond to these leaders with the same balance of respect and challenge they would give White leaders. The persons in this book achieved and lived out that balance. Anne Braden committed herself through her work to always work under multiracial leadership. Despite being actively involved in the civil rights movement from the beginning, Myles Horton always remained supportive but in the background. Mary White Ovington promoted the

---

[15] Peggy McIntosh, "White Privilege and Male Privilege," in *Critical White Studies: Looking Behind the Mirror*, ed. Richard Delgado and Jen Stefancic (Philadelphia: Temple University Press, 1988), 291–99; Paul Kivel, *Uprooting Racism: How White People Can Work for Racial Justice* (Gabriola Island, BC, Canada: New Society, 2002).

[16] Kivel, *Uprooting Racism*, 98.

ascendancy of African American leadership in the NAACP and was a consistent supporter of W. E. B. Du Bois.

In previous eras, leadership by People of Color was actively repressed except in the pockets of resistance where racial justice activists operated. However, in our own era, acknowledging and supporting the leadership of People of Color is one of the clearest ways in which racial justice allies can work. Curtiss Paul DeYoung and Tim Wise have both written extensively on the importance of Whites accepting and supporting the leadership of People of Color, and have demonstrated these convictions in their personal and professional lives.[17] With the election of Barack Obama, one might think that such actions would be unnecessary; however, what has emerged is a strategy of discrediting the first African American president with seemingly nonracist phrases that are in a fact code words for race. Thus Obama has been accused of not being a US citizen, a covert Muslim, and a radical social liberal, when by most political standards his actions qualify him as a Democratic moderate. Behind these accusations is the persistent fear of Black backlash among some White people, a fear that is as old as Southern plantation owners who feared retaliation and rebellion from the slaves under their control. Instead of examining the injustice behind that fear, Whites have chosen to justify and rationalize that fear away by passing of Jim Crow laws, practicing violent acts of terror, theologizing on the biblical support for slavery, and making economic arguments demanding cheap labor. Although the form of these rationalizations may be different in our present day, they fit a pattern that has been in place for over three hundred years.

A Positive White Antiracist Identity

The purpose of this book has been to tell the stories of antiracist allies through US history in order to provide role models for Whites seeking to understand how to become White allies. My hope is that in telling these stories I might aid the reader in developing a positive White antiracist identity in the ongoing struggle for racial justice in our time.

In the introduction to her book on contemporary White activists during and since the civil rights movement, Becky Thompson discusses

---

[17] See Tim Wise, *White Like Me: Reflections on Race from a Privileged Son* (Brooklyn, NY: Soft Skull Press, 2005); Curtiss Paul DeYoung, *Homecoming: A White Man's Journey through Harlem to Jerusalem* (Minneapolis: Jezi Press, 2009).

the inherent paradox of seeking to develop a positive White identity.[18] Noel Ignatiev and John Garvey have contended that because Whiteness was created in order to oppress and enslave others, the notion of a positive White identity is inherently contradictory.[19] Ian Haney-López asserts that Whiteness as a way of thinking needs to be destroyed and that contemporary Whites wanting to combat racism must become what Noel Ignatiev calls a "race traitor."[20] A race traitor is one who "is nominally classified as White, but who defies the rules of whiteness so flagrantly as to jeopardize his or her ability to draw upon privileges of white skin."[21]

Although appearing to being inherently nihilistic, this argument is not without merit. Critical Whiteness Studies seeks to uncover the dynamics of White power operating in the structures, laws, and policies of culture and systems so as to undermine and dismantle those dynamics in order to move toward a multiracial, just society. There is no question that the legacy of Whiteness bequeathed to contemporary Whites in our various systems—legal, educational, political, economic, and social—is so insidious as to tempt one simply to destroy it all and start over again. However, to do so is also to destroy that which is inherently life affirming from European heritage. African American leaders such as Frederick Douglass and Martin Luther King Jr.[22] framed their arguments for racial justice within the very documents that had been used to exclude them; in a sense they used Whiteness in order to deconstruct and challenge its power. Principles such as freedom of speech and democracy, while grossly distorted when applied to People of Color, are still principles inherently worth preserving.

Furthermore, just as all Whites are not equally privileged (i.e., poor Whites, while having the advantage of being White in this society, do

---

[18] Becky Thompson, *A Promise and a Way of Life: White Antiracist Activism* (Minneapolis: University of Minnesota Press, 2001).

[19] Noel Ignatiev and John Garvey, eds., *Race Traitor* (New York: Routledge, 1996).

[20] Ian Haney-López, *White by Law: The Legal Construction of Race* (New York: University of New York Press, 1996), 189.

[21] Ibid.

[22] For examples, see Frederick Douglass, "The Meaning of July Fourth for the Negro," in *Frederick Douglass: Selected Speeches and Writings*, ed. Philip Foner (Chicago, IL: Lawrence Hill Books, 1999), 188–206; and Martin Luther King Jr., "I Have a Dream (1963)," in *A Testament of Hope: The Essential Writings of Martin Luther King Jr.*, ed. James Melvin Washington (San Francisco: Harper & Row, 1986), 208–216.

not experience privilege in other ways), so too all Whites are not equally powerful. Moreover, as critical feminist scholarship on intersectionality has highlighted, the dynamics of racism cannot be separated from dynamics of classism, sexism, and other forms of discrimination.[23] In destroying Whiteness, one cannot help but unfairly victimize others in the name of justice. Thus the goal of dismantling Whiteness carries within it the inherent threat of destroying that which is evil in pursuit of that which is good, and further injuring those who are innocent.

For this reason, I side with Thompson and Barbara T. Flagg, who see the goal of this work as helping Whites develop positive, though imperfect, White antiracist identities. In discussing her notion of "positive White identity" Flagg views the problem not as being race (i.e., Whiteness), but rather racism (i.e., White power). From her perspective, the goal is to make Whites more consciously aware of the way in which the norms, values, experiences, and perspectives they hold are "White specific" and through which they are rewarded unfairly in the day-to-day workings of society. She invites White decision makers to investigate other racial and cultural norms and values to determine if there are ways to live, think, and act more inclusively.[24] As Thompson says, developing a positive White identity may involve the rigorous self and societal analysis that Ignatiev insists on, but ultimately the goal is not for White people to cease being White, but rather to learn how "becoming activists [goes] hand in hand with accepting themselves as White people."[25]

As a young adult recently out of college, I remember sitting in the back seat of a car, as the two White guys in the front seat discussed how they did not want to be White anymore; they wanted to become Black. I was perplexed and yet intrigued by this conversation, because like them when I first became aware of the ravages that White power and racism had inflicted on the Black people in North Carolina and Massachusetts where I had recently lived, I too had wanted to become something other than White. However, forty-plus years of grappling with these questions has led me to the realization that despite all the

---

[23] See Kimberle Crenshaw, "Mapping the Margins: Intersectionality, Identity Politics, and Violence against Women of Color," *Stanford Law Review* 43, no. 6 (July 1991): 1241–99.

[24] Barbara T. Flagg, "Was Blind But Now I See: White Race Consciousness and the Requirement of Discriminatory Intent," *Michigan Law Review* 91, no. 5 (1993): 953–1017.

[25] Thompson, *Promise*, xxi.

antiracist work I have done, all the antiracism trainings I have attended, and all the courses on race and ethnic relations I have taught, I am still very White. My way of dressing, my concept of time, my way of thinking, and even the music I enjoy is White. At the same time I have learned to listen and take seriously perspectives and ways of thinking and acting that are culturally different and therefore unfamiliar and uncomfortable to me. I have learned to trust in culturally indigenous wisdom that comes out of legacies and experiences of oppression and marginalization. I have learned to appreciate and trust the stories of People of Color whose experiences lie outside my experience and on the surface seem unbelievable to me. I also have come to realize that my way of seeing and being in the world is not shared by all, and that in accepting myself, I must offer equal respect and acceptance to those whose way of seeing and being in the world is vastly different from my own. The challenge has been and continues to be to develop a positive antiracist White identity in the midst of a world of difference. The people whose stories are related here have been some of those who have guided me on my journey. My hope is that they have and will help others on their journeys as well.

Discussion Questions

1. Respond to the five factors that distinguish White allies. Which are most challenging? Which seem most surprising? What other factors would you add that are not discussed in this chapter?
2. Have you ever known a White person who expressed a desire not to be White? What does it meant to be White in American culture?

Bibliography

Bonilla-Silva, Eduardo. *Racism without Racists: Colorblind Racism and the Persistence of Racial Inequality in America*. Lanham, MD: Rowan and Littlefield, 2006.

Cone, James. *The Cross and the Lynching Tree*. Maryknoll, NY: Orbis Books, 2011.

Crenshaw, Kimberle W. "Mapping the Margins: Intersectionality, Identity Politics, and Violence against Women of Color." *Stanford Law Review* 43, no. 6 (July 1991): 1241–99.

DeYoung, Curtiss Paul. *Homecoming: A White Man's Journey through Harlem to Jerusalem*. Minneapolis: Jezi Press, 2009.

Flagg, Barbara T. "Was Blind But Now I See: White Race Consciousness and the Requirement of Discriminatory Intent," *Michigan Law Review* 91, no. 5 (1993): 953–1017.

Fosl, Catherine. *Subversive Southerner: Anne Braden and the Struggle for Racial Justice in the Cold War South*. New York: Palgrave Macmillan, 2002.

Haney-López, Ian. *White by Law: The Legal Construction of Race*. New York: University of New York Press, 1996.

Ignatiev, Noel, and John Garvey, eds. *Race Traitor*. New York: Routledge, 1996.

King, Martin Luther Jr. "I See the Promised Land." In *A Testament of Hope: The Essential Writings of Martin Luther King*, ed. James W. Washington, 279–86. San Francisco: Harper and Row, 1986.

———. "Letter from a Birmingham Jail." In *Why We Can't Wait*, by Martin Luther King Jr., 64–84. New York: Signet Classic, 1963.

Kivel, Paul. *Uprooting Racism: How White People Can Work for Racial Justice*. Gabriola Island, BC, Canada: New Society, 2002.

McIntosh, Peggy. "White Privilege and Male Privilege: A Personal Account to See Correspondence through Work in Women's Studies." In *Critical White Studies: Looking Behind the Mirror*, ed, Richard Delgado and Jen Stefancic, 291–99. Philadelphia: Temple University Press, 1988.

Thompson, Becky. *A Promise and a Way of Life: White Antiracist Activism*. Minneapolis: University of Minnesota Press, 2001.

Warren, Mark. *Fire in the Heart: How White Activists Embrace Racial Justice*. New York: Oxford University Press, 2010.

Wise, Tim. *White Like Me: Reflections on Race from a Privileged Son*. Brooklyn, NY: Soft Skull Press, 2005.

Appendix

Other White Allies for Racial Justice*

The stories told in this book highlight some of the people who have served as allies over the centuries in the cause for racial justice in the United States. But there are many others. What follows is a brief overview of some others whose lives were characterized by a commitment to and search for the "beloved community."

Antislavery Efforts in Colonial Times

Anthony Benezet (1713–1784). A French-born abolitionist who came to the American colonies with his family in 1731 and joined the Quakers. A contemporary of John Woolman, Benezet worked to persuade Quakers to emancipate their slaves and work for the abolition of slavery. He also founded a school to educate Negro children in 1770.

Thomas Hazard (1720–1798). A Quaker farmer from Rhode Island, Hazard defied his family by freeing his slaves and becoming an advocate for the abolition of slavery in Rhode Island, especially among his fellow Quakers. He helped design the legislation that led to the abolition of slavery in Rhode Island in 1784.

Abolitionists

Edward Coles (1786–1868). The son of a wealthy Virginia slave owner, Coles became convinced of the evils of slavery at an early age. When his father died, Coles inherited twenty of his father's slaves along with a sizable amount of property. Because the state of Virginia required that freed slaves leave the state,

---

* Sources for the short descriptions in this section come from Wikipedia; Cynthia Stokes Brown, *Refusing Racism: White Allies and the Struggle for Civil Rights* (New York: Teachers College Press, 2002) 149–58; Robin K. Bertson, *Marching to a Different Drummer: Unrecognized Heroes of American History* (Westport, CT: Greenwood Press, 1994); and the author's personal knowledge of the individuals.

Coles sold his estate in Virginia and moved to Illinois, whereupon he granted freedom to his slaves along with a plot of his land in Illinois. He successfully ran for governor in Illinois on an antislavery platform and served in the administrations of Presidents Madison and Monroe, where he continually argued the abolitionist position.

Thaddeus Stevens (1792–1868). A congressman from Pennsylvania elected in 1858, Stevens became a leading opponent of slavery before and during the Civil War in Congress. He was a leader of the Radical Republicans following the war who advocated that Blacks not only be freed but be given land and a stake in the future of the South.

Lucretia Mott (1793–1880). A Quaker abolitionist from Philadelphia, Mott, along with her husband, founded the American Anti-Slavery Society, and with other White and Black women founded the Philadelphia Female Anti-Slavery Society to promote the abolitionist cause among women. Along with Elizabeth Cady Stanton she founded the Seneca Falls Convention, which pushed for women's rights alongside the abolition of slavery. She was actively involved in antislavery efforts until after the Civil War, at which time she continued her activism in support of women's rights.

John Brown (1800–1859). An abolitionist originally from Massachusetts, Brown believed that armed insurrection was the only way to eradicate the institution of slavery in the United States. He participated in armed antislavery conflicts in Kansas in the mid-1850s. In 1859 he led a group of eighteen men who captured the US Arsenal at Harper's Ferry, Virginia, in what he hoped would spark an antislavery insurrection throughout the South. Instead, Brown and his co-conspirators were captured, and Brown was executed by hanging in December 1859.

William Lloyd Garrison (1805–1879). One of the most prominent abolitionists of his time, Garrison served as the editor of the *The Liberator*. Garrison credited John Rankin's "Letters on Slavery" for drawing him into the antislavery cause. His newspaper and example were major influences on abolitionists, including Sarah and Angelina Grimké.

Susan B. Anthony (1820–1906). A Quaker Social Reformer from the area of Rochester, New York, Anthony began collecting antislavery petitions with her father at age seventeen. She became close friends with Frederick Douglass and was drawn to the abolitionist ideas of William Lloyd Garrison. Later she joined with Elizabeth Cady Stanton to form the Seneca Falls Convention arguing for women's right to vote. Throughout her life she saw the women's suffrage cause as interrelated with the antislavery cause.

Robert Gould Shaw (1837–1863). A Union Army officer in the Civil War, Shaw at the age of twenty-five agreed to lead the Fifty-Fourth Massachusetts Regiment, the first African American regiment in the war. In July 1863, he led his troops into an assault on Fort Wagner, South Carolina, where he and sixty-two Black soldiers died in battle.

Jim Crow Era

Harold Ickes (1874–1952). A journalist, lawyer, and politician from Chicago, Ickes served as president of the Chicago NAACP and later served as Secretary of the Interior under President Franklin D. Roosevelt, where he worked for self-government for Native Americans and sought to include African Americans in the Roosevelt Administration.

Branch Rickey (1881–1965). Rickey was the president and general manager of the Brooklyn Dodgers, which was the first major league baseball franchise to sign an African American player, Jackie Robinson, to their roster in 1945. Rickey's action opened the door for other teams to sign Black players from that point on.

Eleanor Roosevelt (1884–1962). The wife of President Franklin Delano Roosevelt, Eleanor Roosevelt was a champion of civil rights during and after her time in the White House. She worked to promote anti-lynching legislation, advocated for desegregation of the military, worked for African Americans to have jobs in the defense industry, and served on the board of the NAACP from 1945 to 1955.

Vito Marcantonio (1902–1954). A son of Italian immigrants, Marcantonio became a US congressman representing East Harlem. He was an outspoken advocate for freedom who supported anti-lynching legislation and the repeal of Southern poll taxes. He defended the rights of Mexican mine workers and campaigned for Puerto Rican independence. After leaving Congress, he had a private law practice in which he defended W. E. B Du Bois. Du Bois offered the eulogy at Marcantonio's funeral, and called him "the best friend the Negro people ever had."

Civil Rights

Aubrey Williams (1890–1965). Originally from Alabama, Williams became a social worker who was active in the Southern Conference of Human Welfare (SCHW) and the Southern Conference Educational Fund (SCEF). He later was the editor of *Southern Farm and Home*, which promoted farmers' unions and racial integration. He was a close associate of Anne and Carl Braden.

Jim Dombrowski (1897–1983). Dombrowski was a co-founder of Highlander Folk School with Myles Horton and Don West. As a young Methodist minister in 1934, he founded the Conference of Younger Churchmen in the South and later served as the executive director of the SCHW (1942–46) and SCEF (1946–66). Along with Carl Braden, Anne Braden, Myles Horton, and others he was charged with subversion for his civil rights activities.

Glen Smiley (1910–1993). A field secretary with the Fellowship of Reconciliation, Smiley served as an adviser on the practice of Gandhian nonviolence to Dr. Martin Luther King Jr. during the Montgomery bus boycott. Along with James Lawson, he helped organize several nonviolence training sessions for people taking part in the civil rights demonstrations throughout the South, particularly those in the student-led lunch-counter sit-in movement of the early 1960s.

Carl Braden (1914–1975). A journalist and labor organizer from Louisville, Kentucky, Braden, along with his wife, Anne Braden, helped purchase a house for a Black man, Andrew Wade. Along with Anne he was blacklisted and spent six months in jail. Along with his wife he served as an organizer SCEF.

Will Campbell (1924–2013). A Baptist pastor from Mississippi, Campbell repeatedly spoke out in favor of desegregation and civil rights while a pastor in Louisiana and a chaplain at the University of Mississippi. During the integration of Central High School in Little Rock, Arkansas, Campbell accompanied one of the Black students into the school. He later served as a field officer in the National Council of Churches and then as director of the Committee of Southern Churchmen, as an active participant in the civil rights movement. He continued to speak out and write about issues of racism throughout his life in the journal *Katallagete*.

Lois Mark Stalvey (1925–2004). A mother and wife, Stalvey worked for an African American family's right to move into a segregated neighborhood of Omaha, Nebraska, in the late 1950s. After moving to Philadelphia in 1961 she formed the Panel of Philadelphians, an interracial and interreligious group of women that sponsored conversations about racial justice throughout Philadelphia. In 1970 she published *Education of a WASP*, which described her experience as a White person learning about racism in Omaha, and then *Three to Get Ready: The Education of a White Family in Inner City Schools* in 1997 about living in an integrated neighborhood of Philadelphia.

James Reeb (1927–1965). A Unitarian Universalist minister, Reeb went to Selma, Alabama, as a member of the South Christian Leadership Conference to join protests calling for voting rights for African Americans. After eating dinner at a local restaurant he was beaten by White men with clubs. Despite receiving brain surgery he died two days later. The three men arrested for his murder were acquitted by an Alabama jury.

Bob Zellner (1939–). Zellner was the first White field secretary of the Student Nonviolent Coordinating Committee (SNCC). As a young college student in Alabama he began researching the civil rights movement and was challenged by

Dr. King and Rosa Parks to get involved with the movement. With SNCC he tried to organize sympathetic Whites throughout the South and was often the victim of violence for his efforts. Following the civil rights movement he continued to teach organizing skills to poor Whites and Blacks in the rural South and to advocate for racial justice.

James Zwerg (1939–). As a college student from Beloit College in Wisconsin, Zwerg attended Fisk University, a historically Black college in Nashville, Tennessee, on a one-year exchange program. At Fisk he met John Lewis and other students involved in the lunch-counter sit-ins and joined SNCC. In 1961 along with Lewis and eleven other Blacks and Whites, he took part in the first Freedom Ride, which sought to desegregate bus terminals in the South. In Montgomery, Alabama, Zwerg and the other riders were attacked by an angry White mob, which resulted in Zwerg's being hospitalized with severe injuries that nearly killed him.

Casey Hayden (1937–). Born Sandra Cason, Casey Hayden was one of the early White staff members of SNCC. She served as a northern field secretary for SNCC and then as a literacy coordinator in Tugaloo, Mississippi, during the Freedom Summer of 1963. She helped author several papers advocating for full enfranchisement of women in SNCC and the civil rights movement in general. Hayden left SNCC in 1965 as it moved to become an all–African American organization, but she continued her activism in areas of racial and gender justice.

Contemporary

Marshall Ganz (1943–). Ganz left Harvard College in 1964 to help register African American voters in Mississippi. In 1965 he joined the farmworkers' movement under the leadership of Cesar Chavez. He worked as an organizer in the farmworkers' movement until 1981, after which he worked on several political campaigns. He returned to Harvard in 1991 to finish his degree and a doctorate, after which he was a faculty member at the Kennedy School of Government at Harvard University.

Mab Segrest (1949–). Originally from Tuskegee, Alabama, Segrist protested segregation by opposing her parents' efforts to establish all-White schools in opposition to the Supreme Court order to desegregate schools. She is best known for her book *Memoir of a Race Traitor* in which she describes her journey into activism against the KKK and coming to terms with her lesbianism. An English professor at Connecticut College, Segrest continues to illuminate the linkages between homophobia and racism.

Fr. Michael Phleger (1949–). A Roman Catholic priest, Fr. Phleger has served as the pastor of St. Sabina's a predominantly African American parish in Southside Chicago since 1981. Under Fr. Phleger's leadership, St. Sabina's initiated a number of organizations serving the local community. He is a tireless advocate against gun violence, opponent of the illegal drug trade, and proponent of racial justice. Against the wishes of his superiors, Fr. Phleger has adopted and raised two African American foster children.

Chris Rice (1960–). The director of the Center for Reconciliation at Duke Divinity School in Durham, North Carolina. Prior to coming to Duke, Rice lived in Jackson, Mississippi, where he collaborated with Spencer Perkins on promoting racial reconciliation in the Christian church. Following Perkins's untimely death, Rice attended Duke Divinity School, and in 2005 with Emmanuel Katongole from Uganda he co-founded the Center for Reconciliation, which seeks to promote reconciliation work in the United States and around the world, as well as training persons in reconciliation skills.

Index